Theodore Roosevelt and His Library at Sagamore Hill

Theodore Roosevelt and His Library at Sagamore Hill

Mark I. West

Sept. 2022

Larry,

I hope you enjoy this virtual tour of Theodore Roosevelt's library.

Your friend,

Mark

ROWMAN & LITTLEFIELD
Lanham • Boulder • New York • London

Published by Rowman & Littlefield
An imprint of The Rowman & Littlefield Publishing Group, Inc.
4501 Forbes Boulevard, Suite 200, Lanham, Maryland 20706
www.rowman.com

86-90 Paul Street, London EC2A 4NE

British Library Cataloguing in Publication Information Available

Library of Congress Cataloging-in-Publication Data

Names: West, Mark I., author.
Title: Theodore Roosevelt and his library at Sagamore Hill / Mark I. West.
Description: Lanham : Rowman & Littlefield Publishers, [2022] | Includes
    bibliographical references and index.
Identifiers: LCCN 2021060674 (print) | LCCN 2021060675 (ebook) | ISBN
    9781538159354 (cloth) | ISBN 9781538159361 (ebook)
Subjects: LCSH: Roosevelt, Theodore, 1858–1919—Homes and haunts—New York
    (State)—Oyster Bay. | Roosevelt, Theodore, 1858–1919—Books and
    reading. | Private libraries—New York (State)—Oyster Bay. | Sagamore
    Hill National Historic Site (Oyster Bay, N.Y.)—Library.
Classification: LCC F129.O98 W47 2022 (print) | LCC F129.O98 (ebook) |
    DDC 974.7/245—dc23/eng/20211214
LC record available at https://lccn.loc.gov/2021060674
LC ebook record available at https://lccn.loc.gov/2021060675

For all of the administrators and staff members at the
Sagamore Hill National Historic Site

Contents

~

Foreword

When I first spoke on the phone with Mark West, I wondered why a children's literature professor was interested in writing a book about Theodore Roosevelt's love of reading and his books and library at Sagamore Hill. While there are hundreds of volumes of children's books in the Theodore Roosevelt Home, West was not specifically focused on them. Instead, he sought to write a book that explored the centrality of books to Roosevelt's life and family. We work with many researchers and authors at Sagamore Hill National Historic Site, but West is the first to focus on the magic of the books and the library in the Theodore Roosevelt Home.

Theodore Roosevelt and His Library at Sagamore Hill is a welcome addition to the canon of works about Theodore Roosevelt. The book is a fine complement to Thomas Bailey and Katherine Joslin's 2018 book *Theodore Roosevelt: A Literary Life*. While Bailey and Joslin focus on Roosevelt's life as a writer, West explores Roosevelt's life as a reader. Understanding what Roosevelt read and why gives us a window into the words and worlds that captivated and inspired him.

This book is an excellent read for both Roosevelt enthusiasts and visitors to Sagamore Hill. It builds on the work of previous Roosevelt scholars to tell the story of Roosevelt's intimate relationship with reading and his book collection. The book augments a trip to Sagamore Hill by describing the evolution of the library from a family space to an office during the presidential years, and eventually to a space that preserves the Roosevelt family's love for books. The chapter containing the list of books in the Sagamore Hill

National Historic Site collection enables the reader to get a sense of the breadth of works the Roosevelt family read, enjoyed, and treasured. After finishing this book, you will understand why the Roosevelts referred to the library as the heart of the home.

Laura Cinturati
Acting Museum Curator
Sagamore Hill National Historic Site
November 2021

~

Acknowledgments

While researching and writing *Theodore Roosevelt and His Library at Sagamore Hill*, I received help from several people. Laura Cinturati, the acting museum curator at the Sagamore Hill National Historic Site, helped me in many ways. She provided me with an updated list of Roosevelt's books at Sagamore Hill, read drafts of my chapters, and identified photographs to include in the book. Two other staff members at Sagamore Hill also helped update the list of books. They are museum technician Lindsay Davenport and museum technician Kevin Costigan. Susan Sarana, the former museum curator at Sagamore Hill, helped me during the research stage of this project. She answered all of my questions and provided me with much-needed encouragement. I thank all of these people for their assistance and for so generously sharing their expertise with me.

Angie Williams helped tremendously with the time-consuming process of converting the updated list of Roosevelt's books from a lengthy spreadsheet into manuscript pages. I thank her for her assistance and for her attention to details.

My appreciation also goes to the chair of my department, Paula Eckard, and to my colleagues at the University of North Carolina at Charlotte for their ongoing support of my research.

Finally, my thanks go to my wife, Nancy Northcott, and our son, Gavin West, for their love and support. I am sure that there were times when they felt that Theodore Roosevelt had become a boisterous fourth member of our family, but they never seemed to mind. Nevertheless, I am sure they will be glad when TR goes back to Sagamore Hill where he belongs.

~

Introduction

Modern view of the Library at Sagamore Hill. *NPS/© Audrey C. Tiernan Photography, Inc.*

I remember vividly the first time I visited Sagamore Hill, Theodore Roosevelt's home in Oyster Bay, New York. In October 2008, I traveled to Oyster Bay to conduct research for an article I was writing on Roosevelt's interest in children's literature. Like most visitors to Sagamore Hill, I could not help but notice that Roosevelt's home is filled with books. Nearly every room includes

1

bookcases, and all of the bookcases are packed with the actual books that belonged to Roosevelt or his wife, Edith Roosevelt. Both were avid readers, and most of their books are still located at Sagamore Hill. They raised their family and lived out their lives while being surrounded by books that they read and shared on a regular basis. As the writer Edith Warton once said after visiting Sagamore Hill, "The house was like one big library."[1]

During that first visit, I had no idea that I would eventually write a book about Roosevelt's library at Sagamore Hill, but the experience of touring Sagamore Hill sparked my interest in Roosevelt's passion for books. My interest in this topic intensified over the years. As a children's literature specialist, I had much to learn. I revisited Sagamore Hill, interviewed the professional staff members about Roosevelt's library, and studied Roosevelt's life. The result of this research is *Theodore Roosevelt and His Library at Sagamore Hill*.

Although contemporary visitors to Sagamore Hill can see rows upon rows of books when they step into the rooms, the bookshelves are cordoned off to protect the books and the other objects on the shelves. As a result, visitors generally cannot get close enough to the books to read the titles on the spines. For anyone interested in Roosevelt's life, however, knowing what books are on the shelves is a matter that transcends idle curiosity. Roosevelt read books nearly every day of his adult life, and his reading shaped his values, his point of view, and his thinking on the many topics that interested him. In a sense, his books provide a window into the workings of his mind.

Theodore Roosevelt and His Library at Sagamore Hill provides researchers and others interested in Roosevelt's life with a complete list of all of Roosevelt's books that are currently located at Sagamore Hill. This list is drawn from several inventories taken over the years of the books, art objects, and furnishings associated with Sagamore Hill. Although the actual books on this list are not accessible to researchers, the detailed information gleaned from the inventories can help researchers identify titles that mattered to Roosevelt. This list does not include all of the books that Roosevelt ever owned or read, for Roosevelt often gave books away. Also, after his death in 1919, some of his books were taken from Sagamore Hill by family members. Nevertheless, the list includes thousands of books that belonged to Roosevelt. These books reflect his love of classic works of literature, his interest in history, and his fascination with the natural sciences.

This book also includes an overview of Roosevelt's life as a reader, a discussion of the role that reading particular books played in shaping his life and career, and a short history of his personal library. The book concludes with an essay that Roosevelt wrote near the end of his life in which he reflected on his reading habits and commented on some of his favorite books.

For Roosevelt, his library was not just a collection of books. Roosevelt felt that his identity was tied in part to the books that he read. When commenting on his love of books, Roosevelt once said, "I am old-fashioned, or sentimental, or something, about books! Whenever I read one, I want, in the first place, to enjoy myself, and in the next place, to feel that I am a little better and not a little worse for having read it."[2] His library at Sagamore Hill was full of books that he enjoyed reading, and there can be little doubt that he was the better for having read them.

Notes

1. Edith Wharton, *A Backward Glance* (New York: Charles Scribner's Sons, 1933), 316.

2. Edward Wagenknecht, *The Seven Worlds of Theodore Roosevelt* (Guilford, CT: Lyons Press, 2009), 87.

CHAPTER ONE

~

An Overview of Theodore Roosevelt's Life as a Reader

President Theodore Roosevelt called himself a "book lover" and for good reason. From his boyhood days in the 1860s to the very end of his life in 1919, Roosevelt had a deep-seated passion for reading books. Wherever he went, he brought books with him. Whether he was rounding up cattle on his ranch in the Dakota Territory, giving campaign speeches from the back of a train, governing the nation from the White House, hunting big game on an African safari, or exploring an uncharted tributary of the Amazon River, he always made time to read books. According to the Roosevelt scholar Edmund Morris, Roosevelt "consumed, and largely memorized, between three and five hundred books a year."[1] As his longtime friend Owen Wister recalled, Roosevelt often read an entire book over the course of an evening: "Somewhere between six one evening and eight-thirty next morning, beside his dressing and his dinner and his guests and his sleep, he had read a volume of three-hundred-and-odd pages, and missed nothing of significance that it contained."[2]

For Roosevelt, reading was not a passive pastime. He regularly applied what he learned from his reading to his daily life and to his work in politics. When he finished reading a book, he often contacted the author to discuss the implications of the author's main points. A prolific author himself, he frequently wrote about books that he had read in his own books and articles. During the years of his presidency, he invited some of his favorite authors to have dinner with him at the White House. He regularly corresponded with the authors of books that he especially liked, and in some cases, he struck up lifelong friendships with these authors.

Childhood and Early Adulthood

Roosevelt's passion for reading can be traced back to his own childhood. Born in 1858, Roosevelt grew up in an affluent family in New York City. During much of his childhood, he suffered from debilitating asthma that limited his ability to engage in physical activities, and he responded to this limitation by immersing himself in the world of books. He grew up in a house filled with books, and his parents made sure that he always had reading material readily available. As Roosevelt later recounted in his autobiography, "I was given the chance to read books that they thought I ought to read, but if I did not like them, I was then given some other good book that I did like."[3] The stories that he read as a boy left a lasting impression on him. He wrote his autobiography when he was in his mid-fifties, but he was able to write in considerable detail about the books that he read during his childhood.

As a young boy, Roosevelt's favorite author was Thomas Mayne Reid, the author of numerous outdoor adventure books, such as *The Boy Hunters, Or, Adventures in Search of a White Buffalo.* Although Roosevelt was very much a city boy, he liked reading Reid's action-packed stories set in the American wilderness.[4] Douglas Brinkley, the author of *The Wilderness Warrior: Theodore Roosevelt and the Crusade for America,* argues that Roosevelt's lifelong interest in the outdoors as well as his approach to writing about natural history stemmed from his childhood fascination with Reid's books. "Whenever Roosevelt wrote about the wilderness," Brinkley writes, "traces of Reid's hyper-romantic style are easily detectable. Although other naturalist writers captivated young Theodore's imagination . . . [Reid] remained his role model."[5]

Roosevelt's childhood interest in natural history led him to read works of nonfiction as well as Reid's adventure stories. During his boyhood, Roosevelt's favorite nonfiction book about natural history was J. G. Wood's *Homes without Hands: Being a Description of the Habitations of Animals, Classed According to Their Principle of Construction.* Although not intended for children, this scientific book greatly appealed to Roosevelt and inspired him to write an essay about ants when he was just eight years old.[6]

In addition to giving him books, Roosevelt's parents provided him with a subscription to the children's magazine *Our Young Folks,* and he looked forward to getting every issue. In his autobiography, he wrote about how much he enjoyed this publication: "As a small boy I had *Our Young Folks,* which I then firmly believed to be the very best magazine in the world—a belief, I may add, which I have kept to this day unchanged, for I seriously doubt if any magazine for old or young has ever surpassed it."[7]

As he became a more proficient reader, he took to reading longer novels as well as works of poetry. He occasionally read quieter books, such as Louisa May Alcott's *Little Women* and *Little Men*,[8] but his favorite books were adventure stories. He especially liked Frederick Marryat's *Mr. Midshipman Easy*, a seafaring tale about Jack Easy's adventures in the Royal Navy during the Napoleonic Wars.[9] He also liked the adventure stories by R. M. Ballantyne, the Scottish author of such works as *The Young Fur Traders* and *The Coral Island*.[10] His favorite poet during his childhood was Henry Wadsworth Longfellow. As he wrote in his autobiography, "Even in poetry it was the relation of adventures that most appealed to me as a boy. At a pretty early age I began to read certain books of poetry, notably Longfellow's poem, 'The Saga of King Olaf,' which absorbed me."[11]

In September 1876, Roosevelt headed off to Cambridge, Massachusetts, to start his college education at Harvard. Initially, he wanted to study science and become a naturalist like John James Audubon. As a teenager, Roosevelt had read and admired Audubon's *Birds of America*, and he was attracted to the type of field work that Audubon conducted while writing *Birds of America*.[12] However, when he learned that Harvard "treated biology as a science of the laboratory and the microscope," he "abandoned all thought of becoming a scientist."[13] His disillusionment with Harvard's science curriculum, combined with the fact that his father died during his sophomore year, caused Roosevelt to feel somewhat disengaged from his studies at Harvard.

During his four years at Harvard, he lived in a small apartment near campus. His apartment included a study, and he took pride in the new bookcase that he had installed in the study.[14] He filled the bookcase with the books his professors assigned him to read, but these required readings did not resonate deeply with him. In their book *Theodore Roosevelt: A Literary Life*, Thomas Bailey and Katherine Joslin explain that Roosevelt took a range of language and literature courses while at Harvard,[15] and this experience provided him with a solid grounding in classical literature.[16] However, in his autobiography, Roosevelt did not mention any specific books that he read as a college student. In fact, he wrote very little about his Harvard years in his autobiography. He summarized these years by saying, "I thoroughly enjoyed Harvard, and I am sure it did me good, but only in the general effect, for there was very little in my actual studies that helped me in after life."[17]

In his last year at Harvard, he took a strong interest in naval history. He had long enjoyed reading novels about seafaring adventures, and these novels led him to start reading works of nonfiction about naval history. He read James Fenimore Cooper's *History of the Navy of the United States of America*, and this book aroused his intellectual curiosity.[18] After reading several other

Theodore Roosevelt's apartment while he attended Harvard, c. 1877. *Courtesy of Saga-more Hill National Historic Site, National Park Service, Oyster Bay, NY*

books about the history of the American navy, he began writing what would become his first book, *The Naval War of 1812*. Instead of writing an honors thesis during his senior year, he wrote the preliminary drafts of two chapters for this book.[19] After he graduated from Harvard in June 1880, he decided to become a lawyer. He enrolled in Columbia Law School, but he continued to work on his naval history book, spending much of his free time researching naval history at the Astor Library in Manhattan.[20]

Roosevelt finished writing *The Naval War of 1812* in December 1881, and G. P. Putnam's Sons published it in 1882. Reviewers were impressed with Roosevelt's thorough research and his lively depictions of naval battles. In fact, the book went on to become required reading at the Naval Academy in Annapolis. The book's success established Roosevelt as an up-and-coming man of letters even though he was just twenty-three at the time that the book first came out.[21]

Dakota Years

The publication of *The Naval War of 1812* was not the only momentous event that occurred in Roosevelt's life during the first half of the 1880s. He married Alice Hathaway Lee on October 27, 1880, and the two of them took an extended European trip the next year. After taking several courses at Columbia Law School, he decided against pursuing a career in the law. Instead, he entered the world of politics and was elected to the New York State Assembly in November 1881. In early September 1883, he took a break from his burgeoning political career and traveled to the Dakota Territory, where he spent two memorable weeks on a hunting trip. He returned home to his wife at the end of September in time to prepare for the arrival of their first child. Alice Lee Roosevelt was born on February 12, 1884. Tragically, two days later, both his wife and his mother died. The deaths of his wife and mother sent Roosevelt into a period of depression. He disengaged from his family and his political career. After arranging to have his sister Anna (also known as Bamie) take care of his infant daughter, he moved to the Dakota Territory where he established his Elkhorn Ranch in June 1884.[22]

Throughout all of this upheaval, Roosevelt continued to read and write. He arranged for a library to be included in his new Elkhorn Ranch. Edmund Morris includes the following description of this library in *The Rise of Theodore Roosevelt*: "Sturdy shelves groaned with the collected works of Irving, Hawthorne, Cooper, and Lowell."[23] He also immersed himself in Leo Tolstoy's *Anna Karenina*.[24] He often read these books while sitting in his rocking chair on the veranda overlooking his ranch.

During this period in Roosevelt's life, he took a particular interest in reading books about the history of the American West, such as Theodore S. Van Dyke's *Still Hunter* and Richard Irving Dodge's *Plains of the Great West and Their Inhabitants*.[25] He especially liked Francis Parkman's *The Oregon Trail: Sketches of Prairie and Rocky-Mountain Life*, and he decided to use Parkman as a role model for a series of books he wrote about the life in the West. The first of these books, *Hunting Trips of a Ranchman: Sketches of Sport on the Northern Cattle Plains*, came out in 1885. It was followed by *Ranch Life and the Hunting Trail* in 1888, *The Winning of the West* in 1889, and *The Wilderness Hunter* in 1893. Roosevelt dedicated *The Winning of the West* to Parkman.[26] While Roosevelt was researching and writing these books, he continued to correspond with his political contacts in New York, but he did not see himself as a politician. As he wrote in a letter to a friend, "I'm a literary feller, not a politician these days."[27]

New York Years

Roosevelt maintained ownership of Elkhorn Ranch until 1898, but he stopped spending so much time at his "ranch home," as he often called it, in 1886.[28] On December 2, 1886, he married Edith Kermit Carow, a close friend from his childhood, and the next year they took up residence in their new twenty-three-room home called Sagamore Hill. Located near the town of Oyster Bay in Long Island, New York, Sagamore Hill became the permanent home for Roosevelt and his growing family. They had five children between 1887 and 1897.[29]

Sagamore Hill soon took on the appearance of a library with bookshelves in nearly every room. In addition to Roosevelt's books, the shelves included Edith's books. Like her husband, Edith was an avid reader. In the words of Hermann Hagedorn, the author of *The Roosevelt Family of Sagamore Hill*, "She needed books as she needed air and food, consumed them and absorbed them, adding their life to hers."[30] The shelves also included books intended for their children. Just as his parents had done for him, Roosevelt and his wife provided their children with a wide variety of reading material. Among the vast number of books that found their way to Sagamore Hill were hundreds of children's books by such authors Louisa May Alcott, Thomas Bailey Aldrich, Kenneth Grahame, Joel Chandler Harris, Charles Kingsley, Rudyard Kipling, Howard Pyle, and Robert Louis Stevenson. The family library also included anthologies of fairy tales, collections of poetry for children, and many issues of *St. Nicholas*, the famous children's magazine edited by Mary Mapes Dodge.[31]

After marrying Edith and settling into Sagamore Hill, Roosevelt relaunched his political career. He took an active interest in the presidential election of 1888, which Benjamin Harris won. In 1889, Harris appointed Roosevelt to the position of U.S. Civil Service Commissioner, a position he held until 1895 when he resigned in order to become the police commissioner of New York City. He held this position for two years and attracted national attention for his efforts to reform the police department. During this stage in his career, Roosevelt's reading interests moved in new directions. Although he continued reading books about the American West, he began reading books about urban life and the immigrant experience.[32]

The book that had the greatest impact on him at this point in his life was Jacob Riis's *How the Other Half Lives: Studies among the Tenements of New York*, which Roosevelt read shortly after the book came out in 1890. Immediately upon finishing the book, Roosevelt went to Riis's office to talk to him, but Riis was not there. Undeterred, Roosevelt left Riis a note on his desk.[33] This marked the beginning of a long relationship between Roosevelt and Riis during which the two of them worked to improve the living conditions for the impoverished immigrants who lived in the tenements.[34] In his autobiography, Roosevelt wrote about the significance of this relationship:

> The man who was closest to me throughout my two years in the Police Department was Jacob Riis. . . . I already knew Jake Riis, because his book *How the Other Half Lives* had been to me both an enlightenment and an inspiration for which I could never be too grateful. Soon after it was written I had called at his office to tell him how deeply impressed I was by the book, and that I wished to help him in any practical way to try to make things a little better. . . . Jacob Riis had drawn an indictment of the things that were wrong . . . with the tenement homes. In his book he had pointed out how the city government, especially those connected with the departments of police and health, could aid in remedying some of the wrongs.[35]

Roosevelt's response to Riis's book underscores a benefit that Roosevelt gained from his voluminous reading. By reading about people whose lives were so different from his own, Roosevelt developed a sense of empathy for these people. Through reading Riis's book, Roosevelt began to empathize with the difficult lives of the immigrants who came to America hoping for a new start, and this sense of empathy played a role in his political career.

Military Career and Governorship of New York

Roosevelt's two years as the police commissioner of New York City came to an end in April 1897 when President William McKinley appointed him to the position of assistant secretary of the navy. Given Roosevelt's long-standing interest in naval history, the position appealed to him. Serving as the assistant secretary of the navy required him to focus on America's standing as naval power. One of the books that shaped his views on this topic was Alfred Thayer Mahan's *The Influence of Sea Power upon History*. Roosevelt corresponded with Mahan, and he cited Mahan's writings when he advocated for a stronger U.S. Navy.[36]

With the outbreak of the Spanish-American War in April 1898, Roosevelt resigned as the assistant secretary of the navy and volunteered to fight in the war. He accepted a commission as lieutenant colonel and took charge of organizing the First United States Volunteer Calvary Regiment, better known as the Rough Riders. After training for a few weeks in San Antonio, Texas, Roosevelt and his Rough Riders shipped off to Cuba to engage the Spanish forces stationed there. They landed in Cuba on June 22, 1898.

Roosevelt's time in Cuba came to a head on July 1, 1898, during the Battle of San Juan Hill, one of the most famous battles fought during the Spanish-American War. Roosevelt and his Rough Riders played a key role in helping the American forces win this battle, and his success catapulted him into the national spotlight.[37]

Roosevelt went on to write about his experiences in the Spanish-American War in his book *The Rough Riders*, which came out in 1899. Roosevelt actually dictated this book, and he based most of it on his personal memories of his experiences with the Rough Riders. However, his writing was informed by Richard Harding Davis's news coverage of the Rough Riders. Roosevelt and Davis were friends, and Roosevelt arranged for Davis to accompany the Rough Riders during their time in Cuba. As Doris Kearns Goodwin points out in *The Bully Pulpit: Theodore Roosevelt, William Howard Taft, and the Golden Age of Journalism*, "No public figure of the time understood better than Roosevelt the importance of cultivating reporters."[38] Davis wrote extensively and laudatorily about Roosevelt's exploits during the Spanish-American War, and Roosevelt came across as an action hero in Davis's coverage. Davis's account of the Rough Riders and Roosevelt's *The Rough Riders* dovetail perfectly. In the words of Thomas Bailey and Katherine Joslin, Davis's reports already "made Theodore Roosevelt wildly popular," and Roosevelt's *The Rough Riders* simply reinforced this popularity.[39]

Roosevelt's Rough Rider fame quickly impacted his political career. He was elected governor of New York State in November 1898, and two years later he was elected vice president of the United States under President McKinley. During this two-year period, he remained engaged in literary matters, paying particular attention to biographies of political and military figures. While serving as the governor of New York, he wrote a biography titled *Oliver Cromwell*, which came out in 1900.[40] Of the biographies that he read at this juncture in his career, the one he especially liked was Owen Wister's biography *Ulysses S. Grant*. Roosevelt and Wister attended Harvard together, and Roosevelt often corresponded with Wister. On March 11, 1901, he sent Wister a letter about Wister's biography of Grant. "I have now read through your book again, most carefully," he wrote. "It seems to me that you have written the very best short biography which has ever been written of any prominent American."[41] According to Bailey and Joslin, one of the reasons Roosevelt focused on biographies at this point is that he "was thinking about who should become his own biographer, who could best make his character shine."[42]

Presidency

Roosevelt's life changed dramatically on September 6, 1901, when President William McKinley was shot while visiting the Pan-American Exposition in Buffalo, New York. McKinley died on September 14, at which point Roosevelt was sworn in as the twenty-sixth president of the United States. He was reelected in 1904 and remained in office until March 1909. Soon after assuming the presidency, Roosevelt and his family all took up residence in the White House.[43] At this point in his life, Roosevelt had six children between the ages of three and seventeen. Not since the presidency of Abraham Lincoln had the White House been the home of young children.

The demands and responsibilities associated with serving as the president of the United States caused Roosevelt to take a bit of a respite from his career as an author, but he continued to read widely. When Roosevelt read a book that he especially liked, he occasionally invited the author to join him in the White House. Early in his presidency, for example, he read Booker T. Washington's *Up from Slavery*, which came out in 1901. Washington's autobiography impressed Roosevelt, and he invited Washington to have dinner with him. The dinner took place on October 16, 1901. When news of this dinner hit the papers, it stirred up a controversy.[44] Many editorials criticized Roosevelt for inviting an African American to have dinner at the White House, but Roosevelt did not back down. He invited Washington back to the White House on February 26, 1902.[45]

Another author Roosevelt invited to the White House was his friend Owen Wister. Roosevelt greatly admired Wister's 1902 novel *The Virginian: A Horsemen of the Plains*, which Wister dedicated to Roosevelt. Soon after the book's publication, Roosevelt sent Wister a letter in which he called *The Virginian* "a remarkable novel."[46] At Roosevelt's invitation, Wister and his wife stayed at the White House from January 8 to January 12, 1903. In his book *Roosevelt: The Story of a Friendship*, Wister described the visit at length. In commenting on one of the dinners he had at the White House, he wrote, "It was all easy and informal and gay, as Roosevelt most liked to have it."[47]

Roosevelt also invited Edith Wharton, the author of such works as *The House of Mirth* and *Ethan Frome*, to the White House. On March 16, 1905, Wharton and several other writers joined Roosevelt for a luncheon that resembled a literary salon.[48] In her autobiography, *A Backward Glance*, Wharton recalled that Roosevelt immediately brought up Lewis Carroll's extended poem "The Hunting of the Snark" during this luncheon. Roosevelt knew that Wharton shared his interest in Carroll's writings, so he welcomed her to the luncheon by saying, "At last I can quote 'The Hunting of the Snark' without being asked what I mean." According to Wharton, he then added, "Would you believe it, no one in the administration has ever heard of Alice, much less of the Snark, and the other day when I said to the Secretary of the Navy: 'Mr. Secretary, *What I say three times is true*,' he did not recognize the allusion."[49] Wharton, of course, recognized the line as coming from a stanza from Carroll's famous poem.

Not all of President Roosevelt's meetings with authors took place in the White House. Given Roosevelt's passion for the outdoors, Roosevelt gravitated to the writings of naturalist John Muir. According to Douglas Brinkley, Roosevelt "read all of Muir's works."[50] One of these books was Muir's *Our National Parks*, which was published in 1901. Roosevelt supported Muir's goal to protect and expand the newly designated Yosemite National Park. On March 14, 1903, Roosevelt wrote a letter to Muir, suggesting that the two of them go camping together at Yosemite. He wrote, "I do not want anyone with me but you, and I want to drop politics absolutely for four days and just be out in the open with you."[51] In May 1903, Muir took Roosevelt on a three-day wilderness trip through Yosemite. As Brinkley put it in *The Wilderness Warrior: Theodore Roosevelt and the Crusade for America*, "Oh, what a grand time Roosevelt and Muir had together in Yosemite for those three memorable days. They hiked to and camped in many of the most beautiful spots in Yosemite."[52] This trip played a pivotal role in motivating Roosevelt to expand the Yosemite National Park and create more national parks.[53]

Roosevelt's experiences as a father of young children influenced his reading during his White House years. Roosevelt always made time for his children, often reading aloud to them in the White House library or listening in while his wife read to the children. According to Roosevelt, the children preferred it when their mother read to them, but they liked it when he read outdoor adventure stories to them:

> If their mother was absent, I would try to act as vice-mother—a poor substitute, I fear—superintending the supper and reading aloud afterwards. The children did not wish me to read the books they desired their mother to read, and I usually took some such books as *Hereward the Wake*, or *Guy Mannering*, or *The Last of the Mohicans* or else some story about a man-eating tiger, or a man-eating lion, from one of the hunting books in my library.[54]

When he was traveling on official business or his children were away at school, he wrote letters to them, and he often made references to children's books in these letters. A selection of these letters appeared in a book titled *Theodore Roosevelt's Letters to His Children*, edited by Joseph Bucklin Bishop.

This book came out a few months after Roosevelt's death on January 6, 1919, but Roosevelt assisted Bishop in assembling this book and told Bishop, "I would rather have this book published than anything that has been written about me."[55] As Peggy Sullivan pointed out in an article published in *The Horn Book* in 1959, "What we know of Roosevelt's interest in his children's reading comes mostly from his letters."[56]

Roosevelt had a strong interest in poetry for children, and he especially liked Laura E. Richards's humorous poems.[57] In several of the letters he wrote to his children, he mentioned Richards's poems, including her poem titled "Punkydoodle and Jollapin." This poem appealed to Roosevelt in part because of the following lines referring to the president:

> Oh, Pillykin Willykin Winky Wee!
> How does the President take his tea?
> He takes it in bed, he takes it in school,
> He takes it in Congress against the rule.
> He takes it with brandy, and thinks it no sin.
> Oh, Punkydoodle and Jollapin.[58]

In August 1905, he wrote a letter to his then fifteen-year-old son, Kermit, in which he described the rambunctious experience he had after reading "Punkydoodle and Jollapin" to his two youngest children, Archibald (known as Archie) and Quentin:

> I read them Laura E. Richards' poems, including "How does the President take his tea?" They christened themselves Punkeydoodle and Jollapin, from the chorus of this, and immediately afterwards I played with them on Archie's bed. First I would toss Punkeydoodle (Quentin) on Jollapin (Archie) and tickle Jollapin while Punkeydoodle sprawled and wriggled on top of him, and then reverse them and keep Punkeydoodle down by heaving Jollapin on him, while they both kicked and struggled until my shirtfront looked very much the worse for wear.[59]

In a number of the letters that Roosevelt wrote to his children, he referred to Joel Chandler Harris's Br'er Rabbit stories. Roosevelt's familiarity with Harris's writings considerably predates his years in the White House. In 1894, for example, he praised Harris in an article titled "What 'Americanism' Means," which appeared in the *Forum Magazine*.[60] During his presidency, however, his interest in Harris intensified. He read Harris's *Uncle Remus: His Songs and Sayings* aloud to his children. In the letters that he wrote to his children, he frequently mentioned Br'er Rabbit and other animal characters from Harris's stories. In a letter to Quentin, he wrote, "The other day when out riding what should I see in the road ahead of me but a real B'rer Terrapin and B'rer Rabbit. They were sitting solemnly beside one another and looked just as if they had come out of a book."[61]

Harris also struck up a correspondence with Harris. For his part, Harris regularly provided Roosevelt with copies of his books. Upon receiving an autographed copy of one of Harris's books, Roosevelt sent Harris the following letter dated October 12, 1901:

> It is worth being President when one's small daughter receives that kind of an autographed gift. When I was younger than she is, my Aunt Annie Bulloch, of Georgia, used to tell me some of the brer rabbit stories, especially brer rabbit and the tar baby. But fond though I am of the brer rabbit stories I think I am even fonder of your other writings. I doubt if there is a more genuinely pathetic tale in all of our literature than *Free Joe*. Moreover, I have felt that all that you write serves to bring our people closer together. . . . Your art is not only an addition to our sum of national achievement, but it has also always been an addition to the forces that tell for decency, and above all for blotting out of sectional antagonism.[62]

When Harris started a periodical titled *Uncle Remus's Magazine* in 1907, Roosevelt not only took out a subscription but sent a letter to Harris inviting him to the White House. Roosevelt wrote, "Can't you come up to Washington and give me the very real pleasure of having you dine at the White House? Do try to do this."[63] Harris accepted the invitation. In November 1907, Harris and his oldest son, Julian, visited Roosevelt at the White House. It was one of the few times that Harris traveled away from his native state of Georgia.[64]

Another children's author with whom Roosevelt regularly corresponded was Kenneth Grahame. Roosevelt initiated this correspondence after reading Grahame's *The Golden Age* and *Dream Days*. Upon learning of Roosevelt's interest in these two books, Grahame sent autographed copies of them to Roosevelt in 1907. The next year Grahame sent Roosevelt a copy of *The Wind in the Willows*, which had just been published in Great Britain. Roosevelt sent Grahame a polite thank you note shortly after the book arrived, but when he started reading the book, he found he did not like it as much as he did Grahame's earlier books. A few months later, however, he gave the book a second chance, and this time he fell in love with it. In a letter to Grahame dated January 17, 1909, Roosevelt explained that he initially "could not accept the toad, the mole, the water-rat, and the badger," but upon rereading the book he changed his mind:

Mrs. Roosevelt and two of the boys . . . got hold of *The Wind in the Willows* and took such a delight in it that I began to feel that I might have to revise my judgment. Then Mrs. Roosevelt read it aloud to the younger children, and I listened now and then. Now I have read it and reread it, and have come to accept the characters as old friends; and I am almost more fond of it than your previous books. Indeed, I feel about going to Africa very much as the seafaring rat did when he almost made the water rat wish to forsake everything and start wandering! I felt I must give myself the pleasure of telling you how much we had all enjoyed your book.[65]

Roosevelt let it be known to the public that he liked this book. In part because of Roosevelt's recommendation, Charles Scribner's Sons published *The Wind in the Willows* in the United States in 1909,[66] the same year that Roosevelt's presidency came to an end.

Post-Presidency Years

With the inauguration of President William Howard Taft on March 4, 1909, Roosevelt's time as the president of the United States was officially over. Roosevelt now felt free to embark on what he called his "last chance at something in the nature of a great adventure."[67] On March 23, Roosevelt, his son Kermit, and several naturalists associated with the Smithsonian set out for a year-long hunting safari in Africa.

Although Roosevelt relished the opportunity to hunt big game and spend time outdoors, he knew that he would miss having easy access to his library. He solved this problem by creating what became known as his Pigskin Library, which he took with him on his safari. He and Kermit selected around sixty favorite books, which he had rebound in pig's leather so that they would be more durable. He then packed these books in a specially built aluminum and brass trunk, and this collection of books traveled with Roosevelt throughout the expedition. Roosevelt's Pigskin Library included such classics as *The Iliad* and *The Odyssey* by Homer, *Adventures of Huckleberry Finn* by Mark Twain, *Pilgrim's Progress* by John Bunyan, and *Our Mutual Friend* by Charles Dickens.[68] In addition to reading the books in his Pigskin Library, Roosevelt wrote a series of articles about his African adventures for *Scribner's Magazine*. He brought these articles together in a book titled *African Game Trails: An Account of the African Wanderings of an American Hunter-Naturalist*, which came out in 1910.[69]

After spending around a year abroad, Roosevelt returned home to Sagamore Hill in June 1910, and he soon reengaged in the American political scene. As a leading figure in the Republican Party, he became enmeshed in the party infighting over the presidential nomination process. Some party leaders wanted President Taft to be renominated while others wanted Roosevelt to be the party's nominee. When Taft was renominated, some of the more progressive members of the party split off from the Republican Party and formed the Progressive Party, often called the Bull Moose Party. In August 1912, Roosevelt became the presidential nominee of the Progressive Party. During Roosevelt's involvement with the Progressive Party, he became more outspoken in his support of immigrants and women's suffrage. These stands were tied to his reading.

Roosevelt read Jane Addams's 1910 bestseller, *Twenty Years at Hull-House*, in which she recounted her experiences of working with immigrants living in the Chicago area. Reading this book and interacting with Addams reinforced Roosevelt's pro-immigrant stance and his growing support of the women's suffrage movement. In his autobiography he wrote, "I always favored woman's suffrage, but only tepidly, until my association with women like Jane Addams . . . changed me into a zealous instead of a lukewarm adherent of the cause."[70] Roosevelt also read Mary Antin's 1912 memoir *The Promised Land*. Roosevelt was moved by Antin's story about being a Jewish immigrant who moved from Russia to a Boston slum as a girl and ultimately made a place for herself in America. Roosevelt initiated a correspondence with Antin, and the two became political allies.[71] Both Addams and Antin campaigned for Roosevelt when he ran as the Progressive Party's candidate for president.

On November 5, 1912, Roosevelt's third-party campaign to get reelected as the president of the United States ended in defeat. Woodrow Wilson was declared the winner, and Roosevelt graciously admitted defeat and congratulated Wilson.[72] This turn of events caused Roosevelt to disengage from politics and instead focus his energy on writing his autobiography. In the words of Edmund Morris, "Roosevelt decided to make his autobiography as impersonal as possible" and as a result of this decision he "wrote hundreds of colorless paragraphs."[73] *Theodore Roosevelt: An Autobiography* came out in December 1913, and it received mixed reviews.[74] However, the one part of the autobiography that reviewers loved was the chapter titled "Outdoors and Indoors," in which where he wrote about his love of books. In this chapter, Roosevelt wrote about why he placed such a high value on the reading of literature:

> Now and then I am asked as to "what books a statesman should read," and my answer is, poetry and novels—including short stories under the head of novels.

. . . In the final event, the statesman and the publicist, and the reformer . . . all need more than anything else to know human nature, to know the needs of the human soul; and they will find this nature and these needs set forth as nowhere else by the great imaginative writers, whether of prose or of poetry.[75]

Following the publication of his autobiography, Roosevelt embarked on what would become his last strenuous, outdoor adventure. He wanted to have an exciting experience similar to his African safari expedition, but this time he set out to explore a tributary of the Amazon River. As he did when he went on his African safari, he brought a selection of books to read, including Thomas More's *Utopia* and the last two volumes of Edward Gibbon's *Decline and Fall of the Roman Empire*.[76] However, unlike his African safari, his South American exhibition proved to be a harrowing experience. He injured his leg, and the wound became seriously infected. The infection caused him to suffer from a dangerously high fever, and he started to lose consciousness. However, even as he was teetering on the brink of death, his passion for literature came to the surface. He fought off unconsciousness by repeatedly reciting the opening lines to Samuel Taylor Coleridge's poem "Kubla Khan."[77] Roosevelt survived, but three members of his party did not. He returned to his home in May 1914, and he immediately set to work on a book about his expedition. Titled *Through the Brazilian Wilderness*, the book came out at the end of 1914. It received good reviews, but Roosevelt was disappointed in the sales.[78] On the whole, his journey to South America did not rejuvenate him. He never fully recovered from the leg injury he sustained during the expedition, and his near-death experience forced him to ponder his mortality.

During his final years, Roosevelt experienced a series of disappointments. With the outbreak of World War I in Europe, Roosevelt contacted President Wilson and requested permission to organize a division of volunteers to fight in Europe if needed, but Wilson turned down his request.[79] When America entered the war, Roosevelt was pleased when all four of his sons enlisted, but his pride turned to grief when his youngest son, Quentin, was killed in action in France on July 14, 1918. As the war wore on, Roosevelt's health declined. The war came to an end on November 11, 1918, and on that very day Roosevelt was admitted to Roosevelt Hospital in New York City where he spent the next six weeks.[80] He was discharged on December 23 and spent Christmas with his family at Sagamore Hill. He died in his sleep on January 6, 1919, at the age of sixty.[81]

Although his last years were shaped by disappointments and declining health, he continued to take satisfaction in his writing. One of his last books he wrote was *A Book-Lover's Holidays in the Open*, which came out in

1916.[82] In this book, he celebrated two of his greatest passions—adventuring outdoors and reading books. It was a fitting book to come at the end of his storied life.

Notes

1. Edmund Morris, introduction to *The Seven Worlds of Theodore Roosevelt*, by Edward Wagenknecht (Guilford, CT: Lyons Press, 2009), viii.

2. Owen Wister, *Roosevelt: The Story of a Friendship, 1880–1919* (New York: Macmillan, 1930), 89.

3. Theodore Roosevelt, *Theodore Roosevelt: An Autobiography* (New York: Charles Scribner's Sons, 1913), 15.

4. David McCullough, *Mornings on Horseback* (New York: Simon & Schuster, 2003), 115–16.

5. Douglas Brinkley, *The Wilderness Warrior: Theodore Roosevelt and the Crusade for America* (New York: HarperCollins, 2009), 28.

6. Brinkley, *Wilderness Warrior*, 28.

7. Roosevelt, *Autobiography*, 15–16.

8. Roosevelt, *Autobiography*, 17.

9. Andrew Vietze, *Becoming Teddy Roosevelt: How a Maine Guide Inspired America's 26th President* (Guilford, CT: Down East Books, 2010), 29.

10. Roosevelt, *Autobiography*, 17.

11. Roosevelt, *Autobiography*, 18.

12. Brinkley, *Wilderness Warrior*, 55.

13. Roosevelt, *Autobiography*, 26–27.

14. McCullough, *Mornings*, 198.

15. Thomas Bailey and Katherine Joslin, *Theodore Roosevelt: A Literary Life* (Lebanon, NH: ForeEdge, 2018), 24.

16. Edward Wagenknecht, *The Seven Worlds of Theodore Roosevelt* (Guilford, CT: Lyons Press, 2009), 56.

17. Roosevelt, *Autobiography*, 24.

18. Bailey and Joslin, *Literary Life*, 31.

19. Wagenknecht, *Seven Worlds*, 35.

20. Edmund Morris, *The Rise of Theodore Roosevelt* (New York: Modern Library, 2001), 119–20.

21. Bailey and Joslin, *Literary Life*, 37–39.

22. Roger L. Di Silvestro, *Theodore Roosevelt in the Badlands* (New York: Walker and Co., 2011), 112.

23. Morris, *Rise*, 294.

24. Di Silvestro, *Badlands*, 206.

25. Bailey and Joslin, *Literary Life*, 47.

26. Bailey and Joslin, *Literary Life*, 78.

27. Morris, *Rise*, 394.

28. Di Silvestro, *Badlands*, 250.

29. Nathan Miller, *Theodore Roosevelt: A Life* (New York: William Morrow, 1992), 190–95.

30. Hermann Hagedorn, *The Roosevelt Family of Sagamore Hill* (New York: Macmillan, 1954), 16.

31. Mark I. West, "Theodore Roosevelt and the Golden Age of Children's Literature," *Journal of American Culture* 33, no. 2 (June 2010): 122.

32. Bailey and Joslin, *Literary Life*, 92–93.

33. Morris, *Rise*, 502.

34. Edward P. Kohn, *Heir to the Empire City: New York and the Making of Theodore Roosevelt* (New York: Basic Books, 2014), 152.

35. Roosevelt, *Autobiography*, 173–74.

36. Henry J. Hendrix, *Theodore Roosevelt's Naval Diplomacy: The U.S. Navy and the Birth of the American Century* (Annapolis: Naval Institute Press, 2009), 8.

37. Morris, *Rise*, 641–60.

38. Doris Kearns Goodwin, *The Bully Pulpit: Theodore Roosevelt, William Howard Taft, and the Golden Age of Journalism* (New York: Simon & Schuster, 2013), 228.

39. Bailey and Joslin, *Literary Life*, 123.

40. Bailey and Joslin, *Literary Life*, 134.

41. Wister, *Story of a Friendship*, 80–81.

42. Bailey and Joslin, *Literary Life*, 139.

43. Hagedorn, *Roosevelt Family*, 126–28.

44. Deborah Davis, *Guest of Honor: Booker T. Washington, Theodore Roosevelt, and the White House Dinner That Shocked a Nation* (New York: Atria Books, 2012), 203–17.

45. Bailey and Joslin, *Literary Life*, 143–44.

46. Wister, *Story of a Friendship*, 105.

47. Wister, *Story of a Friendship*, 107.

48. Bailey and Joslin, *Literary Life*, 170.

49. Edith Wharton, *A Backward Glance* (New York: Charles Scribner's Sons, 1933), 312.

50. Brinkley, *Wilderness Warrior*, 537.

51. Edmund Morris, *Theodore Rex* (New York: Random House, 2001), 230.

52. Brinkley, *Wilderness Warrior*, 545.

53. Brinkley, *Wilderness Warrior*, 547.

54. Roosevelt, *Autobiography*, 345–46.

55. Theodore Roosevelt, *Theodore Roosevelt's Letters to His Children*, ed. Joseph Bucklin Bishop (New York: Charles Scribner's Sons, 1919), 10.

56. Peggy Sullivan, "Theodore Roosevelt and Children's Books," *The Horn Book*, February 1959, 25–27.

57. Roosevelt, *Autobiography*, 15.

58. Laura E. Richards, *In My Nursery: A Book of Verse* (Boston: Little Brown, 1890), 58.

59. Roosevelt, *Letters to His Children*, 135.

60. Theodore Roosevelt, "What 'Americanism' Means," *Forum Magazine*, April 1894, 199.

61. Roosevelt, *Letters to His Children*, 101.

62. Roosevelt, *Letters to His Children*, 67–68.

63. Julia Collier Harris, *The Life and Letters of Joel Chandler Harris* (Boston: Houghton Mifflin, 1918), 511.

64. Roosevelt, *Autobiography*, 332.

65. Patrick R. Chalmers, *Kenneth Grahame: Life, Letters and Unpublished Work* (London: Methuen, 1933), 139–40.

66. Peter Hunt, *The Wind in the Willows: A Fragmented Arcadia* (New York: Twayne, 1994), xiii.

67. Miller, *A Life*, 490.

68. Patricia O'Toole, *When Trumpets Call: Theodore Roosevelt after the White House* (New York: Simon & Schuster, 2005), 57–58.

69. Morris, *Theodore Rex*, 112.

70. Roosevelt, *Autobiography*, 167.

71. Evelyn Salz, ed., *Selected Letters of Mary Antin* (Syracuse, NY: Syracuse University Press, 2000), xiii–xxii.

72. Morris, *Theodore Rex*, 252.

73. Morris, *Theodore Rex*, 275–76.

74. Bailey and Joslin, *Literary Life*, 265.

75. Roosevelt, *Autobiography*, 346–47.

76. Candice Millard, *The River of Doubt: Theodore Roosevelt's Darkest Journey* (New York: Doubleday, 2005), 311–12.

77. Millard, *River of Doubt*, 297.

78. Bailey and Joslin, *Literary Life*, 294.

79. O'Toole, *When Trumpets Call*, 311.

80. O'Toole, *When Trumpets Call*, 400–401.

81. O'Toole, *When Trumpets Call*, 402–4.

82. Bailey and Joslin, *Literary Life*, 298.

~

CHAPTER TWO

Fourteen Books That Shaped Theodore Roosevelt's Life and Career

At one point in his autobiography, Theodore Roosevelt wrote, "I have always had a horror of words that are not translated into deeds, of speech that does not result in action."[1] He made this comment when recalling his initial response to Jacob Riis's *How the Other Half Lives*. Roosevelt explained that after reading Riis's book he wanted to do something tangible to improve the horrible living conditions in the tenement homes as described by Riis. However, Roosevelt's point about translating words into deeds also shaped his responses to some other key books that he read over the course of his life. Of the thousands of books that he read, a handful stand out for having had a direct impact on his life and career. These books were not necessarily his all-time favorite books, for he loved many books simply because of the aesthetic pleasure they provided or the intriguing information and insights they contained. Still, some of the books that Roosevelt read caused him to take immediate action or alter the course of his life.

Books That Shaped Roosevelt's Boyhood and Adolescence

Roosevelt's tendency to take action as a result of reading a book can be traced back to his childhood. As an eight-year-old boy, he took an interest in the lives of animals, so his father gave him a copy of John George Wood's *Homes without Hands: Being a Description of the Habitations of Animals, Classed according to Their Principle of Construction*, a scientific treatise that originally came out in 1866. Wood, a British scholar and naturalist, intended for this book to be used as an introductory text for university biology and zoology courses, but the book's many engravings appealed to young Roosevelt. He also enjoyed reading about how animals construct burrows and other habitats.[2] As he later recalled in his autobiography, he came to regard this book as one of his "cherished possessions."[3] He especially liked the parts of the book in which Wood wrote about ant nests and tunnels. After reading these passages, Roosevelt decided to observe the behavior of ants and write down his observations. Douglas Brinkley discusses this decision in his book *The Wilderness Warriors: Theodore Roosevelt and the Crusade for America*:

> Roosevelt marveled at passages in this weighty 632-page tome about ant nests and tunnels, deciding on the spot to emulate the author. The eight-year-old Roosevelt sat down and wrote a short essay, his first known written work, titled "The Foraging Ant." . . . Proud of "The Foraging Ant," which was about the workaholism of ants, Roosevelt read the essay out loud to his parents, who were complimentary about the pseudoscientific earnestness of his naturalist prose.[4]

Roosevelt's decision to emulate Wood after reading *Homes without Hands* persisted throughout his childhood and adolescence. Reading this book served as a catalyst that sparked Roosevelt's decision to pursue a career in the natural sciences.

Roosevelt read many works of natural history during his childhood and adolescence, but he especially liked John James Audubon's *The Birds of America*. Originally published as a multi-volume work between 1827 and 1838, *The Birds of America* made history for its detailed illustrations of more than four hundred birds native to North America. Roosevelt's introduction to this work occurred in November 1872 during a family trip to Europe. While visiting relatives in Liverpool, he borrowed his aunt's copy of *The Birds of America*, and he spent hours examining every page.[5] He so loved Audubon's work that he ended up obtaining his own copy of *The Birds of America*. His fascination in Audubon's approach to ornithology led him to take an interest in taxidermy. As a teenager, he studied taxidermy with John Graham Bell, a taxidermist who worked closely with Audubon when Audubon was collecting bird specimens that he depicted in *The Birds of America*.[6]

Roosevelt became so interested in Audubon's work that he decided that he wanted to pursue a career doing the type of field work that Audubon conducted while creating *The Birds of America*. When he entered Harvard, he brought his copy of *The Birds of America* with him with the hopes of using it as an inspiration for his studies. Initially, he wanted to study the natural sciences and become an ornithologist like Audubon, but he was disappointed to learn that the Harvard science curriculum did not support the type of field research that appealed to him.[7] Although Roosevelt did not focus on studying the natural sciences at Harvard, his interest in Audubon resulted in his first publication. After finishing his freshman year at Harvard, he and a college friend named Henry Minot spent the summer writing a booklet titled *The Summer Birds of the Adirondacks*, which was privately printed in 1877.[8]

Roosevelt did not pursue a career as an ornithologist, but he remained interested in Audubon and the field of ornithology for the rest of his life. He helped George Bird Grinnell found the Audubon Society in 1886, and he supported Grinnell's efforts to protect endangered birds.[9] Early in his presidency, he signed an executive order establishing Pelican Island off the coast of Florida as the first federal bird reservation. He then went on to establish fifty other bird preserves over the course of his presidency.[10]

In addition to reading books about the natural sciences, Roosevelt read many novels during his childhood and adolescent years. Of these novels, the two that had an especially significant impact on his later life were Thomas Mayne Reid's *The Boy Hunters; or, Adventures in Search of a White Buffalo* and Frederick Marryat's *Mr. Midshipman Easy*. Both of these novels appealed to young Roosevelt's taste for escapist adventure stories, but they also had a lasting impact on his adult interests and views.

Reid, an Irish-American novelist and veteran of the Mexican-American War, took an interest in the American West not long after he immigrated to America from Ireland in 1840. He traveled throughout Texas and other areas in the Southwest, and he often used western settings in his novels. He published his first novel, *The Rifle Rangers*, in 1850, and he went on to write seventy-five novels, including Roosevelt's favorite, *The Boy Hunters; or, Adventures in Search of a White Buffalo*, which came out in 1853.[11] *The Boy Hunters* is about three brothers who travel across the Texas prairie in pursuit of a rare white buffalo. The novel is a combination of an adventure story and a travelogue, and it includes lots of details about the flora and fauna found in this part of Texas. Reid's depiction of the American West resonated with Roosevelt. In his autobiography, he recalled that Reid's novel "strengthened my instinctive interest in natural history. I was too young to understand much of Mayne Reid, excepting the adventure part and the natural history part—these enthralled me."[12] As Douglas Brinkley argues in *The Wilderness Warrior*, Roosevelt's boyhood love of *The Boy Hunters* played a role in shaping Roosevelt's lifelong love of the wilderness and his deep-seated interest in the history of the American West.[13]

Another adventure story that Roosevelt especially liked as a boy was Frederick Marryat's *Mr. Midshipman Easy*. First published in 1836, this nautical novel is set during the Napoleonic Wars, and it is based in part on the author's experiences as a retired captain in the Royal Navy. Marryat's depictions of life in the Royal Navy greatly appealed to Roosevelt, and it helped spark his interest in naval history. On another level, this novel played a role in his efforts to overcome his childhood insecurities associated with his chronic asthma. Andrew Vietze elaborates on this point in his book *Becoming Teddy Roosevelt*:

> He didn't want to be confined to the sickroom, he didn't want to be afraid of the bigger boys, and he didn't want to be so shy. In later years he often referred to an incident in Frederick Marryat's *Mr. Midshipman Easy* where a sea captain on a British man-of-war is counseling a sailor who is struggling with his fears. The captain tells him that he, too, used to be afraid heading into action, but made up his mind to act unafraid. Despite how he felt inside he would give the outward appearance of courage—and after a while that was how he actually felt. It was a lesson that stuck in TR's mind—whatever circumstances he confronted he was determined to act courageous.[14]

History Books That Shaped Roosevelt's Career

Roosevelt's interest in naval history intensified during his years at Harvard. He read a wide variety of books related to naval history while still a college student, but he took a special interest in books about the history of the U.S. Navy. His interest in this topic led him to read James Fenimore Cooper's *Naval History of the United States*, which first came out in 1839. As a boy, Roosevelt had read many of Cooper's novels, including *The Last of the Mohicans*, so he already had an appreciation for Cooper's contributions to American literature.[15] Roosevelt liked Cooper's literary approach to writing about naval history. Also, since Cooper served in the U.S. Navy as a young man, he was able to write from his own experiences, and this aspect of Cooper's book appealed to Roosevelt. However, Roosevelt felt that Cooper's account of the U.S. Navy's role in the War of 1812 did not pay sufficient attention to the "British side of the question" and that that it was written "without great regard for exactness."[16] He therefore set out to write a more impartial account based on the naval records from both sides of the war. Thus, even though Roosevelt questioned Cooper's approach and methodology, it was in part because of his response to Cooper's *Naval History of the United States* that

Roosevelt wrote *The Naval War of 1812*, the book that launched his career as a published author.

Roosevelt remained interested in naval history long after the publication of his book *The Naval War of 1812* in 1882. When new works came out on the topic, he often read them shortly after their publication. One such book was Alfred Thayer Mahan's *The Influence of Sea Power upon History*. Little, Brown published Mahan's book in the spring of 1890, and Roosevelt read it that May over the course of a weekend. As Edmund Morris writes in *The Rise of Theodore Roosevelt*, Roosevelt was intrigued with Mahan's analysis of "the intricate relationship between political power and sea power, warfare and economics, geography and technology. Roosevelt flipped the book shut a changed man."[17] As soon as he finished the book, he sent Mahan a letter praising the book, and soon thereafter they began corresponding on a regular basis. Persuaded by Mahan's argument that national greatness is tied to maintaining a strong navy, Roosevelt became a tireless and vocal advocate for building a larger and more modern U.S. Navy. His advocacy resulted in Roosevelt being named the assistant secretary of the navy in 1897. During the time he served in this position, he often consulted with Mahan about naval matters, and he often recommended that the leaders of the U.S. Navy read and take to heart Mahan's *The Influence of Sea Power upon History*.[18]

Roosevelt's passion for reading works of history extended well beyond the field of naval history. He also enjoyed reading books about the history of the American West. His interest in this topic intensified after he moved to the Dakota Territory in 1884 and tried his hand at raising cattle on his Elkhorn Ranch. Of the many books that he read about the history of the West during this period in his life, the book that had the greatest impact on him was Francis Parkman's *The Oregon Trail: Sketches of Prairie and Rocky-Mountain Life*. Parkman's *Oregon Trail* is a first-person account of the author's adventures traveling through what are now the states of Nebraska, Wyoming, Colorado, and Kansas during the summer of 1846, when the author was a twenty-three-year-old recent graduate of Harvard. The book came out in 1849 after first being serialized in *Knickerbocker's Magazine*. In the words of Douglas Brinkley, the book deeply resonated with Roosevelt: "It electrified Roosevelt that Parkman, a fellow Harvard alumnus (class of 1846), had used his classical education to honor the western frontier in serious historical prose. Roosevelt adopted Parkman—a devoted naturalist and horticulturalist, with expertise in roses and lilies—as his guiding light in history studies."[19] In recognition of his respect for Parkman's work, Roosevelt dedicated his four-volume history of the American frontier, *The Winning of the West*, to Parkman.[20]

During Roosevelt's time in the Dakota Territory, he also read Henry Cabot Lodge's *Daniel Webster*, which Houghton, Mifflin and Company published in 1883 as part of their American Statesmen Series. Roosevelt enjoyed reading Lodge's account of Webster's career as a constitutional lawyer, U.S. senator, and secretary of state, and he let Lodge know that he would be interested in trying his hand at writing a similar volume for the American Statesmen Series. Since Roosevelt and Lodge were friends, Lodge, to quote Edmund Morris, "pulled a few strings, with the result that Roosevelt received a commission to write an American Statesmen book. His biography was to be of Senator Thomas Hart Benton, the Western expansionist."[21] In a letter Roosevelt sent to Lodge in May 1886, he praised Lodge's biography of Webster and made it clear that he was using Lodge's biography as a model for his biography of Benton.[22] While writing this biography in the near solitude of his Dakota ranch, Roosevelt found it difficult to conduct research on Benton. He sent a letter to Lodge's Boston residence in which he asked Lodge for help with a series of questions about dates related to Benton's life. "I hate to trouble you," he wrote, "but the Bad Lands have much fewer books than Boston has."[23] With assistance from Lodge, Roosevelt's *Thomas Hart Benton* came out in 1887. Roosevelt went on to write several other biographies, including *Gouverneur Morris*, which was also part of the American Statesmen Series.[24] Roosevelt and Lodge remained interested in the lives of American statesmen, and this interest resulted in them co-writing a children's book titled *Hero Tales from American History*, which came out in 1895.[25]

Issue-Oriented Books That Shaped Roosevelt's Career

Roosevelt often read books about social problems and issues, and one such book was Jacob A. Riis's *How the Other Half Lives: Studies among the Tenements of New York*, which came out in 1890. Riis was a Danish immigrant who moved to New York City as a young man. After landing a job as a police reporter for the *New York Tribune*, he spent more than twenty years writing about crime in New York City. His work as a reporter brought him into close contact with the immigrants who lived in New York's crowded tenements, and he was appalled at the living conditions that these people faced. In *How the Other Half Lives*, Riis not only wrote about this problem, but he also included photographs that he took himself. Roosevelt read *How the Other Half Lives* soon after its publication, and the book so impressed him that he immediately contacted Riis.[26] Some years later, Riis wrote about how they became acquainted:

He came to my office one day when I was out and left his card with the simple words written upon it: "I have read your book, and I have come to help." That was the beginning. The book was *How the Other Half Lives*, in which I tried to draw an indictment of the things that were wrong, pitifully and dreadfully wrong, with the tenement homes of our wage-workers. It was like a man coming to enlist for a war because he believed in the cause, and truly he did.[27]

The two men became close friends and steadfast political allies. Inspired by Riis's writings, Roosevelt set out to improve the living conditions in New York's tenements. During Roosevelt's time as the New York police commissioner, Roosevelt relied on Riis to help him with his on-site investigations and his efforts to initiate reforms.[28] In his autobiography, Roosevelt credited Riis for providing him with the information he needed to carry out his reform agenda: "I used to visit the different tenement-house regions, usually with Riis, to see for myself what the conditions were. . . . The trips that Riis and I took enabled me to see what the Police department was doing, and also gave me personal insight into some of the problems of city life."[29] For his part, Riis wrote a supportive biography titled *Theodore Roosevelt, the Citizen*, which came out in 1904. Riis remained a stalwart supporter of Roosevelt right up until his death in 1914.[30]

Another issue that concerned Roosevelt was the threat to America's wilderness areas. Of the many books he read on this topic, John Muir's *Our National Parks* had a particularly strong impact on him. Originally published by Houghton, Mifflin in 1901, *Our National Parks* consists of ten essays that first appeared as individual articles in the *Atlantic Monthly*. In these essays, Muir described the national parks that existed at that time, including Yosemite National Park, which Muir helped create in 1892. After reading this book, Roosevelt reached out to Muir for advice about expanding the national park system. Roosevelt shared Muir's desire to protect the timberlands in and around the Yosemite National Park, and he wrote to Muir suggesting that they go camping together in Yosemite so that they could formulate a plan to expand the national forest reserves. In May 1903, Roosevelt and Muir hiked through Yosemite together and camped out for three nights. During this camping trip, Roosevelt and Muir forged an alliance that had tangible results. Soon after their meeting, Roosevelt set into motion a plan that resulted in a tremendous expansion of the land set aside for national forests and the creation of five additional national parks.[31]

Shortly after Muir's death on December 24, 1914, Roosevelt celebrated Muir's life in an essay titled "John Muir: An Appreciation." He concluded his essay by praising Muir's books: "He wrote well, and while his books have not the peculiar charm that a very, very few writers on similar subjects have had, they will nevertheless last long. Our generation owes much to John Muir."[32]

Roosevelt's desire to preserve national forests led him to take an interest in the writings of Gifford Pinchot, who is widely recognized as America's first professionally trained forester. After graduating from Yale in 1889, Pinchot went to Europe and studied forestry. Upon his return to America, he wrote several technical works about forestry, including A *Primer of Forestry*, the first volume of which came out in 1899. Pinchot's forestry publications came to Roosevelt's attention, and Roosevelt ended up agreeing with Pinchot about the importance of professional forest management. In 1899 the two of them met while Roosevelt was serving as the governor of New York, and they forged a lasting friendship and political alliance at this meeting.[33] During the early years of his presidency Roosevelt often consulted with Pinchot about conservation issues, and in 1905 Roosevelt named Pinchot to the position of chief of the U.S. Forest Service.[34]

Of Pinchot's various books, the one that had the greatest impact on Roosevelt was *The Fight for Conservation*, which was published in 1910. Unlike Pinchot's more technical publications, *The Fight for Conservation* took the form of a political manifesto. It starts with an appeal to action:

> The most prosperous nation of to-day is the United States. Our unexampled wealth and well-being are directly due to the superb natural resources of our country, and to the use which has been made of them by our citizens, both in the present and in the past. We are prosperous because our forefathers bequeathed to us a land of marvelous resources still unexhausted. Shall we conserve those resources, and in our turn transmit them, still unexhausted, to our descendants? Unless we do, those who come after us will have to pay the price of misery, degradation, and failure for the progress and prosperity of our day. When the natural resources of any nation become exhausted, disaster and decay in every department of national life follow as a matter of course. Therefore, the conservation of natural resources is the basis, and the only permanent basis, of national success. There are other conditions, but this one lies at the foundation.[35]

Roosevelt so liked the book's activist message that he wrote a public letter promoting the book and its author. In the letter, he praised Pinchot for being "fearless in opposing wrong, whether by a great corporation or by a mob; by a wealthy financier, or by a demagogue."[36] The book played a pivotal role in launching the conservation movement.[37] Moreover, *The Fight for Conservation* helped persuade Roosevelt to make conservation a cornerstone of his campaign as the Progressive Party candidate for the presidency.[38] Although Roosevelt lost this campaign, he never lost his admiration for Pinchot's contributions to the conservation movement. In his autobiography, Roosevelt wrote, "Gifford Pinchot is the man to whom the nation owes most for what has been accomplished as regards the preservation of the natural resources of our country."[39]

Autobiographies That Shaped Roosevelt's Career

Throughout his adult life, Roosevelt often read autobiographies and memoirs of people he admired, and in some cases, the experience of reading these works influenced his career. Such was the case when he read Booker T. Washington's *Up from Slavery*. Washington provided Roosevelt with an advance copy of the book, and Roosevelt read it as soon as it arrived. He then recommended it to his wife, and she read it, too. On March 21, 1901, Roosevelt sent Washington a thank-you note in which he wrote, "Mrs. Roosevelt is as much pleased as I am with your book. I shall not try to tell you what I think about it, my dear sir, for I do not want to seem to flatter you too much. . . . I do not know who could take your place in the work you are doing."[40]

Roosevelt especially liked the chapters in the book about the Tuskegee Institute, which Washington founded in 1881. After reading *Up from Slavery*, Roosevelt resolved to do what he could to support Washington's Tuskegee Institute. Roosevelt met with Washington in Roosevelt's office in New York City on April 1, 1901, and the two of them made plans for Roosevelt to visit Tuskegee later in the year. Since Roosevelt was the vice president of the United States at the time, this planned visit was seen as an opportunity for Roosevelt to draw national attention to the Tuskegee Institute and its educational programs.[41] However, when the assassination of William McKinley elevated Roosevelt to the presidency, Roosevelt had to cancel his upcoming visit to Tuskegee. Instead, Roosevelt invited Washington to have dinner with him at White House, which took place on October 16, 1901. Some racist editorial writers condemned Roosevelt for having dinner with Washington, but Roosevelt did not back down. In a letter he sent to a friend, he wrote, "There are certain points where I would not swerve from my views if the entire people was a unit against me, and this is one of them. I would not lose my self-respect by fearing to have a man like Booker T. Washington to dinner if it cost me every political friend."[42] Roosevelt eventually made good on his commitment to visit Tuskegee. On October 24, 1905, Roosevelt visited Tuskegee Institute where he delivered a speech in which he proclaimed, "I will do all I can to help Tuskegee."[43]

Another autobiographical work that had an impact on Roosevelt was Jane Addams's *Twenty Years at Hull House*, which was first published in 1910. As this memoir recounts, Addams founded Hull House in Chicago in 1889. Intended as a settlement house to help recent immigrants adapt to life in America, Hull House became famous for its innovative support services and educational programs. Roosevelt already knew Addams before reading *Twenty Years at Hull House*. In fact, he had visited Hull House several times during his presidency and publicly supported Addams's efforts to help immigrants.[44] At one point, for example, he gave a speech at the Chicago Armory to a group of naturalized citizens associated with Hull House. It was during this visit that he informed Addams of his plan to come out in favor of women's suffrage.[45] As he stated in a letter that he sent to Addams, he admired the "eminent sanity, good humor and judgment you always display."[46] After reading *Twenty Years at Hull House*, he reached out to Addams and solicited her support for his 1912 presidential campaign. Addams was pleased with Roosevelt's pro-immigrant positions and his support for women's suffrage, and she agreed to support his candidacy. She not only campaigned for him; she seconded his nomination during the Progressive Party's convention in August 1912.[47]

Mary Antin's 1912 memoir *The Promised Land* also shaped Roosevelt's interest in supporting immigrants to the United States. Roosevelt was moved by Antin's story about being a Jewish immigrant who moved from Russia to Boston as a thirteen-year-old girl and ultimately made a place for herself in America. After reading *The Promised Land*, Roosevelt contacted Antin, and the two quickly became political allies. Antin strongly argued for unrestricted immigration, and she felt encouraged when Roosevelt and his Progressive Party took a stand in favor of open immigration. Like Addams, Antin campaigned for Roosevelt and continued to support the Progressive Party even after Roosevelt's defeat in the 1912 election.[48]

After the election, Roosevelt and Antin continued to exchange letters. In 1913, Roosevelt sent Antin a letter in which and asked her to contribute a photograph of herself for a collection of photographs he was compiling of "ideal Americans." He wrote, "You are an American in whom I so deeply believe that I should be sorry if I could not include your photograph with those of Jane Addams and Miss [Frances Alice] Kellor [a lawyer who worked on behalf of immigrants]."[49] In 1914, Antin sent Roosevelt a specially bound edition of *The Promised Land*, and Roosevelt responded by writing, "It will occupy, as long as I live, one of the most honored places in my library."[50]

The aforementioned books are just a tiny sliver of the thousands of books that Roosevelt read over the course of his life, but Roosevelt's responses to these fourteen books provide good examples of how Roosevelt's reading often informed his actions. Moreover, his responses to several of these books suggest that reading contributed to Roosevelt's sense of empathy. His love of reading autobiographies, for example, gave him insights into the lives of people whose experiences differed vastly from his own, and these insights helped him forge meaningful connections with Americans from many walks of life.

Notes

1. Theodore Roosevelt, *Theodore Roosevelt: An Autobiography* (New York: Charles Scribner's Sons, 1913), 174.

2. Douglas Brinkley, *The Wilderness Warrior: Theodore Roosevelt and the Crusade for America* (New York: HarperCollins, 2009), 29.

3. Roosevelt, *Autobiography*, 18.

4. Brinkley, *Wilderness Warrior*, 28–29.

5. Thomas Bailey and Katherine Joslin, *Theodore Roosevelt: A Literary Life* (Lebanon, NH: ForeEdge, 2018), 16–17.

6. David McCullough, *Mornings on Horseback* (New York: Simon & Schuster, 2003), 118.

7. Brinkley, *Wilderness Warrior*, 101.

8. Bailey and Joslin, *Literary Life*, 22.

9. Brinkley, *Wilderness Warrior*, 189.

10. Brinkley, *Wilderness Warrior*, 828–29.

11. Roy W. Meyer, "The Western Fiction of Mayne Reid," *Western American Literature* 3, no. 2 (Summer 1968), 115–132.

12. Roosevelt, *Autobiography*, 15–16.

13. Brinkley, *Wilderness Warrior*, 26–27.

14. Andrew Vietze, *Becoming Teddy Roosevelt: How a Maine Guide Inspired America's 26th President* (Guilford, CT: Down East Books, 2010), 29.

15. Brinkley, *Wilderness Warrior*, 40–41.

16. Bailey and Joslin, *Literary Life*, 31.

17. Edmund Morris, *The Rise of Theodore Roosevelt* (New York: Modern Library, 2001), 433–34.

18. Henry J. Hendrix, *Theodore Roosevelt's Naval Diplomacy: The U.S. Navy and the Birth of the American Century* (Annapolis: Naval Institute Press, 2009), 8–17.

19. Brinkley, *Wilderness Warrior*, 128.

20. Morris, *Rise*, 393.

21. Morris, *Rise*, 316.

22. Henry Cabot Lodge, *Selections from the Correspondence of Theodore Roosevelt and Henry Cabot Lodge, 1884–1918* (New York: Charles Scribner's Sons, 1925), 40.

23. Lodge, *Correspondence*, 41.

24. Bailey and Joslin, *Literary Life*, 76.

25. Bailey and Joslin, *Literary Life*, 333.

26. Doris Kearns Goodwin, *The Bully Pulpit: Theodore Roosevelt, William Howard Taft, and the Golden Age of Journalism* (New York: Simon & Schuster, 2013), 204–6.

27. Jacob A. Riis, *Theodore Roosevelt, the Citizen* (New York: Macmillan, 1904), 131–32.

28. H. W. Brands, *T. R.: The Last Romantic* (New York: Basic Books, 1997), 274.

29. Roosevelt, *Autobiography*, 204–5.

30. Alexander Alland, *Jacob Riis: Photographer and Citizen* (New York: Aperture, 1974), 33–34.

31. Thurman Wilkins, *John Muir: Apostle of Nature* (Norman: University of Oklahoma Press, 1995), 214–18.

32. Theodore Roosevelt, "John Muir: An Appreciation," *Outlook* 109 (January 6, 1915), 28.

33. Timothy Egan, *The Big Burn: Teddy Roosevelt and the Fire That Saved America* (New York: Mariner Books, 2009), 24–26.

34. Gifford Pinchot, *Breaking New Ground* (New York: Harcourt, Brace & Company, 1947), 150–62.

35. Gifford Pinchot, *The Fight for Conservation* (New York: Doubleday, Page & Company, 1910), 3–4.

36. Brinkley, *Wilderness Warrior*, 805.

37. Jason R. Holley, "Gifford Pinchot and *The Fight for Conservation*," *Journalism History* 42, no. 2 (2016): 91–99.

38. Martin L. Fausold, *Gifford Pinchot: Bull Moose Progressive* (Westport, CT: Greenwood Press, 1961), 41–42.

39. Roosevelt, *Autobiography*, 409.

40. Deborah Davis, *Guest of Honor: Booker T. Washington, Theodore Roosevelt, and the White House Dinner That Shocked a Nation* (New York: Atria Books, 2012), 120.

41. Davis, *Guest of Honor*, 120–21.

42. Bailey and Joslin, *Literary Life*, 144.

43. Robert J. Norrell, *Up from History: The Life of Booker T. Washington* (Cambridge, MA: Harvard University Press, 2009), 10.

44. James Weber Linn, *Jane Addams: A Biography* (New York: D. Appleton-Century, 1935), 260.

45. Leslie Leighninger, "Jane Addams and the Campaign of Theodore Roosevelt," *Journal of Progressive Human Services* 15, no. 2 (2004): 57.

46. H. W. Brands, ed., *Selected Letters of Theodore Roosevelt* (Lanham, MD: Rowman & Littlefield, 2001), 405.

47. Edmund Morris, *Colonel Roosevelt* (New York: Random House, 2010), 221–22.

48. Evelyn Salz, ed., *Selected Letters of Mary Antin* (Syracuse, NY: Syracuse University Press, 2000), xvii.

49. Salz, *Selected Letters of Mary Antin*, 151–52.

50. Salz, *Selected Letters of Mary Antin*, 152.

CHAPTER THREE

~

Theodore Roosevelt's Library at Sagamore Hill

Theodore Roosevelt's books, like Theodore Roosevelt himself, were well traveled. He acquired books wherever he went, and always brought books with him when he was away from home. Even while living in temporary residences, he surrounded himself with books. During the years of his presidency, for example, he maintained a book-lined study on the second floor of the White House, and he held most of his official meetings in this study.[1] The books from this study and most of the other books he accumulated over the course of his momentous life eventually came to rest at Sagamore Hill, Roosevelt's permanent home located near the town of Oyster Bay in Long Island, New York.

At the time of Roosevelt's death on January 6, 1919, Sagamore Hill contained approximately twelve thousand books. This number does not include all of the books that Roosevelt ever owned and read. He often gave his books to friends and family members. For example, he gave his daughter Ethel Roosevelt Derby his famous Pigskin Library that he took with him on his African safari in 1909, and her family eventually donated these books to the Theodore Roosevelt Collection at the Harvard College Library.[2] Still, the twelve thousand books included the majority of the books that Roosevelt owned as an adult.

Roosevelt's wife, Edith Roosevelt, continued to live at Sagamore Hill until her death in 1948, and during this period, about four thousand of the books were given away or claimed by various members of the family. When the Roosevelt Memorial Association acquired the house in 1948, it came with approximately eight thousand books. These books remained in the home when it was eventually transferred to the National Park Service in 1963.[3]

Sagamore Hill was opened to the public in 1953, and ever since visitors have marveled at all the books that are scattered throughout the home. Roosevelt's presence comes through clearly when one sees the books that he read. These books reflect his love of classic works of literature, his interest in history, and his fascination with the natural sciences. Because many of these books are shelved in the same bookcases that he and his family used so many decades ago, the arrangement of the books also speaks to his tastes and intellectual proclivities. One can see how he grouped books, how he favored certain books by giving them prime bookshelf space, and how he displayed his books with other objects that had meaning for him. Roosevelt was an avid reader, and his library captures this important side of his life.

Sagamore Hill as a Family Home

The history of Roosevelt's library at Sagamore Hill can be traced back to 1880, the year he married his first wife, Alice Hathaway Lee. They lived in a brownstone home in Manhattan, but they had long-term plans to move to Oyster Bay. He had many positive associations with Oyster Bay since his family often spent their summers there during his growing-up years.[4] In 1880, he purchased more than a hundred acres of farmland on the Cove Neck peninsula near Oyster Bay, and he and his wife began making plans to build a Queen Anne–style home on the land.[5] Roosevelt initially intended to call their home Leeholm in honor of his wife and her family. He made a few preliminary sketches of his plans for the interior of this house, which included a first-floor library.[6] However, he and his wife did not initiate the construction of this envisioned home during their time together.

On February 14, 1884, Roosevelt's wife died from kidney failure shortly after giving birth to their daughter (named Alice after her mother). Roosevelt's mother, Martha Bulloch Roosevelt, died from typhoid fever on this same day, and these deaths caused him to sink into a period of depression. Immediately after the death of his wife, he decided to vacate their brownstone home in Manhattan and implement their plan to build a new home in Oyster Bay. Two weeks after her death, he signed a contract with a builder to start construction. A few months later, he headed off for the Dakota Territory and left it to his sister Anna, generally known as Bamie, to take care of his infant daughter and oversee the construction of the home.[7] Roosevelt saw the completed home for the first time in the summer of 1885, and at that point he decided to rename it Sagamore Hill in honor of Sagamore Mohannis, an Indian chieftain whom he admired.[8]

Even after the completion of Sagamore Hill, the house remained vacant most of the time until after Roosevelt married Edith Kermit Carow in December 1886. After taking an extensive honeymoon trip in Europe, the couple moved into Sagamore Hill in May 1887.[9] Although they and their growing family sometimes spent extended periods of time away from Sagamore Hill, it functioned as their permanent home for the entirety of their marriage.

The Library at Sagamore Hill

Of the many rooms in Sagamore Hill, Roosevelt's favorite was his library. Located just off the front hall, the library housed hundreds of books, a large writing desk, a painting of Roosevelt's father, and many personal items. As Bill Bleyer points out in *Sagamore Hill: Theodore Roosevelt's Summer White House*, Roosevelt "chose the library across the hall as his personal space, where he could write under the gaze of a portrait of his father."[10] For several years, the library also functioned as a family room where Roosevelt and his wife would gather their children together and read aloud to them.[11]

The Library at Sagamore Hill, 1904. *Courtesy of Sagamore Hill National Historic Site, National Park Service, Oyster Bay, NY*

These read-aloud sessions were an important family tradition. According to Amy Verone, Roosevelt and his wife associated reading aloud to their children with a larger effort to educate their children.[12] The experience of being read to left a lasting impression on the Roosevelt children. In her memoir titled *Crowded Hours*, Alice Roosevelt Longworth (the oldest of the Roosevelt children) wrote, "Both Father and Mother read aloud to us a great deal when we were children." As she recalled, this ritual usually took place "after supper."[13] Her brother Theodore Roosevelt III also wrote about these reading-aloud sessions in his memoir titled *All in the Family*. He wrote, "When father read to us, we all interrupted him continually with questions . . . [and] soon the reading almost stopped. Father hit on a device to save the situation. He said he would answer all questions, but not until the reading was finished for the day."[14]

After Roosevelt became president in 1901, his library at Sagamore Hill took on a new role, especially during the summer months. As president, Roosevelt often spent his summers at Sagamore Hill, which is why it came to be known as the Summer White House. Roosevelt transformed the library into the main place where he conducted the nation's business during these summer months. He arranged to have a telephone installed in the library, and he used the library as an official meeting room. Nearly every morning, he met with his office staff in the library, and in the afternoons, he often welcomed cabinet members and diplomats to the library for high-level meetings. When he was not conducting meetings, he sat at his desk in the library where he read reports and correspondence and dictated letters. In quiet moments, however, he selected a book from the shelves in the library and immersed himself in its pages. During the Summer White House years, Roosevelt's family members seldom gathered in the library, but once Roosevelt's presidency came to an end, the library once again doubled as a family room.[15]

Roosevelt kept the core of his book collection in his library at Sagamore Hill, but the library was by no means the only room in the home that contained books. Once the shelves in his library reached capacity, he started shelving books in the north room, an addition constructed in 1905 to serve as a receiving room for important guests. After Roosevelt's presidency ended, he moved many of the books from his study in the White House to the north room. This room is also where he set up two of the large bookcases from his White House study. These bookcases were given to Roosevelt by Charles McKim, the architect who worked with Roosevelt during the remodeling of the White House in 1902.[16]

He kept many of his books about science and natural history in a spacious, third-floor room that he called the gun room since he also used it to store his rifles and other firearms. Roosevelt was particularly proud of his extensive "big game library," which he believed was one of the largest collections of hunting books in America.[17] Fittingly, he kept many of these books in the gun room. Roosevelt also used this room as a study. He kept a large desk in this room, and he wrote several of his books there, including his scholarly biography of Gouverneur Morris (an American statesman and signatory of the U.S. Constitution) and *The Rough Riders*.[18] When he was working on *The Rough Riders*, he dictated the text to a stenographer and then had a secretary type it. He arranged to have a second desk installed in the gun room for his secretary to use.[19]

The drawing room, which the family sometimes called the parlor, functioned as Edith Roosevelt's personal space, and she kept many of her books in this room. As Lewis L. Gould comments in *Edith Kermit Roosevelt: Creating the Modern First Lady*, she shared her husband's love of reading, but she did not always read the same books that he read:

> Theodore Roosevelt was a prodigious reader, but his wife may well have equaled his devotion to literature and commitment to reading. . . . While she and Theodore read many books in common, . . . their tastes in literature differed. . . . Edith preferred authors such as William Makepeace Thackeray and other nineteenth-century British writers.[20]

She was also interested in collecting "elusive editions" of her favorite books, and she enjoyed going on book-hunting expeditions at Loudermilk's Bookstore in Washington, D.C.[21] The books in the drawing room reflected her literary tastes and collecting interests.

The children's bedrooms on the second floor also included bookcases. The six Roosevelt children often moved from bedroom to bedroom over the course of their growing-up years, and the boys sometimes shared rooms. As a result, the books located in these bedrooms were not always easily identified as belonging to a particular Roosevelt child. However, Alice Roosevelt, the oldest of the Roosevelt children, was the first to have her own bedroom, so the books in her bedroom clearly belonged to her. In general, the books in the children's bedrooms were tied to the evolving reading interests of children.[22]

In his autobiography, Roosevelt included a chapter titled "Outdoors and Indoors" in which he celebrated his family's shared passion for books. This passion, he wrote, resulted in books being scattered throughout Sagamore Hill:

> The books are everywhere. There are as many in the north room and in the parlor—is drawing-room a more appropriate name than parlor?—as in the

library; the gun-room at the top of the house, which incidentally has the love-
liest view of all, contains more books than any of the other rooms; and they
are particularly delightful books to browse among, just because they have not
much relevance to one another, this being one of the reasons why they are
relegated to their present abode. But the books have overflowed into all of the
other rooms too. . . . Let me add that ours is in no sense a collector's library.
Each book was procured because some one of the family wished to read it. We
could never afford to take overmuch thought for the outsides of books; we were
too much interested in their insides.[23]

Roosevelt was not the only person who commented on all the books in
Sagamore Hill. Edith Wharton, one of Roosevelt's author friends, visited
Roosevelt for a luncheon at Sagamore Hill not long after he had completed
his term as president. In her autobiography, A Backward Glance, she recounted her impressions of Roosevelt and his house during this visit, which
proved to be the last time she saw him. She described him as being "absorbed
in books and nature, and in the quiet interests of country life." She then
commented on Sagamore Hill: "The house was like one big library, and the
whole tranquil place breathed of the love of books and of the country, so that
I felt immediately at home there."[24]

Roosevelt's post-presidency years were action packed. He took a year-long
safari in Africa, ran for president as a third-party candidate, and explored an
uncharted tributary of the Amazon River. However, even up to the very end of
his life, he found time to read books. As Thomas Bailey and Katherine Joslin
state in their book Theodore Roosevelt: A Literary Life, during Roosevelt's last
year of life, he "kept up his intense schedule of reading almost anything that
came into his hands, forever having a book going, learning, disagreeing, sometimes just reading for pleasure."[25] He not only read the books from his own
personal library, but he also read books that he obtained from his local town library. Shortly before he died, he asked his wife to go to the Oyster Bay Library
to check out some works of popular fiction that appealed to him.[26] Bailey and
Joslin conclude their book by writing, "He was a man of letters, of language, a
spokesman for human imagination expressed in words, a tireless reader of these
words himself, a believer, finally, in language in all of its forms."[27]

During Roosevelt's final months, he suffered from inflammatory rheuma-
tism, vertigo, and other debilitating ailments, but he continued to read on a
nearly daily basis. Sometimes he would read aloud to his wife, and sometimes
she would read aloud to him. A few days before his death, he struggled out
of his bed, slowly made his way downstairs, and spent the day in his beloved
library, reclining on the sofa while reading a book.[28]

The Preservation of Roosevelt's Library

Roosevelt's funeral took place on January 8, 1919, and shortly thereafter Edith Roosevelt temporarily closed Sagamore Hill and went to live with relatives and then to travel to Europe. During this time, the 1919 probate inventory was conducted, which provided a listing of objects and books associated with Sagamore Hill. She contemplated selling the home, but she eventually decided to return to Sagamore Hill and keep it as "a center for the family."[29] She made some changes to the house over the nearly thirty years that she lived there on her own.[30] However, one room that she did not change was the library. In a letter she wrote to her son Kermit many years after Roosevelt's death, she said that "[s]till I find father" in the library.[31]

Following the death of Edith Roosevelt in 1948, the Roosevelt Memorial Association (renamed the Theodore Roosevelt Association in 1953) purchased Sagamore Hill along with the furnishings and "miscellaneous personal property," which included eight thousand books.[32] The association oversaw a three-year restoration of the home with the plan of eventually opening the home to the public. On June 14, 1953, the association opened Sagamore Hill to the public. President Dwight D. Eisenhower presided over the opening ceremonies. Also in attendance were former president Herbert Hoover, New York governor Thomas Dewey, and numerous members of the Roosevelt family. The first visitors to Sagamore Hill did not have access to the entire home, but they were able to tour the first floor, including Roosevelt's library.[33]

From 1953 to 1963, the Theodore Roosevelt Association (TRA) managed Sagamore Hill. During this time, the TRA opened additional rooms to the public, including the third-floor gun room and two of the upstairs bedrooms.[34] One of these bedrooms had originally been Alice Roosevelt's room. When she married congressman Nicholas Longworth in 1906, one of her younger brothers claimed the bedroom, resulting in the room being redone to appeal to his tastes and interests. All of the original furnishings in the room, including Alice's books, were shipped to Alice, who kept everything. Fifty years later, she donated the contents of her childhood bedroom back to Sagamore Hill. As a result, the TRA was able to refurbish the bedroom so that it perfectly matched its original appearance as part of the 1956 restoration work.[35]

In 1963, the TRA transferred the ownership of Sagamore Hill and the surrounding seventy-eight acres to the National Park Service. During a ceremony to commemorate the event, Stuart L. Udall, the secretary of the interior, commented that "the charm and flavor not only of the home itself, but of the family which inhabited it, have been faithfully and tastefully preserved."[36] The National Park Service has administered the site since then. In coordination with this transfer, the National Park Service designated the home and the surrounding grounds a National Historic Site.[37]

For the management and staff of the Sagamore Hill National Historic Site, overseeing the day-to-day operation of the site was only part of a larger mission to preserve Roosevelt's home so that future generations would be able to visit the site. In 2008, however, the management of Sagamore Hill concluded that this larger mission was in jeopardy because of structural problems with the house, which was showing its age. They formulated a plan to restore the house. Over the next four years, they arranged for consultant reports and obtained the necessary funding to carry out this project. In December 2011, Sagamore Hill was closed to the public, and the $10 million restoration project began.[38]

Nearly all of the objects from the house needed to be relocated before the structural work could start, and it fell to Susan Sarna, the site's museum curator, to oversee this process. The eight thousand books posed a special challenge for Sarna. Given the historical significance of these books, Sarna worked closely with the Northeast Document Conservation Center to devise a plan to protect the books throughout the restoration process. This plan involved cleaning, photographing, and wrapping each book before it was packed. In some cases, the particularly fragile books also needed to be repaired. Sarna entered key information about each book on a spreadsheet. She noted not only the title of each book but also exactly where the book was shelved before it was packed and moved.

The book collection ended up filling five hundred specially designed boxes. She color-coded the boxes by rooms. The Roosevelt family kept books in many of the house's twenty-three rooms, and Sarna made sure that each box was identified with its appropriate room. In February 2012, the movers transported these boxes of books to the Steamtown National Historic Site in Scranton, Pennsylvania, which had sufficient storage space to accommodate such a large collection of books. The books remained at this location for three years.

After the completion of the major restoration work, the movers returned the books to Sagamore Hill in March 2015. Sarna then had four weeks to get the books back on their original shelves. She organized a team of twenty people, some of whom were volunteers, and this team carefully unpacked and shelved all eight thousand books. She also had to make sure that the original furniture, art works, and mounted trophies from Roosevelt's hunting expeditions were returned to their proper places. These other objects combined with the books resulted in a total of approximately twelve thousand objects that had to be packed, moved, stored, and then returned to the house. During this three-year process, not a single object was lost, stolen, or damaged.

Modern exterior view of Sagamore Hill. *NPS/© Audrey C. Tiernan Photography, Inc.*

On July 12, 2015, the National Park Service held a reopening ceremony for the Sagamore Hill National Historic Site, complete with a performance of period music by a twenty-five-piece band. For Sarna, the restoration of Sagamore Hill marked the high point of her career with the National Park Service. She took tremendous satisfaction in the fact that the basic appearance of Sagamore Hill had not changed as a result of the restoration project. "My goal," she said, "was to have TR walk in the front door and feel he was at home."[39] Sarna accomplished her goal. If Roosevelt were to walk through the front door today and take the turn into the library, he could easily find one of his favorite books, remove it from the shelf, and start reading. For Roosevelt, that is how he would feel at home.

Notes

1. William Seale, "Theodore Roosevelt's White House," *White House History* 11 (Summer 2002): 32.

2. Paula Carter, "Lions, Tigers, and Books," *Harvard Gazette*, September 25, 2003.

3. Mark I. West, "Preserving a Presidential Persona," *New York Archives* 15, no. 2 (Spring 2016): 36.

4. David McCullough, *Mornings on Horseback* (New York: Simon & Schuster, 2003), 142–43.

5. Bill Bleyer, *Sagamore Hill: Theodore Roosevelt's Summer White House* (Charleston, SC: History Press, 2016), 21.

6. Bleyer, *Sagamore Hill*, 24.

7. Edmund Morris, *The Rise of Theodore Roosevelt* (New York: Modern Library, 2001), 237.

8. Morris, *Rise*, 297–98.

9. Hermann Hagedorn, *The Roosevelt Family of Sagamore Hill* (New York: Macmillan, 1954), 15.

10. Bleyer, *Sagamore Hill*, 32.

11. Hagedorn, *Roosevelt Family*, 35.

12. Amy Verone, "A Constant Pleasure: Theodore Roosevelt at Sagamore Hill," in *Theodore Roosevelt: Icon of the American Century*, ed. James G. Barber (Washington, DC: Smithsonian Institution, 1998), 105.

13. Alice Roosevelt Longworth, *Crowded Hours* (New York: Charles Scribner's Sons, 1933), 7.

14. Theodore Roosevelt III, *All in the Family* (New York: G. P. Putnam's Sons, 1929), 174.

15. Bleyer, *Sagamore Hill*, 128.

16. Hermann Hagedorn and Gary G. Roth, *Sagamore Hill: An Historical Guide* (Oyster Bay, NY: Theodore Roosevelt Association, 1977), 44.

17. Theodore Roosevelt, *Theodore Roosevelt: An Autobiography* (New York, Charles Scribner's Sons, 1913), 345.

18. Bleyer, *Sagamore Hill*, 131–32.

19. Hagedorn and Roth, *Sagamore Hill: An Historical Guide*, 60.

20. Lewis L. Gould, *Edith Kermit Roosevelt: Creating the Modern First Lady* (Lawrence: University Press of Kansas, 2013), 23.

21. Gould, *Edith Kermit Roosevelt*, 23.

22. Bleyer, *Sagamore Hill*, 131.

23. Roosevelt, *Autobiography*, 344–46.

24. Edith Wharton, *A Backward Glance* (New York: Charles Scribner's Sons, 1933), 316.

25. Thomas Bailey and Katherine Joslin, *Theodore Roosevelt: A Literary Life* (Lebanon, NH: ForeEdge, 2018), 308.

26. Bailey and Joslin, *Literary Life*, 308.

27. Bailey and Joslin, *Literary Life*, 314

28. Bleyer, *Sagamore Hill*, 91.

29. Bleyer, *Sagamore Hill*, 93.

30. Bleyer, *Sagamore Hill*, 99–100.

31. *Sagamore Hill National Historic Site: Home of Theodore Roosevelt* (Lawrence-burg, IN: Creative Company, 2000), 9.

32. Bleyer, *Sagamore Hill*, 105.

33. Bleyer, *Sagamore Hill*, 110.

34. Hagedorn and Roth, *Sagamore Hill: An Historical Guide*, 61.

35. Bleyer, *Sagamore Hill*, 131.

36. Bleyer, *Sagamore Hill*, 113–14.

37. Bleyer, *Sagamore Hill*, 112–14.

38. Bleyer, *Sagamore Hill*, 122–26.

39. West, "Preserving a Presidential Persona," 37.

CHAPTER FOUR

~

A Bibliography of Theodore Roosevelt's Books at Sagamore Hill

Theodore Roosevelt never drew up a list of the books in his personal library at Sagamore Hill, but since his death in 1919, efforts have been made to compile such a list. Shortly after his death, a probate inventory was taken. This initial inventory not only listed some of his books, but it also mentioned the rooms where these books were located. In 1945, his wife, Edith Roosevelt, had an inventory drawn up of the objects in the home, including many books. Following her death in 1948, the Roosevelt family heirs had an additional probate inventory drawn up. This inventory was used to help create the transfer list when the house and its contents were sold to the Roosevelt Memorial Association in 1948–1949. A bill of sale was used to document the objects that the Theodore Roosevelt Association transferred to the National Park Service in 1963. These early inventories listed only some of the books at Sagamore Hill, but they provided a starting point for compiling a more complete listing of the books.

When Sagamore Hill became a National Historic Site (NHS) in 1963, the first curator began the long process of formally cataloging all the objects following National Park Service conventions. Throughout the following decades, the museum staff and volunteers of Sagamore Hill NHS have continued to catalog the objects in the house. This cataloging process has been a daunting task as the book collection itself numbers more than eight thousand volumes.

In preparation for a major rehabilitation of Sagamore Hill in 2012, all the books were individually packed, removed from the home, and put into storage. In that process, several original books were found stored in built-in benches and trunks. These books were cataloged and formally added to the collection. In 2015, following the rehabilitation, each book was unpacked and put into the same room from which it had been removed. Many of the books are in the locations they are documented as being in according to the 1919 probate inventory.

The book list in this chapter represents the cataloged books currently in the Sagamore Hill NHS museum collection. It was formed by exporting information from the collection management database the National Park Service uses called ICMS (Interior Collection Management System). The vast majority of the books on this list are original to the Roosevelt family. Many have the original Theodore Roosevelt or Edith K. Roosevelt bookplate pasted inside the front cover. It is important to keep in mind, however, that the Roosevelts added to and subtracted from their collection over the years. Theodore Roosevelt was known to give away books to friends and family members. Any book with a published date after 1948 was removed from the list, as both the Theodore Roosevelt Association and the National Park Service added some books to the home that are not original to the family. Also removed from this list are duplicate copies of the same book. This list retains the formatting style consistent with the National Park Service's cataloging system.

Theodore Roosevelt's book-plate with family crest. *Courtesy of Sagamore Hill National Historic Site, National Park Service, Oyster Bay, NY*

The List of the Roosevelt Books at Sagamore Hill

Abbey, Edwin Austin. *An American Soldier*. 1918.

Abbott, Charles. *A Naturalist's Rambles about Home*. 1884.

Abbott, Charles. *Howard Pyle / A Chronicle*. 1925.

Abbott, Clinton G. *The Home Life of the Osprey*. 1911.

Abbott, Frances M. *Birds and Flowers about Concord N.H.* 1906.

Abbott, Lawrence F. *Impressions of Theodore Roosevelt*. 1919.

Abbott, Lawrence F. *Impressions of Theodore Roosevelt*. 1920.

Adam, Paul. *Princesses Byzantines* (in French). 1893.

Adams, Adeline. *Daniel Chester French*. 1932.

Adams, Charles Francis. *Charles Francis Adams*. American Statesmen. 1900.

Adams, Charles Francis, and Henry Cabot Lodge (1850–1924). Intro. *Charles Francis Adams: An Autobiography*. 1916.

Adams, Dr. Charles C. *Suggestions for Research on North American Big Game*. 1917.

Adams, Henry (1838–1918). *The Life of George Cabot Lodge*. 1911.

Adams, Henry (1838–1918). *John Randolph* (American Statesmen Series), vol. 16. 1898.

Adams, Henry (1838–1918). *History of the United States*. 1890.

Adams, Henry (1838–1918). *John Randolph* / American Statesmen. 1884.

Adams, Henry (1838–1918), and Henry Cabot Lodge (1850–1924). *The Education of Henry Adams*. 1907.

Adams, John Quincy (1767–1848). *The Wants of Man (A Poem)*. 1841.

Adams, Joseph Quincy. *The Folger Shakespeare Library*. 1933.

Adams, Leith A. *Field and Forest Rambles*. 1873.

Adams, Rev. William. *The Cherry Stones*. 1891.

Adams, W., Rev. *The Shadow of the Cross*. 1844.

Addams, Charles. *Drawn and Quartered*. 1942.

Admiral Kennedy. *Sporting Sketches in South America*. 1892.

Aesop, Washington. *Fables Out of the World*. 1878.

Agar, Herbert. *A Time for Greatness*. 1942.

Agar, Wilfred Eade (1882–1951). *Transmission of Environmental Effects*. 1912.

Agassiz, Prof., and Mrs. Louis. *A Journey in Brazil*. 1868.

Aiken, Dr., and Mrs. Barbauld, revised by Cecil Hartley. *Evenings at Home Illustrated*. N.d.

Akeley, Carl E. *Bibi Na Tembe*. 1907.

Alaskan Boundary Tribunal. *Alaskan Boundary Tribunal Atlas*. 1903.

Alcott, Louisa May (1832–1888). *An Old-Fashioned Girl*. 1873.

Alcott, Louisa May (1832–1888). *Little Women*. 1869.

Alcott, Louisa May (1832–1888). *Work: A Story of Experience*. 1873.

Alcott, Louisa May (1832–1888). *Little Women* (2 vols.). 1880.

Alcott, Louisa May (1832–1888). *Jack and Jill*. 1893.

Alcott, Louisa May (1832–1888). *Cupid and Chow-Chow and Other Stories*. 1873.

Alcott, Louisa May (1832–1888). *Eight Cousins.* 1909.

Alcott, Louisa May (1832–1888). *Old Fashioned Girl.* 1911.

Aldin, Cecil. *A Sporting Garland.* c. 1903.

Aldrich, Mrs. Thomas Bailey. *Crowding Memories.* 1920.

Aldrich, Thomas Bailey (1836–1907). *The Story of a Bad Boy.* 1877.

Alexander, De Alva Stanwood. *A Political History of the State of New York* (3-vol. set) (1774–1832, –1861, –1883). 1906–1909.

Alexander, E. P. *Military Memoirs of a Confederate.* 1907.

Alexander, James W. *Life of Dr. Alexander.* 1854.

Alexander, Lt. Boyd. *From the Niger to the Nile,* vols. 1 and 2. 1907.

Alexander, Major General Sir James Edward. *Bush Fighting the Maori War.* 1873.

Alexander, Mrs. *Hymns for Little Children.* Unknown.

Alger, George William (1872). *Moral Overstrain.* 1906.

Alighieri, Dante. *The Inferno of Dante Alighieri.* 1900.

Alighieri, Dante. *The Divine Comedy of Dante* (vol. 1, Hell; vol. 2, Purgatory). 1892.

Alighieri, Dante (1265–1321), and Henry Wadsworth Longfellow (1807–1882). *Dante Alighieri,* vols. 1–3. 1867.

Alison, Archibald, LL.D. *The Life of John, Duke of Marlborough* (2-vol. set). 1852.

Allan, William. *The Army of Northern Virginia in 1862.* 1892.

Allen, Glover M. (1879–1942). *Memoirs of the Boston Society of Natural History,* vol. 8, Number 2, *Monographs of the Natural History of New England, The Whalebone Whales of New England.* 1916.

Allen, Glover M., and Thomas Barbour. *Narrative of a Trip to the Bahamas.* December 1904.

Allen, Hervey. *Israfel; The Life and Times of Edgar A. Poe* (2-vol. set). 1926.

Allen, Hervey, and Thomas Ollive Mabbott. *Poe's Brother: The Poems of William Henry Leonard Poe.* 1926.

Allen, Joel Asaph. *US Geological Survey EF Hayden, Monograph of North American Pinnipeds.* 1880.

Allen, Joel T. *The Influence of Physical Conditions in the Genesis of Species.* 1907.

Allen, John. *Principles of Modern Riding 1825.* 1825.

Allen, Lieutenant Henry T. *Reconnaissance in Alaska.* 1887.

Allen, Paul. *History of the Expedition under the Command of Captains Lewis and Clark,* 2 vols. 1814.

Allen, T. A., James Chapin, and Herbert Lang. *The American Museum Congo Expedition Collection of Bats.* September 29, 1917.

Allier, Roger (1890–1914). *Roger Allier* (in French). 1910–1918.

Allman, T. and J. *The Life, Voyages and Sea Battles of Paul Jones.* 1829.

Allyn, Charles. *Battle of Groton Heights and Its Centennial.* 1882.

American Museum of Natural History. *Journal of the American Museum of Natural History, January 1919.* 1919.

Ammen, Daniel. *The Atlantic Coast: The Navy in the Civil War.* 1883.

Amory, Copley Jr. *Persian Days.* 1928.

Amory, Thomas. *Life of John Buncle*. 1770.

Amundsen, Roald. *The South Pole: An Account of the Norwegian Antarctic Expedition in the "Fram" 1910–1912*. 1913.

Andersen, Hans Christian (1805–1875). *The Nightingale*. 1898.

Andersen, Hans Christian (1805–1875). *Hans Andersen's Fairy Tales*. N.d.

Anderson, Robert Gordon. *Leader of Men*. 1920.

Anderton, Isabella M. *Fairy Tales from Tuscany*. 1907.

Andre, Eugene. *A Naturalist in the Guianas*. 1900.

Andre, John, edited by H. C. Lodge. *Andre's Journal 1777–1778*. 1903.

Andrews, Byron. *Facts about the Candidate*. 1904.

Andrews, Edward L. *Napoleon and America*. 1909.

Angier, Belle Sumner. *A Garden Book of California*. 1906.

Annin, Robert Edwards. *Woodrow Wilson; A Character Study*. 1924.

Anson, W. S., and Edward Latham. *Who Wrote What and Who Said That* (2 vols.). 1905.

Anthony, Katharine. *Louisa May Alcott*. 1938.

Appleton. *The Christian Year (Thoughts in Verse)*. 1848.

Appleton, Morgan. *Plays of Mr. William Shakespeare*. 1908.

Appleton, Nathan, Capt. Brevet. *Russian Life and Society*. 1904.

Appleton, Thomas G. *Chequer-Work*. 1879.

Archer, William. *The Thirteen Days*. 1915.

Archer, William. *Through Afro-America: An English Reading of the Race Problem*. 1910.

Arliss, George. *Up the Years from Bloomsbury: An Autobiography*. 1928.

Armes, Ethel. *Stratford on the Potomac*. 1928.

Armstrong, Hamilton Fish. *The Calculated Risk*. 1947.

Armstrong, Margaret, and J. J. Thurber. *Western Wild Flowers*. 1915.

Arnaud, M. *One Day in A Baby's Life*. 1886.

Arnold, Matthew. *Poems*. 1883.

Arnold, Matthew. *Matthew Arnold's Poems: Lyric and Elegiac*. 1885.

Asbjornsen, Peter Christen (1812–1885). *Fairy Tales from the Far North*. 1897.

Asbjornsen, Peter Christen (1812–1885). *Tales from the Field: A Second Series of Popular Tales*. 1874.

Ashe, Elizabeth. *Intimate Letters from France*. 1918.

Ashmead-Bartlett, Ellis. *With the Turks in Thrace*. 1913.

Audubon, John James (1785–1851). *Birds of America*. 1859.

Audubon, John James (1785–1851), and Rev. John Bachman (1790–1874). *Quadrupeds of North America*. 1845.

Audubon, Maria, and Elliott Coues (1842–1899). *Audubon and His Journal*. 1897.

Auer, Harry A. *Camp Fires in the Yukon*. 1916.

Auerbach, Berhold. *Barfüßele*. Unknown.

Auerbach, Joseph S. *Theodore Roosevelt: An Appreciation*. 1923.

Augusta Fox Riggs Foundation. *Miss Emily Tuckerman, Memorial Drawn Up for the Augusta Fox*. 1924.

Aurelius, Marcus (121–180). *Thoughts of Marcus Aurelius*. Unknown.

Austin, Alfred. *The Garden That I Love*. 1898.

Austin, Jane G. *Moon Folk: A True Account of the Home of the Fairy Tales*. 1874.

Austin, Mary. *The Land of Little Rain*. 1903.

Avebury, Lord. *Prehistoric Times*. 1913.

Aymar, Benjamin. *Aymar of New York*. 1903.

Bacheller, Irving. *The Story of a Passion*. 1899.

Bacon, Francis (1561–1626), and Richard Whatley. *Bacon's Essays with Annotations*. 1892.

Bacon, Leonard. *Rhyme and Punishment*. 1936.

Bacon, Robert. *Bacon's Essays*. 1903.

Bade, William Frederic. *John Muir the Life and Letters*. 1923.

Baedeker, Karl. *Baedeker's Berlin and Its Environs*. 1905.

Baedeker, Karl (1801–1859). *Baedeker's Northern Italy*. 1913.

Bagehot, Walter. *Literary Studies*, vols. 1, 2, 3. 1910.

Bagehot, Walter. *Biographical Studies*. 1907.

Bagehot, Walter (1826–1877). *Shakespeare, the Man: An Essay*. 1901.

Bailey, Cyril (Editor). *The Legacy of Rome*. 1923.

Bailey, Florence Merriam. *Handbook of Birds of the Western United States*. 1902.

Bailey, Vernon. *North American Fauna #17 Review of American Moles*. 1900.

Bailey, Vernon. *North American Fauna #25 Biological Survey of Texas*. 1905.

Bailey, Vernon. *North American Fauna #35, Life Zones and Crop Zones of New Mexico 1913*. 1913.

Bailey, Vernon (1864–1942). *North American Fauna #39, Pocket Gophers, Genus Thomomys*. 1915.

Bailey, Vernon (1864–1942) and Florence Merriam Bailey (1863–?). *Wild Animals of Glacier National Park*. 1918.

Bailey, W. F. *The Slavs of the War Zone*. 1917.

Baillie-Grohman, William A. *Camps in the Rockies*. 1884.

Baily, Francis, F. R. S. *Journal of A Tour in Unsettled Parts of America in 1796 and 1797*. 1856.

Bain, Francis William (1863–1940). *Bubbles of the Foam*. 1912.

Bain, R. Nisbet. *Heroes of the Nations Charles XII*. 1895.

Baird, S. F., T. M. Brewer, and R. Ridgway. *North American Birds Water Birds*. 1874.

Baird, S. F., T. M. Brewer, and R. Ridgway. *North American Birds*. 1874.

Baker, E. O., and C. V. Finch. *Geography of the World's Agriculture by VC Finch and OE Baker*. 1917.

Baker, Samuel White. *Albert N'yanza, Great Basin of the Nile*. 1866.

Baker, Sir Samuel White (1821–1893). *Wild Beasts and Their Ways, Reminiscences of Europe, Asia, Africa, and America*. 1890.

Baker, Sir Samuel White (1821–1893). *Ismailia; A Narrative of the Expedition to Central Africa for the Suppression of the Slave Trade; Organized by the Ismail, Khedive of Egypt.* 1874.

Baker, Sir Samuel White (1821–1893). *Ismailia; A Narrative of the Expedition to Central Africa for the Suppression of the Slave Trade; Organized by Ismail, the Khedive of Egypt.* 1875.

Baker, Samuel W., Sir. *The Nile Tributaries of Abyssinia.* 1907.

Baldwin, Joseph G. *The Flush Times of Alabama and Mississippi.* 1853.

Baldwin, William Charles. *Hunting in South Africa.* 1863.

Balfour, Arthur, James, M.P. *Decadence.* 1908.

Balfour, Rt. Hon. Arthur James (1848–1930). *Theism and Humanism: Being the Gifford Lectures Delivered at the University of Glasgow 1914.* 1915.

Ball, J. Dyer. *Things Chinese / Or Notes Connected with China.* 1925.

Ballantyne, R. M. *Coral Island / A Tale of the Pacific Ocean.* 1923.

Bancroft, George. *Bancroft's History of the United States,* vol. 1. 1852.

Bancroft, George. *Bancroft's History of the United States,* vol. 2. 1852.

Bancroft, George. *Bancroft's History of the United States,* vol. 3. 1858.

Bancroft, George. *Bancroft's History of the United States,* vol. 4. 1852.

Bancroft, George. *Bancroft's History of the United States,* vol. 5. 1852.

Bancroft, George. *Bancroft's History of the United States,* vol. 7. 1858.

Banks, Charles Eugene, and Leroy Armstrong. *Theodore Roosevelt; A Typical American.* 1901.

Barack, Max. *Barack Reineke Fuchs.* Unknown.

Barbauld, Mrs. *Hymns in Prose for Children.* 1866.

Barbour, Thomas. *Bulletin of the Museum of the Comparative Zoology, Harvard,* vol. 52, no. 15. *Notes of the Herpetology of Jamaica, May 1910.* 1910.

Barclay, George C. *Harvard College; Class of 1919, Second Report.* 1923.

Baretti, Giuseppe. *Dizionario Delle Lingue Italiana Ed Inglese,* vol. 1. 1839.

Baretti, Joseph. *Dictionary of the English and Italian Languages.* 1839.

Barham, Richard H. *The Life and Letters of the Rev. Richard Harris Barham.* 1870.

Baring-Gould, S. (1834–1924). *Court Royal: A Story of Cross Currents,* vol. 1 of 2 vols. 1886.

Barker, Lady. *Station Amusements in New Zealand (Station Life in New Zealand).* 1874.

Barlow, Joel. *The Columbiad: A Poem.* 1807.

Barnard, M. R. *Sport in Norway.* 1864.

Barnes, James. *Through Central Africa from Coast to Coast.* 1915.

Barney, Mary. *A Biographical Memoir of Commodore Joshua Barney.* 1832.

Barr, Matthias. *The Child's Garland of Little Poems.* N.d.

Barrett, S. M. *Geronimo's Story of His Life.* 1906.

Barrie, Sir James Matthew (1860–1937). *Farewell Miss Julie Logan.* 1932.

Barrie, Sir James Matthew (1860–1937). *The Little Minister.* 1898.

Barrie, Sir James Matthew (1860–1937), and Mabel L. Attwell. *Peter Pan and Wendy.* 1924.

Barringer, Daniel Moreau. *Some Rules of Conduct for My Children and Their Children.* 1916.

Barrow, Frances Elizabeth Mease (1822–1894). *The Mitten Series.* 1869.

Barrow, Frances Elizabeth Mease (1822–1894). *Nightcaps.* 1860.

Barrow, Frances Elizabeth Mease (1822–1894). *The New Night-Caps; Told to Charley.* 1860.

Barrow, Frances Elizabeth Mease (1822–1894). *The First Little Pet Book with Ten Short Tales, in Words of Three and Four Letters.* 1863.

Barrow, Frances Elizabeth Mease (1822–1894). *Little Pet Book* (3 vols.). 1863

Barrows, Walter Bradford. *Michigan Bird Life.* 1912.

Barth, Henry. *Discoveries in North and Central Africa,* vols. 1 and 2. 1857.

Bartholomew, John. *The Handy Reference Atlas.* 1927.

Bartholomew, John. *Zoogeography,* vol. 5. 1911.

Bartlett, John. *Familiar Quotations.* 8th Ed. 1882.

Bartlett, Captain Robert A. *The Log of "Bob" Bartlett.* 1928.

Bartlett, Robert A., Capt. *The Last Voyage of the Karluk Flagship of Vilhjalmur.* 1916.

Barzini, Luigi. *La Battaglia Di Mukden.* 1907.

Batcheller, Irving. *A Man for the Ages: A Story of the Builders of Democracy.* 1919.

Bates, Arlo. *Talks on the Study of Literature.* 1897.

Bates, E. Stuart. *Inside Out: An Introduction to Autobiography.* 1937.

Bates, Oric. Editor. *Harvard African Studies, Varia Africana I,* vol. 1. 1917.

Baum, L. Frank (1856–1919), and Alberta Hall. *The Songs of Father Goose.* 1900.

Baumbach, Rudolf. *Sommermarchen* (in German). 1904.

Baumbach, Rudolf. *Neue Marchen* (in German). 1903.

Baumbach, Rudolf. *Es War Einmal* (in German). 1901.

Baumbach, Rudolf. *Erzahlungen U. Marchen* (in German). 1904.

Baxter, M. J. *Medical Statistics of the Provost Marshal General's Bureau,* vol. 1. 1875.

Baynes, Ernest Harold. *Wild Bird Guests.* 1915.

Bazalgette, Leon. *Theodore Roosevelt.* 1905.

Beale, Harriet S. Blaine. *Letters of Mrs. James G. Blaine.* 1908.

Beamish, North Ludlow, Arthur Middleton Reeves, and Hon. Rasmus B. Anderson. *The Norse Discovery of America.* 1906.

Beard, Dan. *Dan Beard's Animal Book.* 1907.

Beazley, Raymond C. *The Dawn of Modern Geography: A History of Exploration.* 1906.

Beck, James M. *The Evidence in the Case as to the Moral Responsibility for the War.* 1915.

Beck, James M. *The War and Humanity.* 1917.

Beck, L. Adams. *The Ghost Plays of Japan.* 1933.

Beck, Lewis Caleb (1798–1853). *Natural History of New York Part III Mineralogy.* 1842.

Becke, Louis. *Pacific Tales.* 1896.

Bedell and Gardner. *Household Mechanics.* 1945–6.

Beebe, William. *Edge of the Jungle.* 1921.

Beebe, William. *Jungle Peace*. 1918.

Beebe, William. *Monograph of the Pheasants*, vols. 1–4. 1918.

Beebe, William, G. I. Hartley, and P. G. Howes. *Tropical Wildlife in British Guiana*, vol. 1. 1917.

Beerbohm, Sir Max (1872–1956). *Poet's Corner*. 1904.

Beerbohm, Sir Max (1872–1956). *A Christmas Garland*. 1937.

Belloc, Hilaire. *Marie Antoinette*. 1924.

Bemporad, R. and F. *Le Avventure di Pinocchio*. 1934.

Bendire, Charles. *Life Histories of North American Birds*. 1892.

Bendire, Charles. *Life Histories of North American Birds*. 1895.

Benet, Stephen Vincent. *The Devil and Daniel Webster*. 1937.

Benet, Stephen Vincent. *James Shore's Daughter*. 1934.

Benn, Alfred William (1843–1915). *Modern England: A Record of Opinion and Action from the Time of the French Revolution to the Present Day*, vol. 1. 1908.

Benn, William, Alfred. *Spanish Gold*. 1908.

Bennett, Arnold. *The Grim Smile of the Five Towns*. 1907.

Benson, E. F. *Charlotte Bronte*. 1933.

Benson, Robert Hugh. *The Light Invisible*. Unknown.

Benton, Thomas Hart (1782–1858). *"Thirty Years in the U.S. Senate 1820–1850."* 1885.

Berard, Victor. *Les Pheniciens et L'odyssee* (2-vol. set). 1902.

Bercy, Paul. *Simples Notions de Francais*. 1894.

Berger, Dr. A. *In Afrikas Wildkammern*. 1910.

Bergson, Henri. *Laughter*. 1912.

Besant, Sir Walter (1836–1901). *All Sorts and Conditions of Men*. 1889.

Besant, Walter. *The Eulogy of Richard Jefferies*. 1888.

Besso, Marco. *Roma Il Papa*. 1903.

Beston, Henry (1888–1968). *The Book of Gallant Vagabond*. 1925.

Beston, Henry (1888–1968). *The St. Lawrence*. 1942.

Beston, Henry (1888–1968). *The Firelight Fairy Book*. Unknown.

Bever, Lavinia Silliman. *The Quest of Bells*. 1917.

Beveridge. Albert J. *The Life of John Marshall*. 1916.

Beyer, Thomas (1876–). *The American Battleship and Life in the Navy*. 1908.

Bickerstaff, Isaac Esq. *The Tatler*. 1709.

Biddle, Anthony J. Drexel. *The Madeira Islands*. 1896.

Bigelow, Samuel. *Samuel Bigelow*. 1915.

Bilibin, Iwan Jakowlewitsch. *Iwan Jakowlewitsch Bilibin*. 1904.

Bill, Buffalo (1846–1917). *The True Tales of the Plains*. 1908.

Bingham, Hiram. *Across South America*. Unknown.

Bingham, Theo. A. *Annual Report upon the Improvement and Care of Public Buildings*. 1898.

Birch, W., and Son. *Interior Views of Philadelphia*. 1799.

Birkenhead, Sheila. *Against Oblivion / The Life of Joseph Severn*. 1944.

Birmingham, G. A. *Spanish Gold*. N.d.

Bishop, Joseph Bucklin. *John Hay: Scholar, Statesman: An Address Delivered before Brown University Alumni Association*. 1906.

Bishop, Joseph Bucklin. *Notes and Anecdotes of Many Years*. 1925.

Bishop, Joseph Bucklin. *The Panama Gateway*. 1913.

Bishop, Joseph Bucklin. *Our Political Drama*. 1904.

Bishop, Joseph Bucklin. *Charles Joseph Bonaparte / His Life and Public Services*. 1922.

Bishop, Joseph Bucklin. *Theodore Roosevelt and His Time*. 1920.

Bishop, William Henry. *The Faience Violin*. 1893.

Bismarck, Prince Otto Von. *Bismarck: The Man and the Statesman*, vol. 1. 1899.

Bjerregard, C. H. A. *Sufi Interpretation of the Quatrains of Omar Khayam and Fitzgerald*. 1902.

Blackwell, I. A., and Benjamin Thorpe. *The Eddas*. 1906.

Blaikie, Garden, W. *The Personal Life of David Livingstone*. Unknown.

Blaine, James Gillespie (1830–1893). *Twenty Years of Congress 1861–1881*, vol. 1. 1884

Blanchan, Neltje. *The ECSR Library Birds*. 1907.

Blanchard, Newton C. *Proceedings of a Conference of Governors in the White House*. 1909.

Blaze, Elzear. Preface. *Livre du Roy Modus*. 1839.

Bliss, Gerald. *The Fated Five*. 1910.

Blom, Alfred. *Photographs from the Royal Danish National Museum*. 1937.

Blome, Richard. *The Gentleman's Recreation*. 1686.

Blumenburg, M. W. (Reported by). *Official Proceedings of the Twelfth Republican National Convention*. 1900.

Bodenheim, Nelly. *Het Regent–Het Zegent*. c. 1907–1909.

Bohm, Henry G. *The Parables of Fredrich Adolphus Krummacher*. 1858.

Bohn, Henry G. *The Zoology of Captain Beechey's Voyage*. 1839.

Boissier, Gaston. *La Conjuration de Catilina*. 1905.

Bok, Edward William (1863–1930). *The Americanization of Edward Bok*. 1920.

Bolles, Frank. *At the North of Bearcamp Water*. 1893.

Bolton, Charles Knowles. *The Private Soldier under Washington*. 1902.

Bolton, Herbert Eugene. *Rim of Christendom: A Biography of Eusebio Francisco Kino, Pacific Coast Pioneer*. 1936.

Bomberger, Maude A. *Colonial Recipes*. 1907.

Bonaparte, Carlo L. Principe. *Fauna Italica: Mammalia Aves*. 1832–1841.

Bonaparte, Charles Lucian. *American Ornithology*. 1825.

Bonaparte, Charles Lucian (1803–1857). *Bonaparte's Ornithology Plates*. N.d.

Bonsal, Stephen. *Unfinished Business*. 1944.

Bonsal, Stephen. *Edward Fitzgerald Beale*. 1912.

Boone and Crockett Club. *Trail and Camp Fire*. 1897.

Bordeaux, Henry. *La Petite Mademoiselle*. 1905.

Borzini, Luigi. *Peking to Paris in a Motor Car*. 1908.

Boswell, James (1740–1795). *The Life of Samuel Johnson, LL.D.* 1831.

Bouchor, Maurice. *Les Chansons Joyeuses Poesies.* 1874.

Bourke, John G. *On the Border with Crook.* 1891.

Bourne, George. *William Smith Potter and Farmer 1790–1858.* 1920.

Boutroux, Emile. *Science and Religion in Contemporary Philosophy.* 1911.

Bowen, Catherine Deinker. *Yankee from Olympus.* 1944.

Bowen, Clarence (Editor). *History of the Centennial of the Inauguration of Washington.* 1892.

Bowman, Ann. *The Young Exiles or the Wild Tribes of the North.* 1858.

Bowman, Isaiah. *The Military Geography of Atacama.* 1911.

Bowman, Isaiah (1878–1950). *The Andes of Southern Peru.* 1916.

Bowring, John. *Ancient Poetry and Romances of Spain.* 1824.

Bowring, John. *Poetry of the Magyars.* 1830.

Boyer, Lieutenant. *Journal of Wayne's Campaign.* 1866.

Boyle, Frederick. *On the Borderland.* 1884.

Bradly-Birt, F. B. *Persia (Oriental Series): Through Persia from the Gulf to the Caspian,* vol. 20. 1910.

Brady, Matthew. *Original Photographs Taken on the Battlefields during the Civil War of the US.* 1907.

Brand, Gerhard. *Life of Michaels De Ruiter* (Old German Script). 1687.

Brandt, Gerard. *La Vie De Ruiter Duc. Chevalier, Lieutenant Admiral General, De Hollande and Deoueft-Frife Ou Eftcomprife L Historie Maritime.* 1647.

Bray, Dr. Thomas (1658–1730). *Various Writings of and Related to Thomas Bray.* 1916.

Brazil, Dr. Vital. *La Defense Contre E'ophidisme.* 1911.

Breasted, James Henry (1865–1935). *Ancient Times: A History of the Early World.* 1916.

Breasted, James Henry (1865–1935). *The Dawn of Conscience.* 1934.

Brewer, David J. *The World's Best Essays from the Earliest Period to the Present Time.* 1900.

Brewer, Rev. E. Cobham LL.D. *The Reader's Handbook.* 1881.

Brewer, Rev. E. Cobham LL.D. *Dictionary of Phrase and Fable.* N.d.

Brewster, H. B. *The Prison.* c. 1908.

Brewster, William. *Birds of the Cambridge Region.* 1906.

Brigham, Willard I. Tyler. *The Tyler Genealogy: Descendants of Job Tyler of Andover, Massachusetts,* vol. 1. 1912.

Brinkley, F., Captain. *Oriental Series Japan Its History, Arts and Literate* (12 vols.) 1901.

Bronson, Edgar Beecher. *Cowboy Life on the Western Plains: The Reminiscences of a Ranchman.* 1913.

Brooks, Charles S. *Journeys to Bagdad.* 1925.

Brooks, Charles S. *There's Pippins and Cheese to Come.* 1917.

Brooks, N. C. *A Complete History of the Mexican War: Its Causes, Conduct, and Consequences.* 1849.

Brooks, Phillips. *Twenty Sermons*. 1903.

Brooks, Phillips. *Christmas Songs and Easter Carols*. 1904.

Brooks, Sidney. *Theodore Roosevelt*. 1910.

Broughton, Urban H. *The British Empire at War*. 1916.

Brown, A. Samler. *The South and East African Yearbook and Guide with Atlas, 27th Issue*. 1897.

Brown, A. Samler. *Brown's Madeira Canary Islands and Azores*. 1932.

Brown, Audrey Alexandra. *A Dryad in Nanaimo*. 1934.

Brown, Caroline. *Knights in Fustian*. 1900.

Brown, John. *The Self-Interpreting Bible*, vols.1 and vol. 2. 1792.

Brown, John, M.D. *Spare Hours*, vols. 1 and 2. 1866.

Brown, Josephine C. *The Rural Community and Social Case Work*. 1933.

Brown, William Garrott. *The Lower South in American History*. 1902.

Browne, D. J. *Trees of America*. 1846.

Browne, Frances. *Granny's Wonderful Chair and Its Tales of Fairy Times*. 1891.

Brownell, Henry Howard. *The Lines of Battle*. 1912.

Browning, Elizabeth Barrett (1806–1861). *Mrs. Browning Poems*. 1887.

Bruce, Robert. *Art and Sculpture of James Edward Kelly*. 1934.

Bruce, Robert. *Art and Sculpture of James Edward Kelly 1855–1933*. 1934.

Bruce, Miner Wait. *Alaska, History and Resources, the Gold Fields Routes and Scenery*. 1895.

Brush, Edward Hale. *Rufus King and His Times*. 1926.

Bruxelles G. *Van Oest and C Notre Pays*. 1909.

Bryan, William Jennings (1860–1925). *The Speeches of William Jennings Bryan* (in two vols.) vol. 2. 1909.

Bryant, Harold C. *The Horned Lizards of California and Nevada of the Geneva Phrynosoma and Anota*. 1911.

Bryant, Sara Cone. *Stories to Tell the Littlest Ones*. Unknown.

Bryant, William Cullen (1794–1878). *Poems*. 1876.

Bryce, Viscount James (1838–1922). *The Relations of the Advanced and the Backward Races of Mankind*. 1902.

Bryce, Viscount James (1838–1922). *The Relations of the Advanced and the Backward Races of Mankind*. 1903.

Bryce, Viscount James (1838–1922). *The Holy Roman Empire*. 1871.

Bryce, Viscount James (1838–1922). *South America Observations and Impressions*. 1912.

Bryce, Viscount James (1838–1922). *The American Commonwealth* (2 vols.). 1910.

Bryce, Viscount James (1838–1922). *Studies in History and Jurisprudence*. 1901.

Bryden, H. A. *Kloof and Karroo*. 1889.

Bryden, H. Anderson. *Gun and Camera in Southern Africa*. 1893.

Brymner, Douglas. *Report on Canadian Archive*. 1889.

Buchheim, C. A. *Deutsche Lyrik*. 1875.

Buckland, Frank. *Log Book of a Fisherman and Zoologist*. N.d.

Buckley, Harold. *Squadron 95*. 1933.

Buckman, George Rex. *Colorado Springs and Its Famous Scenic Environs*. 1893.

Budge, Wallis A. E. *Osiris and the Egyptian Resurrection*. 1911.

Buell, Augustus C. *History of Andrew Jackson* (2-vol. set). 1904.

Buffon, Count de. *Buffon's Natural History of Birds*, vols. 1–2. 1793.

Buhler, M. E. *The Grass in the Pavement*. 1918.

Bulloch, J. G. B. *A History and Genealogy of the Families of Bulloch and Stobo and of Irving of Cults*. 1911.

Bulloch, J. G. B. *Genealogical and Historical Records of the Bailles of Inverness, Scotland and Some of Their Descendants in the United States of America*. 1923.

Bulloch, J. G. B. *A Biographical Sketch of Hon. Archibald Bulloch, President of Georgia 1776–1777*. N.d.

Bulloch, Joseph G. B., M.D. *A History of the Glen Family of South Carolina and Georgia*. Nov. 1923.

Bulloch, Joseph G. B., M.D. *The Cuthberts: Barons of Castle Hill and Their Descendents in South Carolina and Georgia*. 1908.

Bulloch, Joseph G. B., M.D. *A History and Genealogy of the Family of Baillie of Dunain*. 1898.

Bulwer-Lytton, Edward George (1st Baron Lytton) 1803–1873. *My Novel*. N.d.

Bulwer-Lytton, Edward George (1st Baron Lytton) 1803–1873. *Rienzi: The Last of the Tribunes*, vol.1. 1836.

Bunau-Varilla, Philippe. *The Great Adventure of Panama*. 1920.

Bunner, H. C. *Zadoc Pine and Other Stories*. 1891.

Bunyan, John (1628–1688). *The Pilgrim's Progress*. 1926.

Bunyan, John (1628–1688). *Bunyan's Select Works*. 1861.

Bunyan, John (1628–1688). *The Pilgrim's Progress*. 1892.

Burger, Gottfried August. *Burger's Sammtliche Werke*. 1844.

Burgess, Gelett (1866–1951). *Book, the Romance of the Commonplace*. 1902.

Burgess, Thornton W. *The Burgess Book for Children*. 1919.

Burghclere, Lady. *Strafford*, vols. 1 and 2. 1931.

Burke, Edmund (1729–1797). *Reflections on the French Revolution*. 1912.

Burke, Edmund (1729–1797). *Burke's Speeches and Letters on American Affairs Everyman Edition*. 1911.

Burke, Thomas. *More Limehouse Nights*. 1921.

Burnard, F. C. *Pictures from Punch* (in 4 vols.). c.1900.

Burne-Jones, Edward. *Letters to Katie*. 1925.

Burne-Jones, Edward (1833–1898). *The Song of Songs*. 1902.

Burne-Jones, Sir Edward. *Pictures of Romance and Wonder*. 1902.

Burney, Miss. *Cecilia*. Unknown.

Burnham, Frederick Russell. *Scouting on Two Continents*. 1927.

Burns, Robert. *To Mary in Heaven*. 1916.

Burroughs, John (1837–1921). *Bird and Bough*. 1906.

Burroughs, John (1837–1921). *Songs of Nature*. 1901.

Burroughs, John (1837–1921). *Fresh Fields*. 1901.
Burroughs, John (1837–1921). *Leaf and Tendril*. 1908.
Burroughs, John (1837–1921). *Riverby*. 1894.
Burroughs, John (1837–1921). *Far and Near*. 1904.
Burroughs, John (1837–1921). *The Breath of Life*. 1915.
Burroughs, John (1837–1921). *Time and Change*. 1912.
Burroughs, John (1837–1921). *The Summit of the Years*. 1913.
Burroughs, John (1837–1921). *Under the Apple Trees*. 1916.
Burroughs, John (1837–1921). *Ways of Nature*. 1905.
Burroughs, John (1837–1921). *Locusts and Wild Honey*. 1902.
Burroughs, John (1837–1921). *Winter Sunshine*. 1901.
Burroughs, John (1837–1921). *Pepacton*. 1900.
Burroughs, John (1837–1921). *Wake-Robin*. 1871.
Burroughs, John (1837–1921). *Camping and Tramping with Roosevelt*. 1907.
Burroughs, John (1837–1921). *Birds and Poets*. 1901.
Burton, Hill, John. *The Book Hunter*. 1882.
Bury, J. B. *History of Freedom of Thought*. 1913.
Busch, William. *Max and Maurice*. 1899.
Butler, Amos. *Birds of Indiana*. 1906.
Butler, Capt. Alban B. Jr. *Happy Days*. 1928.
Butler, Lt. General Sir William Francis (1838–1910). *Sir William Butler: An Autobiography*. 1911.
Butler, Major William Francis (1833–1910). *The Wild Northland*. 1881.
Butler, Major William Francis (1833–1910). *The Great Lone Land*. 1881.
Butler, Samuel Hudibras. *A Poem in Three Cantos* (2-vol. set). 1793.
Butler, Samuel. *Notes on Hudibras*. 1793.
Butler, William Allen (1825–1902). *Nothing to Wear: An Episode of City Life*. 1857.
Butler, William Allen (1825–1902). *Nothing to Wear and Other Poems*. 1899.
Butt, Archie. *The Letters of Archie Butt*. 1924.
Butterworth, Hezekiah. *Zigzag Journeys in Classic Lands*. 1881.
Cable, George W. *Old Creole Days*. 1885.
Cadena, Mariano Velazquez de la. *Seoane's Neuman and Baretti's Spanish Pronouncing Dictionary*. 1884.
Cahun, David-Leon (1841–1900). *Les Mercenaires*. 1894.
Cahun, Leon. *La Banniere Bleue*. 1897.
Caine, Hall. *The Eternal City*. 1901.
Calverley, Charles Stuart. *Verses and Fly Leaves*. 1896.
Camp Fire Club of America. *Honors Awarded to Theodore Roosevelt by the Camp Fire Club of America, 1911*. April 3, 1911.
Camp, Walter. *Walter Camp's Book of College Sports*. 1893.
Campion, J. S. *On the Frontier*. 1878.
Campion, Thomas. *Thomas Campion; A Book of Airs*. 1885.
Camusso, N. *La Selvaggina*. 1887.

Cane, Claude, Colonel. *Summer and Fall in Western Alaska.* 1903.

Carey, Agnes. *Empress Eugenie in Exile.* 1920.

Carey, H. Lansing. *Power for Peace.* Unknown.

Carleton, James Henry. *The Battle of Buena Vista with Operations of the "Army of Occupation" for One Month.* 1848.

Carleton, John William. *Carleton's Sporting Sketch Book.* 1842.

Carlson, Earl R. *Born That Way.* 1941.

Carlyle, Thomas (1795–1881). *Oliver Cromwell's Letters and Speeches* (5 vols.). 1845.

Carlyle, Thomas (1795–1881). *Critical and Miscellaneous Essays* (4 vols.). 1879.

Carlyle, Thomas (1795–1881). *The French Revolution* (2-vol. set). 1887.

Carman, (William) Bliss (1861–1929). *Ode on the Coronation of King Edward.* 1902.

Carman, (William) Bliss (1861–1929). *Poems by Bliss Carman* (in 2 vols.). 1905.

Carman, Bliss (Bill). *The Rough Rider and Other Poems.* 1909.

Carnegie, Andrew. *The Roosevelt Policy: Introduction by Andrew Carnegie.* 1908.

Carpenter, F. B. *Six Months at the White House with Abraham Lincoln.* 1867.

Carpenter, William. *A Poem on the Execution of William Shaw.* 1916.

Carrigan, Thomas Charles. *The Law and the American Child, Reprinted from the Pedagogical Seminary.* June 1911.

Carroll, Lewis (Pen Name of Charles Dodgson, 1832–1898). *Sylvie and Bruno.* 1889.

Carroll, M. *How Marjory Helped.* 1875.

Cary, Merritt. *North American Fauna #33, A Biological Survey of Colorado.* 1911.

Case, Carleton B. *Good Stories about Roosevelt.* 1920.

Castellamonte, Amedeo D. *La Venarla Reale.* 1674.

Castiglione, Count Baldesar. *The Book of the Courtier.* 1901.

Cather, Willa Sibert (1876–1947). *The Professor's House.* 1925.

Catlin, George (1796–1872). *Catlin's Indians.* N.d.

Catlin, George (1796–1872). *North American Indians,* 2 vols. 1851.

Catlin, George (1796–1872). *Catlin's North American Indian Portfolio: Hunting Scenes and Amusements of the Rocky Mountains and Prairies.* 1885.

Cavendish, George. *The Life and Death of Cardinal Wolsey.* 1905.

Cawein, Madison Julius (1865–1914). *Nature Notes and Impressions in Prose and Verse.* 1906.

Cawein, Madison Julius (1865–1914). *The Vale of Temple Poems.* 1905.

Cawein, Madison Julius (1865–1914). *An Ode in Commemoration of the Founding of the Massachusetts Bay Colony.* 1908.

Cawein, Madison Julius (1865–1914). *The Shadow Garden.* 1910.

Cawein, Madison Julius (1865–1914). *The Poems of Madison Cawein,* vols. 1–5. 1907.

Cawein, Madison Julius (1865–1914). *Kentucky Poems.* 1903.

Cawein, Madison Julius (1865–1914). *New Poems.* 1909.

Cawein, Madison Julius (1865–1914). *The Poet and the Fool and the Faeries.* 1912.

Cawein, Madison Julius (1865–1914). *The Cup of Comus.* 1915.

Cecil. *Records of the Chase and Sporting Anecdotes.* 1854.

Cecil, Gwendolen. *Life of Robert, Marquis of Salisbury,* vols. 1 and 2. 1871.

Cellini, Benvenuto. *The Life of Benvenuto Cellini Written by Himself*. 1906.

Chadwick, French Enser. *The Relations of the United States and Spain Diplomacy*. 1909.

Chadwick, French Enser. *Relations of the United States and Spain: The Spanish-American War*, vol. 2. 1911.

Chambers, Robert W. (1865–1933). *Iole*. 1905.

Chambers, Robert W. (1865–1933). *Lorraine*. 1898.

Chapman, Abel. *Wild Norway*. 1897.

Chapman, Abel F. Z. S. *Bird-Life of the Borders on Moorland and Sea with Faunal Notes Extending over Forty Years*. 1907.

Chapman, Frank M. *The Travels of Birds*. 1916.

Chapman, Frank Michler (1864–1945). *Autobiography of a Bird Lover*. 1933.

Chapman, Frank Michler (1864–1945). *The Habitat Bird Groups*. 1909.

Chapman, Frank Michler (1864–1945). *Camps and Cruises of an Ornithologist*. 1908.

Chapman, Frank Michler (1864–1945). *The Warblers of North America*. 1907.

Chapman, Frank Michler (1864–1945). *Birds of Eastern North America*. 1907.

Chapman, Frank Michler (1864–1945). *The Distribution of Bird-Life in Colombia*. 1917.

Chapman, Frank Michler (1864–1945). *Color Key to North American Birds*. 1903.

Chapman, Frank Michler (1864–1945). *Handbook of Birds of Eastern North America*. 1912.

Charles, Oman. *The Art of War*. 1898.

Charlesworth, Maria Louisa (1819–1880). *Ministering Children–A Tale*. 1857.

Charlesworth, Maria Louisa (1819–1880). *A Sequel to Ministering Children*. 1867.

Charnwood, Lord. *Theodore Roosevelt*. 1923.

Chase, Mary Justice. *Benjamin Lee 2nd Ensign U.S. Naval Reserve Flying Corps*. 1920.

Chellis, Mary Dwinell. *Out of the Fire*. 1873.

Cherubini, E. *Pinokio En Afrique*. Unknown.

Chesterton, Gilbert Keith (1874–1936). *The Flying Inn*. 1926.

Cheyney, Edward P. *A Short History of England*. 1904.

Childe-Pemberton, William S. *The Baroness De Bode 1775–1803*. 1900.

Chirol, Valentine. *Cecil Spring-Rice in Memoriam*. 1919.

Chittenden, F. H. *Insects Injurious to Vegetables*. 1912.

Chittenden, Hiram Martin. *History of the American Fur Trade of the Far West* (3-vol. set). 1902.

Choate, Joseph Hodges (1832–1917). *Boyhood and Youth*. 1917.

Christie, Ella. *A Long Look at Life*. 1940.

Christy, Howard Chandler (1873–1952). *Men of the Army and Navy (Six Pastels in Colors*. 1899.

Church, Alfred J. *The Story of the Nations-Carthage*. 1886.

Church, A. J., M.A. *The Story of the Iliad*. 1891.

Church, John. *A Cabinet of Quadrupeds* (2-vol. set). 1805.

Cist, M., Henry. *Campaigns of the Civil War: The Army of the Cumberland*, vol. 7. 1882.

Clark, Edward B. *Birds of Lakeside and Prairie*. 1901.

Clark, Grenville. *Reprint of the Introduction to World Peace through World Law*. 1958.

Clark, Margery. *The Cook's Surprise*. 1923.

Clark, George Rogers. *Col. George Rogers Clark's Sketch of His Campaign in Illinois in 1778–79*. 1869.

Clarke, M. E. *Paris Waits 1914*. 1915.

Clarke, Rebecca Sophia (Sophie May) (1833–1906). *The Asbury Twins*. 1876.

Clarke, Rebecca Sophia (Sophie May) (1833–1906). *Our Helen*. 1874.

Claybourn, John G. *Dredging on the Panama Canal*. 1931.

Clemenceau, Georges (1841–1929). *Grandeurs et Miseres D'une Victoire*. 1930.

Clemens, Cyril. *Shillaber*. 1946.

Clemens, Cyril. *My Chat with Thomas Hardy*. 1944.

Clemens, Cyril. *Young Sam Clemens*. 1942.

Clement, Marguerite. *Once in France*. 1927.

Clementi, Marie Penelope Rose Eyres (1889–1947). *Through British Guiana to the Summit of Roraima*. 1920.

Clements, Lewis. *Shooting and Fishing Trips in England, France, Belgium, Holland, and Bavaria*. 1878.

Clifford, Mrs. W. K. *Aunt Anne*. 1892.

Clough, A. H. *Plutarch's Lives*, vols. 1–5. 1899.

Clough, Arthur Hugh. *Poems*. 1877.

Clouston, J. Storer. *The Adventures of M. D'Haricot*. 1902.

Clouston, J. Storer. *The Spy in Black*. 1918.

Clowes, William Laird. *The Royal Navy: A History*. 1898.

Coates, Henry T. *Fireside Encylopaedia of Poetry*. 1878.

Coates, Joseph H. *History of the Civil War in America* (4 vols.) 1876.

Cobb, Irvin S. *Speaking of Operations*. 1915.

Coffin, Allen. *The Life of Tristram Coffin*. 1881.

Coffin, Gardner I. *The Oldest House on Nantucket Island, Part I*. 1905

Coffin, Miriam. *Miriam Coffin or the Whale Fisherman*. 1834.

Coffin, Robert P. Tristram. *Saltwater Farm*. 1937.

Coggeshall, George. *History of the American Privateer*. 1856.

Coggeshall, George. *Coggeshall Voyages*. 1852–1853.

Cole, Fay-Cooper (1881–1961). *The Wild Tribes Davao District, Mindanao Field Museum of Natural History #170*. 1913.

Cole, Samuel Valentine. *The Great Grey King*. 1914.

Coleridge, Mary E. *Poems* (by Mary E. Coleridge). 1918.

Coleridge, Samuel Taylor (1772–1834). *The Rime of the Ancient Mariner*. 1876.

Coles, Russell J. *Copeia #4*, vol. 4. 1914.

Coles, Russell J. *Copeia #32*, vol. 32. 1916.

Coles, Russell J. *Copeia #5*. 1914.

Coles, Russell J. *Copia #30*. 1916.

Coles, Russell J. *Observations on the Habits and Distribution*. American Museum of Natural History. 1910.

Coles, Russell J. *Notes on the Embryos . . . American Museum of Natural History*. 1913.

Coles, Russell J. *Copeia #17*. 1915.

Coles, Russell J. *Copeia #24*. 1915.

Collier, Jeremy (1650–1726). *Essays upon Several Moral Subjects*. 1700.

Collins, William. *The Poetical Works of William Collins*. 1830.

Collinswood, W. G. *Cormac*. 1902.

Collodi, C. *Les Adventures de Pinokie*. Unknown.

Colmar, Baron Von der Goltz. *Kriegseschichte Deutschlands Im Nevnzehnten Jahrhundert*. 1910.

Colombian Nationalist Association. *I Took the Isthmus*. 1911.

Colquhoun, John. *The Moor and the Loch* (in 2 vols.). 1878.

Colum, Padraic. *The King of Ireland's Son*. 1916.

Commissioners. *Fisheries, Game and Forests*. 1899.

Committee on Home Nurture in Religion. *Family Prayers for Every Home*. N.d.

Compton, Herbert. *A Free Lance in a Far Land*. 1902.

Comte Desequr. *Histoire De Napoleon et de La Grande-Armee* (2-vol. set). 1820.

Comyn, D. C. E. A. *Service and Sport in the Sudan*. 1911.

Conipiler, Baxter H. J. *Statistics, Medical and Anthropological of Provost Marchal-General's Bureau*, vol. 2. 1875.

Conklin, Edwin Grant. *Heredity and Environment in the Development of Men*. 1916.

Conklin, Prof. Geo. W. *Conklin's Peerless Manual of Useful Information and Atlas of the World*. 1902.

Connolly, James Brendan (1868–1957). *The Trawler*. 1914.

Connolly, James Brendan (1868–1957). *The U-Boat Hunters*. 1918.

Conrad, Joseph (1857–1924). *The Shadow Line: A Confession*. 1917.

Conrad, Joseph (1857–1924). *Youth and Two Other Stories: Youth, A Narrative, Heart of Darkness, the End of the Tether*. 1903.

Constable, W. G. *Paintings in the Lee Collection by W. G. Constable*. 1930.

Cooke, Wells W. *Bulletin of the US Department of Agriculture, Distribution and Migration of North American Rails and Their Allies, No. 128, Sept 25, 1914*. 1914.

Coolidge, Harold J., Jr., and Theodore Roosevelt. *Three Kingdoms of Indo-China*. 1933.

Coolidge, Susan. *Clover*. 1927.

Cooper, Duff. *Talleyrand*. 1932.

Cooper, James Fenimore (1789–1851). *Afloat and Ashore; A Sea Tale*. 1876.

Cooper, James Fenimore (1789–1851). *Pioneer*. 1876.

Cooper, James Fenimore (1789–1851). *Prairie*. 1876.

Cooper, James Fenimore (1789–1851). *Deerslayer*. 1876.

Cooper, James Fenimore (1789–1851). *The Water Witch or the Skimmer of the Seas*. N.d.

Cooper, James Fenimore (1789–1851). *Two Admirals*. N.d.

Cooper, James Fenimore (1789–1851). *Spy.* N.d.

Cooper, James Fenimore (1789–1851). *Pathfinder.* Unknown.

Cooper, James Fenimore (1789–1851). *Mohicans.* Unknown.

Cooper, James Fenimore (1789–1851). *Miles Wallingford: A Sequel to Afloat and Ashore.* Unknown.

Cooper, James Fenimore (1789–1851). *Wyandotté.* Unknown.

Cooper, James Fenimore (1789–1851). *Redskins.* Unknown.

Cooper, James Fenimore (1789–1851). *The Pilot: A Tale of the Sea.* Unknown.

Cooper, James Fenimore (1789–1851). *The Chainbearer; Or the Little Manuscript.* Unknown.

Cooper, James Fenimore (1789–1851). *The Prairie.* 1827.

Cooper, James Fenimore (1789–1851). *Pioneers.* 1823.

Cooper, James Fenimore (1789–1851). *The History of the Navy of the United States of America,* vols.1 and 2. 1839.

Cooper, James Fenimore (1789–1851). *The Wing and Wing.* 1882.

Cooper, James Fenimore (1789–1851). *The Water Witch or the Skimmer of the Seas.* 1863.

Cooper, James Fenimore (1789–1851). *The Deerslayer.* N.d.

Cooper, Rev. Mr. *The History of North America.* 1789.

Cope, E. D. *Primary Factors of Organic Evolution.* 1904.

Corban, E. B. *No Meat? Then What? Wartime Cooking Try These.* 1943.

Corbett, Julian S. *Drake and the Tudor Navy,* vols. 1 and 2. 1898.

Corbett, Sir Julian Stafford (1854–1922). *The Successors of Drake.* 1900.

Corelli, Marie. *A Christmas Greeting.* 1902.

Corson, Juliet. *Cooking School Text Book.* 1881.

Cory, Charles B. *Hunting and Fishing in Florida.* 1895.

Coubertin, Pierre, Baron. *France Since 1814.* 1900.

Coue, Emile. *Self-Mastery through Autosuggestion.* 1922.

Coues, Elliott (1842–1899). *The History of the Lewis and Clark Exposition* (4-vol. Set). 1893.

Coues, Elliott (1842–1899). *The Expeditions of Zebulon Montgomery Pike* (3-vol. set). 1895.

Coues, Elliott (1842–1899). *The Coues Check List and Ornithological Dictionary.* 1882.

Coues, Elliott (1842–1899). *Key to North American Birds.* 1872.

Coues, Elliott (1842–1899). *Birds of the Colorado Valley.* 1878.

Coues, Elliott (1842–1899). *Birds of the Northwest: A Handbook of the Ornithology of the Region Drained by the Missouri River and Its Tributaries.* 1874.

Coues, Elliott (1842–1899). *Birds of the North-West.* 1877.

Coulton, G. G. *From St. Francis to Dante.* 1908.

Coulton, G. G. *The Main Illusions of Pacificism a Criticism of Mr. Norman Angell and of the Union of Democratic Control.* 1916.

Cox, Jacob D. *Atlanta: Campaigns of the Civil War.* 1882.

Cox, Jacob D. *The March to the Sea / Franklin and Nashville / Campaigns of the Civil War*. 1882.

Cox, Nicholas (1673–1731) and John Manwood. *Gentlemen's Recreation*. 1697.

Cox, Palmer. *Palmer Cox's Brownies*. Unknown.

Cox, Palmer (1840–1924). *Queer People with Wings and Stings and Their Queer Kapers*. N.d.

Coxe, Arthur Cleveland. *The Daily Round / Meditation Prayer and Praise*. 1882.

Coxe, William. *History of the House of Austria* (vols. 1–4). 1876.

Craddock, Charles Egbert. *Down the Ravine*. 1885.

Crane, Nathalia. *The Janitor's Boy*. 1924.

Crane, Walter (1845–1915). *The Baby's Own Aesop*. 1887

Crane, Walter (1845–1915). *A Masque of Days*. 1901

Crane, Walter (1845–1915). *The Forty Thieves*. N.d.

Crane, Walter (1845–1915). *Pothooks and Perseverance*. 1886.

Crane, Walter (1845–1915). *Aladdin and the Wonderful Lamp*. N.d.

Crane, Walter (1845–1915). *The Baby's Opera*. N.d.

Crane, Walter (1845–1915). *Bluebeard's Picture Book*. 1899.

Crane, Walter (1845–1915). *This Little Pig's Picture Book*. 1895.

Cranmer-Byng, L. *The Vision of Asia*. 1932.

Cranmer-Byng, L. Introduction. *A Lute of Jade: Being Selections from the Classical Poets of China*. 1917.

Crawford, Francis Marion (1854–1909). *Saracinesca*. 1887.

Crawford, Francis Marion (1854–1909). *Cicilia: A Story of Modern Rome*. 1902.

Crawford, F. Marion. *Greifenstein*. 1889.

Crawford, Francis Marion (1854–1909). *With the Immortals*. 1888.

Crawley, Howard (1869–?). *Two New Sarcosporidia*. 1914.

Crawley, Howard (1869–?). *The Evaluation of Sarcocystis Muris in the Intestinal Cells of a Mouse*. 1914.

Crockett, David. *Adventures*. 1836.

Crockett, W. S. *The Scott Country*. 1902.

Croker, John Wilson. *Croker's Correspondence and Diaries* (vols. 1–3). 1884.

Cromer, Earl of. *Modern Egypt* (2-vol. set). 1908.

Cromer, Earl of. *Ancient and Modern Imperialism*. 1910.

Crook, Col. William H. *Through Five Administrations*. 1910.

Crook, Colonel W.H. *Memories of the White House: The Homelife of Our Presidents from Lincoln to Roosevelt*. 1911.

Crothers, Samuel Mcchord. *Meditations on Votes for Women*. 1914.

Crothers, Samuel Mcchord (1857–1927). *The Convention of Books*. 1911.

Crothers, Samuel Mcchord (1857–1927). *Among Friends*. 1910.

Crownshield, Benjamin W. *A Private Journal*. 1941.

Cruikshank, George (1792–1878), and Laman Blanchard. *George Cruikshank's Omnibus*. 1862.

Cuenoud, Edmond. *Une Histoire Qui Finit Mal*. N.d.

Culbertson, William S. *Alexander Hamilton*. 1916.

Cullom, Shelby M. *Fifty Years of Public Service: Personal Recollections of Shelby M. Cullom*. 1911.

Cunningham, Graham. A. *Vanished Arcadia: Being Some Account of the Jesuits in Paraguay 1607–1767*. 1901.

Cupples, George, Mrs. *The Story of Miss Dollkins*. 1870.

Cureau, Adolphe Louis. *Savage Man in Central Africa*. 1915.

Curtin, Jeremiah. *The Mongols in Russia*. 1908.

Curtis, Edward S. *The North American Indian*. 1915.

Curtis, Edward S. *The North American Indian*, vol. 18. 1915.

Curtis, Francis. *The Republican Party* (2-vol. set). 1904.

Curtis, George William. *The Correspondence of John Lothrop Motley*. 1889.

Curtis, Natalie (1875–1921). *An American Indian Composer*. N.d.

Curtis, Natalie (Editor). *The Indians' Book (Indian Lore, Music and Narrative from American Indians)*. 1907.

Curzon, Marquess George (Curzon of Kedleston) (1859–1925). *Modern Parliamentary Eloquence*. 1913.

Cushing, Otho. *The Teddyssey*. 1907.

Cutting, Mary Stewart. *More Stories of Married Life*. 1920.

Cutting, Mary Stewart. *Refractory Husbands*. 1920.

Cutting, Mary Stewart. *Little Stories of Married Life*. 1920.

Cutting, Mary Stewart. *Little Stories of Courtship*. 1920.

Cutting, Suydam (1889–?). *The Fire Ox and Other Years*. 1940.

Cuyás, Arturo. *Appleton's New Spanish Dictionary*. 1913.

Da Ricaldone, Stefano Tolice. *La Commedia di Dante Alighieri*. 1874.

Da Silva Rondon, Col. Candido. *The Roosevelt-Rondon Scientific Expedition and the Telegraphic Line Commission*. 1916.

Da Silva Rondon, Col. Candido. *The Roosevelt-Rondon Scientific Expedition and the Telegraph Line Commission*. 1915.

Da Silva Rondon, Col. Candido. *Lectures on the Roosevelt-Rondon Scientific Expedition and the Telegraph Line Commission*. 1916.

Dalberg-Acton, John Emerich. *Lectures on the French Revolution*. 1910.

Dalberg-Acton, John Emerich. *History of Freedom and Other Essays*. 1907.

Dampier, Captain William. *Dampier's Voyages*. 1906.

Daniel, William B. *Daniel's Rural Sports* (4-vol. set). 1801–1813.

Daniels, Hon. Josephus (1862–1948), and C. C. Marsh. *Official Records of the Union and Confederate Navies in the War of the Rebellion* (series 2, vol. 2). 1921.

Daniels, Hon. Josephus (1862–1948), and Charles Stewart. *Official Records of the Union and Confederate Navies in the War of the Rebellion* (series 2, vol. 1). 1921.

Daniels, Hon. Josephus (1862–1948), and Charles Stewart. *Official Records of the Union and Confederate Navies in the War of the Rebellion* (series 1, vol. 26). 1914.

Danielson, Florence H., and Charles B. Davenport. *Eugenics Record Office, Memoir No.1, The Hill Folk, Report on A Rural Community of Hereditary Defectives.* Aug 1912.

Dark, Sidney, and Rowland Gray. *W. S. Gilbert: His Life and Letters.* 1923.

Darley, Felix O. C. *Compositions in Outline by Felix O. C. Darley from Judd's Margaret.* 1856.

Darley, Felix O. C. *Rip Van Winkle.* 1848.

Darley, Felix O. C. *The Legend of Sleepy Hollow.* 1849.

Darwin, Charles Robert (1809–1882). *Naturalists Voyage around the World.* 1860.

Darwin, Charles Robert (1809–1882). *The Descent of Man.* 1871.

Darwin, Charles Robert (1809–1882). *The Origin of Species,* vol.1. 1910.

Darwin, Charles Robert (1809–1882), and Francis Darwin (Editor). *The Life and Letters of Charles Darwin,* (vol. 1 and vol. 2). 1911.

Dasent, Sir George Webbe (1817–1896). *Norroena Norse / Anglo Saxon Classics / Norse Popular Tales.* 1906.

Dasent, Sir George Webbe (1817–1896). *Vikings of the Baltic: A Tale of the North in the Tenth Century* (3 vols.). 1875.

Dasent, Sir George Webbe (1817–1896). *Popular Tales.* 1859.

Dasent, Sir George Webbe (1817–1896). *The Story of Burnt Njal.* 1861.

Dasent, Sir George Webbe (1817–1896). *The Story of Gisli the Outlaw.* 1866.

Dasent, Sir George Webbe (1817–1896). *The Prose of Younger Edda Commonly Ascribed to Snorri Sturluson.* 1842.

Dasent, Sir George Webbe, D.C.L. *The Story of Burnt Njal.* 1906.

D'aubigne, J. H. Meele. *History of the Reformation of the Sixteenth Century* (vols. 1–5). 1847.

Dauncey, Mrs. Campbell. *The Philippines (Oriental Series): An Account of Their People, Progress and Condition,* vol. 15. 1910.

D'aurriche, vol. ante Louis. *Fuilles vol. ante D'abazia.* 1887.

Davenport, Russell W. *My Country.* 1924.

David. *The Psalms of David; Also Prayers.* 1767.

Davies, Theodore, and Sir Gaston Maspero. *The Tomb of Siphtah.* 1908.

Davies, Theodore, and Sir Gaston Maspero. *The Tomb of Queen Tiyi.* 1910.

Davis, Gherardi. *Regimental Colors of the War of the Revolution.* 1907.

Davis, Robert H., and Perley Poore Sheehan. *Efficiency: A Play in One Act (Appreciation: By Theodore Roosevelt).* 1917.

Davis, H. W. Carless. *Charlemagne: The Hero of Two Nations.* 1900.

Davis, King Oscar. *Released for Publication.* 1925.

Davis, M. E. M. *A Christmas Mass of Saint Roche. Peri Dagobert and Throwing the Wanga.* 1896.

Davis, Reuben. *Recollections of Mississippi and Mississippians.* 1891.

Davis, Richard Harding. *Her First Appearance.* 1901.

Davis, Richard Harding. *The Notes of a War Correspondent.* 1910.

Davis, Richard Harding (1864–1916). *The Cuban and Porto Rican Campaigns.* 1898.

Davis, Theodore. *The Tombs of Harmhabi and Touatankhamanow.* 1912.

Dawson, Moses. *Memoirs of General Harrison.* 1824.

Dawson, William Leon (1873–1928). *The Birds of Washington.* 1908.

Day, Clarence. *Life with Father.* 1935.

Day, Michael. *The History of Sanford and Merton* (2 vols.). N.d.

De Angeli, Marguerite (1889– ?). *Henner's Lydia.* 1937.

De Bornier, Henri. *La Fille De Roland.* 1895.

De Bosis, Lauro. *Icare.* 1933.

De Buffon, Count. *Buffon's Natural History.* 1791.

De Canteleu, Baron Le Couteu. *La Venerie Francaise.* 1758.

De Cervantes, Miguel. *Don Quixote of La Mancha.* 1906.

De Filippi, Filippo. *Ruwenzori: An Account of the Expedition of H.R.H. Prince Luigi Amedeo of Savoy.* 1908.

Defoe, Daniel (1659?-1731). *La Vie Et Les Aventures De Robinson Crusoe.* 1913.

Defoe, Daniel. *The Life and Adventures of Robinson Crusoe* (vols. 1 and 2). 1790.

De Gomara, Francisco Lopez. *Annals of Charles V (Spine) (Annals of the Emperor Charles V) Title Page.* 1912.

De Kay, James Ellsworth. *Natural History of New York Part 1 Zoology, Reptiles and Fishes.* 1843.

De Kay, James Ellsworth. *Natural History of New York Part 1 Zoology.* 1843.

De Kay, James Ellsworth. *Natural History of New York Part I Zoology and Ornithology.* 1843.

De Kay, James Ellsworth. *Natural History of New York Part 1 Zoology, Reptiles, and Fishes.* 1842.

De Koven, Anna Farwell (Mrs. Reginald) (1860–1953). *The Life and Letters of John Paul Jones* (in 2 vols.). 1913.

De La Conterie, Leverrier. *L'ecole de la Chasse aux Chiens Courants ou Venerie Normande.* 1845.

De La Mare, Walter John (1873–1956). *Memoirs of a Midget.* 1926.

De Lamartine, A. *Histoire De La Turquie,* vol. 1. 1854.

De Lamartine, A. *Histoire De La Turquie,* vol. 2. 1854.

De Lamartine, A. *Histoire De La Turquie,* vol. 4. 1854.

De Lamartine, A. *Histoire De La Turquie.* 1854–1855.

De Liefde, Jacob. *The Great Dutch Admirals.* 1874.

De Lima, J. C. Alves. *Recordacoes De Homens E Cousas Do Meu Tempo.* 1926.

De Monvel, M. B. *La Fontaine: Fables Choises Pour Les Enfants.* N.d.

De Musset, Alfred. *Poesies Nouvelles 1836–1852.* N.d.

De Nolhac, Pierre (1859–1936). *Versailles and the Trianons.* 1906.

De Paris, Comte. *The Battle of Gettysburg.* 1886.

De Paula, Antonio Joaquim. *The Lisbon Guide: Or an Historical and Descriptive View of the City of Lisbon.* 1853.

De Pressense, E. *Une Joyeuse Nichee.* 1913.

De Pressense, E. *Bois-Gentil.* 1913.

De Quincey. *Confessions of an English Opium-Eater*. 1822.

De Saint-Simon, Duc. *Memoires De Saint-Simon*. 1904–1913.

De Suckau, Henri. *Le Robinson Suisse*. c. 1872.

De Toreno, El Conde. *Levantamiento Guerra Y Revoluccion De Espana*. 1851.

De Trobriand, Regis (1816–1897). *Four Years with the Army of the Potomac*. 1889.

De Wolfe, Van (and G. Hermans, Photographer). *Antverpia*. c. 1910.

Dean, Arthur H. *William Nelson Cromwell 1854–1948: An American Pioneer in Corporate Comparative and International Law*. 1937.

Dean, Bashford. *Handbook of Arms and Armor including the William H. Riggs Donation*. 1916.

Deforest, Emily Johnston. *James Colles, 1788–1883: Life and Letters*. 1926.

Delarue, Sidney. *The Land of the Pepper Bird, Liberia*. 1930.

Delbruck, Hans. *Geschichte der Kriegskunst*. 1901.

Deledda, Grazia. *I Giuochi Della Vita*. 1905.

Delke, Charles W. *Problems of Greater Britain*. 1890.

Delong, Emma. *The Voyage of the Jeanette / The Ship and Ice Journals of George W. Delong*, vol. 1. 1883.

Delong, Emma. *The Voyage of the Jeanette / The Ship and Ice Journals of George W. Delong*, vol. 2. 1883.

Demille, James. *The Dodge Club*. 1869.

Deming, Clarence. *By-Ways of Nature and Life*. 1884.

Deming, Edwin-Willard and Therese O. Deming. *American Animal Life*. 1916.

Demontaigne, Michel. *Les Essais de Michel Demontaigne* (vols. 1 and 2). 1906.

Denley, Hon. Edwin, and Col. Harry Kidderwhite. *Official Records of the Union and Confederate Navies in the War of the Rebellion* (series 2, vol. 3). 1922.

Dennis, Alfred L. P. *Adventures in American Diplomacy 1896–1906*. 1928.

Dension, Lt. Col. George. *A History of Cavalry*. 1877.

Department of Commerce and Labor Bureau of the Census. *A Century of Population Growth 1790–1900*. 1909.

Department of State. *Register of officers and Agents*. 1816.

Deperet, Charles. *Transformations of the Animal World*. 1909.

Derby, Capt. George Horatio. *Phoenixiana* (vols. 1 and 2). 1897.

Detmold, Maurice, and Edward Detmold. *16 Illustrations of Subjects from Kipling's "Jungle Book."* 1903.

Dewar, Douglas. *Glimpses of Indian Birds*. 1913.

Dewar, Douglas, and Frank Finn. *The Making of Species*. 1909.

Diaz, A. M. *Christmas Morning: Little Stories for Little Folks*. 1880.

Diaz, Abby Morton. *Cats Arabian Nights*. 1881.

Diaz, Abby Morton. *Polly Cologne*. 1881.

Diaz, Anna M. *The Entertaining Story of King Bronde: His Lily and His Rosebud*. 1869.

Dickens, Charles (1812–1870). *Pickwick Papers*. 1887.

Dickens, Charles (1812–1870). *Pickwick Club*, vol. 2. 1842.

Dickens, Charles (1812–1870). *Dombey and Son*. 1879.

Dickens, Charles (1812–1870). *Great Expectations: Pictures from Italy: American Notes.* 1879.

Dickens, Charles (1812–1870). *A Tale of Two Cities and Christmas Books.* 1879.

Dickens, Charles (1812–1870). *Old Curiosity Shop: Master Humphrey's Clock and Miscellanies.* 1879.

Dickens, Charles (1812–1870). *Barnsby Rudge: Edwin Drood.* 1879.

Dickens, Charles (1812–1870). *The Pickwick Club.* 1879.

Dickens, Charles (1812–1870). *Nicholas Nickleby.* 1879.

Dickens, Charles (1812–1870). *Sketches by Boz: Hard Times: Reprinted Pieces.* 1879.

Dickens, Charles (1812–1870). *Little Dorrit.* 1879.

Dickens, Charles (1812–1870). *David Copperfield.* 1879.

Dickens, Charles (1812–1870). *Oliver Twist: Uncommercial Traveller.* 1879.

Dickens, Charles (1812–1870). *Martin Chuzzlewit.* 1879.

Dickens, Charles (1812–1870). *Our Mutual Friend.* 1879.

Dickens, Charles (1812–1870). *A Child's History of England and Miscellanies.* 1879.

Dickens, Charles (1812–1870). *Pickwick Papers.* 1838.

Dickens, Charles (1812–1870). *Nicholas Nickleby: Original Parts 1838–39.* 1839.

Dickens, Charles (1812–1870). *David Copperfield.* 1850.

Dickens, Charles (1812–1870). *Our Mutual Friend,* vols. 1–20. 1865.

Dickens, Charles (1812–1870). *Our Mutual Friend, Charles Dickens, Original Parts,* vols. 1–20. 1865.

Dickens, Charles (1812–1870). *Bleak House.* 1879.

Dickins, Frederick V. (Translator). *The Loyal League a Japanese Romance.* 1908.

Dielitz, Theo. *The Hunters of the World.* 1866.

Dineflage, Friedrich F. Von. *Deutsche Reiter in Sudwest (Deeds of German Roughriders in Southwest Africa).* N.d.

Ditmars, Raymond L. *Reptiles of the World.* 1910.

Divine, Charles. *City Ways and Company Streets.* 1918.

Dixon, Samuel G. *Benjamin Lee.* N.d.

Dobson, Austin. *Vignettes in Rhyme.* 1883.

Dobson, Austin. *At the Sign of the Lyre.* 1885.

Dodd, William. *Sermons "On the Duties of the Great."* 1770.

Dodd, William E. *Statesmen of the Old South.* 1911.

Dodge, Col. Richard Irving. *Our Wild Indians.* 1882.

Dodge, Harrison Howell. *Mount Vernon Its Owner and Its Story.* 1932.

Dodge, Major-General Grenville M. *Personal Recollections.* 1914.

Dodge, Mary Mapes. *Rhymes and Jingles.* 1930.

Dodge, Mary Mapes. *Donald and Dorothy.* 1906.

Dodge, Mary Mapes. *St. Nicholas.* 1880.

Dodge, Mary Mapes. *Rhymes and Jingles.* 1930.

Dodge, Theodore A. *The Campaign of Chancellorsville.* 1881.

Dodge, Theodore A. *Army and Other Tales.* Unknown.

Dodge, Theodore Ayrault. *Great Captains: Alexander: A History of the Origin and Growth of the Art of War*. 1890.

Dodge, Theodore Ayrault. *Great Captains Napoleon*. 1904.

Dodge, Theodore Ayrault. *Patroclus and Penelope: A Chat in the Saddle*. 1886.

Dodge, Theodore Ayrault. *Riders of Many Lands*. 1894.

Dodge, Theodore Ayrault. *Patroclus and Penelope*. 1885.

Dodge, Theodore Ayrault. *A Bird's Eye View of Our Civil War*. 1883.

Dodge, Theodore Ayrault. *Great Captains*. 1889.

Donovan, Mike. *The Roosevelt That I Know*. 1909.

Doubleday, Abner (1819–1893). *Chancellorsville and Gettysburg*. 1882.

Doubleday, Abner (1819–1893). *Chancellorsville and Gettysburg: Campaigns of the Civil War*. 1882.

Douglas, Hudson. *A Million a Minute: A Romance of Modern New York and Paris*. 1908.

Downing, J. *Letters of J. Downing*. 1834.

Doyle, Dr. C. W. *The Taming of the Jungle*. 1899.

Doyle, Richard. *The Doyle Fairy Book: Consisting of Twenty-Eight Fairy Tales*. 1893.

Doyle, Sir Arthur Conan (1859–1930). *Memories and Adventures*. 1924.

Doyle, Sir Arthur Conan (1859–1930). *A History of the Great War the British Campaign in France and Flanders 1914*. 1916.

Drake, Benjamin. *Life of Tecumseh*. 1850.

Draper, John William (1811–1882). *History of the Intellectual Development of Europe*, vol. 2. 1876.

Drayson, Alfred W. *Sporting Scenes amongst the Kaffirs of South Africa*. 1860.

Dresser, Horatio W. *Living by the Spirit*. 1908.

Drewes, William K. *Fine Arts Insurance*. 1938.

Drinkwater, John. *Robert E. Lee: A Play*. 1923.

Drugard, Samuel. *A Discourse of Having Many Children*. 1695.

Drummond, Henry. *Tropical Africa*. 1890.

Dryden, John (1631–1700). *Dryden's Virgil*. 1880.

Dryden, John (1631–1700). *The Dramatic Works of John Dryden Esq.* (6 vols.) 1857.

Du Buisson, Mr. *La Vie Du Vicomte De Turenne*. 1685.

Du Livre, Journees. *Aux Quatre Coins De Chez Nous*. 1931.

Du Maurier, George (1834–1896). *Trilby / A Novel*. 1894.

Dubriguf, Hans. *Geschichte Der Kriegskunst*. 1900.

Dugmore, A. Radclyffe. *The Romance of the Beaver*. N.d.

Duke, Basil W. *History of Morgan's Cavalry*. 1867.

Duke, Basil W. *Morgan's Cavalry*. 1906.

Duke, Basil W. *Reminiscences of General Basil W. Duke*. 1911.

Dukes, Paul. *Red Dusk and the Morrow / Adventures and Investigations in Red Russia*. 1922.

Dumas, Alexandre (1802–1870). *Les Louves De Machecoul*, vols. 1–3. 1892.

Dunbar, Mary F. P. (Editor). *The Shakespeare Birthday Book*. 1886.

Dunbar, Seymour. *The History of Travel in America*, vols. 1–4. 1915.

Dunlap, William. *Bibliographica Americana and Bibliographical Checklist by William Dunlap*, vol. 1. 1916.

Dunn, J. P., Jr. *Massacres of the Mountains: A History of the Indian Wars of the Far West*. 1886.

Dunn, Jacob Platt. *True Indian Stories with Glossary of Indiana Indian Names*. 1908.

Dunn, Martha Baker. *Cicero in Maine*. 1905.

Dunne, Finley Peter (1867–1936). *Mr. Dooley in Peace and War*. 1899.

Dunraven, Earl of. *The Great Divide: Travels in the Upper Yellowstone in the Summer of 1874*. 1876.

Duveen, James Henry. *Art Treasures and Intrigue*. 1932.

Dymock, John. *Ainsworths Dictionary, English and Latin*. 1876.

Earle, Alice Morse. *Old Time Gar-Dens*. 1901.

Eastman, Julia A. *Young Rick*. 1875.

Eaton, Elon Howard. *Birds of New York* (2 vols.). 1910.

Eaton, Oliver B. A. *Norroena Anglo-Saxon Classics Saxo Grammaticus*. 1906.

Eaton, Seymour. *Shakespeare Rare Print Collection*. 1900.

Eaton, Seymour. *The Roosevelt Bears*. 1906.

Eaton, Seymour. *More about the Roosevelt Bears*. 1907.

Eaton, Seymour. *The Roosevelt Bears Abroad*. 1908.

Eaton, W. D. *Great Poems of the World War*. 1922.

Eberlein, Harold Donaldson. *Manor Houses and Historic Homes of Long Island and Staten Island*. 1928.

Echard, Laurence. *The Gazetteer's or Newsman's Interpreter in Europe*. 1732.

Eddington, Sir Arthur Stanley (1882–1944). *The Expanding Universe*. 1933.

Eddington, Sir Arthur Stanley (1882–1944). *New Pathways in Science*. 1935.

Eddington, Sir Arthur Stanley (1882–1944). *The Nature of the Physical World*. 1929.

Eddington, Sir Arthur Stanley (1882–1944). *Science and the Unseen World*. 1929.

Edgeworth, Maria. *Novels and Tales: Belinda (Spine: Belinda)*, vol. 6. 1833.

Edgeworth, Maria (1767–1849). *Simple Susan Told to the Children by Louey Chisholm*. N.d.

Edgeworth, Maria (1767–1849). *Early Lessons*. 1866.

Edgeworth, Maria (1767–1849). *Tales and Novels*, vols. 1–4, vols. 7–10. 1832.

Edward-Dalberb, John Emerich, Baron Acton (1834–1902). *Lord Acton and His Circle*. 1906.

Edwards, Annie. *A Ballroom Repentance*. 1882.

Edwards, George Wharton. *The Jackdaw of Rheims*. 1919.

Edwards, Harry Stillwell. *The Blue Hen's Chickens*. 1924.

Edwards, Harry Stillwell. *Eneas Africanus*. 1872.

Edwards, Jonathan. *A History of the Work of Redemption*. 1792.

Edwards, Rev. Jonathan (1703–1758). *The Treatise on Religious Affections*. N.d.

Edwards, Rev. Jonathan (1703–1758). *Life of the Late Rev. David Brainerd*. 1749.

Edwards, Rev. Jonathan (1703–1758). *Two Dissertations: 1. Concerning the End for Which God Created the World. 2. The Nature of Pure Virtue.* 1765

Edwards, Rev. Jonathan (1703–1758). *Sermons on Important Subjects Collected from a Number of Ministers in Some of the Northern States of America.* 1797.

Edwards, Rev. Maurice Dwight. *Richard Edwards and His Wife Catherine Pond May / Their Ancestors Lives and Descendants.* 1931.

Edwards, William. *Memoirs of Col. William Edwards (William Edwards 1770–1851).* 1847.

Edwards, Wm. H. *Compiler Edwards Genealogy, The Descendants of Timothy Edwards of Stockbridge, Ma,* 2 vol. 1903.

Egan, Maurice Francis. *Confessions of a Book-Lover.* 1922.

Eggleston, Edward (1837–1902). *Queer Stories for Boys and Girls.* 1884.

Eigenmann, H. Carl. *The American Characidae.* 1918.

Einstein, Lewis. *The Relation of Literature to History.* 1903.

Einstein, Lewis. *Roosevelt: His Mind in Action.* 1930.

Einstein, Lewis. *The Italian Renaissance in England.* 1902.

Einstein, Lewis. *Erasmus Against War.* 1907.

Eliot, Daniel Gerand. *A Monograph of the Felidae.* 1883.

Eliot, George. *Essays and Leaves from A Note Book.* 1884.

Eliot, George. *Impressions of Theophrastus Such.* N.d.

Elliot, Daniel Giraud. *A Monograph of the Felidae; Or Family of the Cats.* 1883.

Elliot, Daniel Giraud. *Monograph of the Tetraoninae.* 1865.

Elliot, Daniel Giraud. *Synopsis of the Mammals of North America.* 1910.

Elliot, Daniel Giraud. *A Review of the Primates.* 1913.

Elliot, Elizabeth Shippen Green (Illustrated by). *Some Colonial and Revolutionary Landmarks Manhattan 1609–1800.* 1932.

Ellis, Edward S. *From Ranch to White House: Life of Roosevelt.* 1906.

Ellis, Edward S. *From Ranch to White House. Life of TR.* 1927.

Ellis, S. M. *George Meredith: His Life and Friends in Relation to His Work.* 1920.

Ellis, William. *Polynesian Researches* (2-vol. set). 1829.

Elmer, Ebenezer. *An Elegy on Francis Barber, Esq.* 1917.

Ely, Helena Rutherford. *A Woman's Hardy Garden.* 1903.

Emerson, Edward W. *Charles Russell Lowell Life and Letters.* 1907.

Emerson, L. O. *The Golden Wreath: A Collection of Favorite Melodies for School Use.* 1857.

Emerson, Ralph Waldo (1803–1882). *Poems.* 1918.

Emerson, Ralph Waldo (1803–1882). *The Conduct of Life.* c. 1888.

Emerson, Ralph Waldo (1803–1882). *Representative Men.* 1888.

Emerson, Ralph Waldo (1803–1882). *Works of Ralph Waldo Emerson,* vol. 1. *Essays.* 1879.

Emerson, Ralph Waldo (1803–1882). *Works of Ralph Waldo Emerson,* vol. 2. *Society and Solitude / Representative Men.* 1879.

Emerson, Ralph Waldo (1803–1882). *Works of Ralph Waldo Emerson*, vol. 3. *Conduct of Life*. 1879.

Emerson, Ralph Waldo (1803–1882). *Works of Ralph Waldo Emerson*, vol. 4. *Letters and Social Aims / Poems*. 1879.

Emerson, Ralph Waldo (1803–1882). *Works of Ralph Waldo Emerson*. vol. 5. *Miscellanies*. 1879.

Emerson, Ralph Waldo (1803–1882). *Select Essays*. N.d.

Emmons, Ebenezer (1799–1863). *Natural History of New York Part IV Geology*. 1842.

Emmons, Ebenezer (1799–1863). *Natural History of New York Part V Agriculture*. 1846.

Emmons, Ebenezer (1799–1863). *Natural History of New York Part V Agriculture, Plates*, vol. 3. 1851

Emmons, Ebenezer (1799–1863). *Natural History of New York Part V Agriculture*. 1848.

Emmons, Ebenezer (1799–1863). *Natural History of New York Part V Agriculture*. 1851.

En Poiutou, Gastine. *La Venerie De Jacques Du Fouilloux Seigneur Dudit Lieu Gentil-Homme Du Pays*. 1624.

Endicott, John (1589–1665). *John Endicott's Petition to Charles II*. 1660.

Espey, John J. *Minor Heresies*. 1945.

Estabrook, Arthur H., and Charles B. Davenport. *Eugenics Record Office, Memoir No 2. the Nam Family*. 1912.

Eugene, Prince (1663–1736). *Histoire du Prince Eugene De Savoye* (5-vol. Set). 1770.

Eustis, Celestine. *Cooking in Old Creole Days*. 1901.

Evans, Mary Ann (1819–1880). *Adam Bede*. Unknown.

Evans, Mary Ann (1819–1880). *Felix Holt*. Unknown.

Evans, Mary Ann (1819–1880). *Daniel Deronda*. Unknown.

Evans, Mary Ann (1819–1880). *The Mill on the Floss*. Unknown.

Evans, Mary Ann (1819–1880). *Silas Marner*. Unknown.

Evans, Mary Ann (1819–1880). *Scenes of Clerical Life*. Unknown.

Evans, Mary Ann (1819–1880). *Romola*. Unknown.

Evans, Mary Ann (1819–1880). *Middlemarch: A Study of Provincial Life*. Unknown.

Ewing, Juliana Horatia. *Mrs. Overtheway's Remembrances*. 1888.

Ewing, Juliana Horatia. *Madame Liberality*. 1901.

Fairbridge, Dorothea. *Historic Houses of South Africa*. 1922.

Fairbridge, Dorothea. *Lady Anne Bernard of the Cape of Good Hope*. 1824.

Falconer, William. *The Shipwreck*. 1827.

Farington, Joseph R. A. *The Farington Diary*, vol. 1. 1923.

Farjeon, Eleanor, and Herbert Farjeon. *Kings and Queens*. Unknown.

Farnol, Jeffery. *Our Admirable Betty*. 1918.

Farnol, Jeffery. *Peregrine's Progress*. 1922.

Farnol, Jeffery. *The Amateur Gentleman*. 1913.

Farnol, Jeffery. *The Broad Highway*. 1911.

Farragut, Loyall. *Life and Letters of Admiral D. G. Farragut.* 1879.

Farrer, Reginald J. *The Garden of Asia.* 1904.

Fedden, Katherine Waldo Douglas (d. 1939). *Manor Life in Old France.* 1933.

Federn, Karl. *Dante and His Time.* 1902.

Fedorova, Nina. *The Family.* 1940.

Feke, Robert (1707–1750). *Robert Feke (Exhibition Catalog) (Portrait Painter).* 1946.

Fenollosa, Ernest, and Ezra Pound (1885–). *Noh Or Accomplishment (A Study of the Classical Stage of Japan).* 1917.

Ferber, Edna (1887–1968). *Show Boat.* 1926.

Ferguson, William Scott. *Hellenistic Athens: An Historical Essay.* 1911.

Ferrero, G. *Grandeur et Decadence de Rome III-IV-V.* 1907.

Ferrero, Guglielmo. *Grandezza E Decadenza di Roma,* vols. 1–6. 1907.

Ferrero, Gugliemo. *The Greatness and the Decline of Rome (5 vols).* 1907.

Ferrier, Susan E. *Miss Ferrier's Novels Destiny,* vol. 1–4. 1894.

Feuchtwanger, Lion. *Jew Süss.* 1927.

Fibbleton, George. *Travels in America.* 1833.

Field, Eugene. *A Little Book of Profitable Tales.* 1889.

Field, Eugene and Reginald De Koven. *Songs of Childhood: Verses by Eugene Field.* 1896.

Field, Eugene (1850–1895). *Second Book of Verse.* 1892.

Field, Eugene (1850–1895). *Verse and Prose.* 1917.

Figuier, Louis. *La Terre Et Les Mers.* 1866.

Findlater, Mary. *Betty Musgrave.* 1913.

Finerty, John F. *War-Path and Bivouac or the Conquest of the Sioux.* 1890.

Finley, William Lowell. *American Birds.* 1907.

Finn, Francis. *Indian Sporting Birds.* 1915.

Fisher, A. K., M.D. *The Hawks and Owls of the United States in Their Relation to Agriculture.* 1893.

Fisher, H. A. L. *James Bryce.* 1927.

Fisher, A. K. *North American Fauna #7 The Death Valley Expedition; A Biological Survey of Parts of California, Nevada, Arizona, and Utah Part II.* 1893.

Fisher, A. K., Leonhard Stejneger, et al. *North American Fauna #7 Part 2 the Death Valley Expedition.* 1893.

Fiske, John. *The Discovery of America (vol. 1 of 2-vol. set).* 1892.

Fiske, John. *Old Virginia and Her Neighbours,* vol. 1. 1900.

Fiske, John. *The Old Virginia and Her Neighbours,* vol. 2. 1900.

Fiske, John (1842–1901). *Excursions of an Evolutionist.* 1884.

Fiske, Rear Admiral Bradley A. (1854–1942). *The Navy as a Fighting Machine.* 1916.

Fitch, George Hamlin. *Comfort Found in Good Old Books.* 1911.

Fitzgerald, Edward (1809–1883). *Works of Edward Fitzgerald (2 vols.).* 1887.

Flandreysy, Jeanne De. *La Venus d'Arles et le Museum Arlaten.* 1903.

Flaubert, Gustave (1821–1880). *The Temptation of St. Anthony.* 1910.

Flaubert, Gustave (1821–1880). *Salammbo.* 1901.

Flecker, James Elroy. *Hassan: The Story of Hassan of Bagdad and How He Came to Make the Golden Journey to Samarkand.* 1924.

Fleischman, Max Charles (1877–1951). *After Big Game in Arctic and Tropic.* 1909.

Fleming, Hanns Friedrich Von. *Des vollkommen (Deutsch Senticher Fagers)* (2-vol. set), vol. 1. 1719; vol. 2 1724. 1724.

Fleming, Thomas. *Around the Capital.* 1902.

Fletcher, L. R. C. *An Introductory History of England.* 1904.

Flourens, M. *Ceuvres' Completes De Buffon,* vols. 1–12. N.d.

Focillon, Henri. *Moyen Age Survivances et Reveils.* 1943.

Focillon, Henri (1881–1943). *Maitres de L'estampe: Pein Tres Graveures.* 1930.

Foerster, Wolfgang. *Prinz Friedrich Karl Von Preuszen (1858–1885)* (2-vol. set) (in German). 1910.

Fogazzaro, A. M. *Pereat Rochus (From Reune Bleue).* 1896.

Fogazzaro, Antonia (1842–1911). *The Patriot.* 1906.

Fogazzaro, Antonia (1842–1911). *The Sinner.* 1907.

Fogazzaro, Antonio. *The Saint.* 1906.

Foley, James William (1874–1939). *Tales of the Trail.* 1912.

Foley, James William (1874–1939). *The Voices of Song.* 1916.

Fontaine, C. B. L. *Les Poetes Francais de Xixe Siecle.* 1889.

Forbes, Archibald. *Memories and Studies of War and Peace.* 1895.

Forbush, Edward Howe. *Useful Birds and Their Protection.* 1907.

Forbush, Edward Howe. *A History of the Game Birds.* 1912.

Force, M. F. *From Fort Henry to Corinth: Campaigns of the Civil War.* 1881.

Ford, Lauren. *The Ageless Story.* 1939.

Ford, Lauren. *The Little Book about God.* 1944.

Ford, Paul Leicester. *The Story of an Untold Love.* 1897.

Ford, Worthington C. (Editor). *Jasper Mauduit 1762–1765.* 1918.

Ford, Worthington C. (Editor). *Letters of Henry Adams 1858–1891.* 1930.

Forest, Mrs. Robert De. *A Walloon Family in America: Lockwood De Forest and His Forbears 1500–1848.* 1914.

Forman, Buxton H. *Notebooks of Percy Bysshe Shelley,* vols. 1–3. 1911.

Foronda and Aguilera, Don Manuel De. *Manuel de Foronada y Aguilera / Estancias y Viajes Emperador Carlos V.* 1914.

Forster, E. M. *The Celestial Omnibus and Other Stories.* 1920.

Fortescue, Granville. *Forearmed.* 1916.

Foster, Charles. *First Steps for Little Feet in Gospel Paths.* 1885.

Foster, J. J. *French Art from Watteau to Prud'hon,* vols. 1–3. 1905–1907.

Foster, R. F. *Foster's Russian Bank (Or Crapette): A Game for Two Players.* 1920.

Fothergill, Jessie. *Kith and Kin.* 1881.

Fouilloux, Jacques Du. *La Venerie.* 1650.

Foulke, William Dudley (1848–1935). *A Hoosier Autobiography.* 1922.

Foulke, William Dudley (1848–1935). *Lucius B. Swift; A Biography.* 1930.

Foulke, William Dudley (1848–1935). *Protean Papers.* 1903.

Foulke, William Dudley (1848–1935). *A Random Record of Travel during Fifty Years.* 1925.

Foulke, William Dudley (1848–1935). *Fighting the Spoilsmen.* 1919.

Foulke, William Dudley (1848–1935). *Roosevelt and the Spoilsmen.* 1925.

Fox, Emmett (1886–1951). *Power through Constructive Thinking.* 1932.

Fox, John, Jr. *Book, Christmas Eve on Lonesome and Other Stories.* 1904.

Fox, John, Jr. *The Little Shepherd of Kingdom Come.* 1903.

Fox, William F. *Regimental Losses in the Civil War.* 1889.

Fox, William F. *Regimental Losses in the American Civil War.* 1898.

Francesco, S. *Fioretti di S. Francesco*, vols. 1 and 2. 1883.

Franck, Louis. *President Roosevelt Karakterschets.* 1924.

Frankfurter, Felix (1882–1965). *The Public and Its Government.* 1930.

Franklin, Benjamin. *The Autobiography of Benjamin Franklin.* 1906.

Frazer, J. G. *Totemism and Exogamy*, vol. 2, 3, and 4. 1910.

Frederica Sophia. *Wilhelmina Margravine of Baireuth: Memoirs of Frederica Sophia Wilhelmina* (2 vols.). 1877.

Frederick, Adolphus, the Duke of Mecklenburg. *From the Congo to the Niger and the Nile.* 1913.

Frederick, Adolphus, the Duke of Mecklenburg (Translator). *In the Heart of Africa.* 1910.

Freeman, B. Austin. *The Vanishing Man.* 1912.

Freeman, Edward A. *The History of the Norman Conquest of England / Its Causes and Its Results*, vol. 1. 1873.

Freeman, Edward A. *The History of the Norman Conquest of England / Its Causes and Its Results*, vol. 4. 1873.

Freeman, Edward A. *The History of the Norman Conquest of England / Its Causes and Its Results*, vol. 5. 1876.

Freeman, Edward A. *The History of the Norman Conquest of England / Its Causes and Its Results*, vol. 6. 1879.

Freeman, Edward A. *Historical Essays—Third Series.* 1879.

Freeman, Edward A. *Historical Essays.* 1875.

Freeman, Edward A. *The Norman Conquest*, vol. 2. 1873.

Freeman, Edward A. *The Norman Conquest*, vol. 3. 1873.

Freeman, Edward A. *The Historical Geography of Europe.* 1881.

Freeman, Mary E. Wilkins. *Six Trees: Short Stories.* 1903.

Freemantle, Hon. Thomas Francis (1862–?). *The Book of the Rifle.* 1901.

French, Mrs. Daniel Chester. *Memories of a Sculptor's Wife.* 1928.

Frick, Childs. *Horned Ruminants of North America.* 1937.

Friedman, I. K. *The Radical.* 1907.

Friswell, Laura Hain. *In the Sixties and Seventies.* 1905.

Froissart, Sir John (1338?–1410?) *Froissart's Chronicles of England, France, Spain and Adjoining Countries* (2 vol.). 1857.

Frolich, L. *Mademoiselle Lili La Campagne.* Unknown.

Frost, A. B. *Stuff and Nonsense*. 1884.

Frost, A. B. *Stuff and Nonsense*. 1888.

Frost, A. B. *The Bull Calf and Other Tales*. 1892.

Frost, John. *The Book of the Navy*. 1895.

Frost, John. *Life of Major General Zachary Taylor*. 1847.

Frost, Matthew. *Matthew Frost or Little Snowdrops Mission*. 1875.

Frost, Robert (1874–1963). *Collected Poems of Robert Frost*. 1930.

Froude, James Anthony. *The English in the West Indies or the Bow of Ulysses*. 1888.

Froude, James Anthony. *Short Studies on Great Subjects* (3-vol. set). N.d.

Froude, James Anthony. *English Seamen of the Sixteenth Century*. 1895.

Froude, James Anthony. *The English in the West Indies*. 1906.

Froude, James Anthony. *Lectures on the Council of Trent: Delivered at Oxford 1892–3*. 1896.

Froude, James Anthony. *Oceana*. 1886.

Fuller, Col. F. C. *The Generalship of Ulysses S. Grant*. 1929.

Fuller, Osgood E. *Ideals of Life*. 1881.

Fullerton, W. Morton. *Problems of Power*. 1914.

Furlong, Charles Wellington. *The Gateway to the Sahara*. 1909.

Furniss, Henry Sanderson. *Memories of Sixty Years*. 1931.

Fyleman, Rose. *The Fairy Green*. 1922.

Fyleman, Rose. *Forty Good-Night Tales*. 1930.

Gade, John A. *All My Born Days / Experiences of a Naval Intelligence Officer in Europe*. 1942.

Gage, Thomas (1721–1787). *A Survey of the Spanish West Indies*. 1702.

Gagnon, Ernest. *Chansons Populaires de Canada*. 1908.

Gallie, Walter W. *American College of Surgeons 1942–1943*. 1942.

Gallois, L. *Vespuce et le Nom D'amerique (Americ Vespuce et les Geographes de Saint-Des / Annales De Geographie #67)*. 1904.

Galsworthy, John. *The White Monkey*. 1924.

Gamoneda, Martin E. *Momumentos Arquitectonicas de Espana Toledo*. 1905.

Gann, Thomas. *In an Unknown Land*. 1924.

Gann, Thomas. *Mystery Cities / Exploration and Adventure Lubaantun*. 1925.

Gardiner, Samuel R. *The Puritan Revolution 1603–1660*. 1898.

Gardner, Constance. *Book, Augustus Peabody Gardner, Major, United States National Guard, 1865–1918*. 1919.

Gardner, Constance (Editor). *Augustus Peabody Gardner*. 1920.

Gardner, Dorsey. *Quatre Bras, Ligny, and Waterloo*. 1882.

Gardner, Herbert. *Come Duck Shooting with Me*. 1917.

Gardner, William Amory. *In Greece with the Classics*. 1908.

Garfield, James Abram (1831–1881). *The Works of James Abram Garfield*. 1883.

Garis, Howard R. (1873–1962). *Uncle Wiggly's Apple Roast*. 1924.

Garland, Hamlin (1860–1940). *Main Travelled Roads*. 1893.

Garland, Hamlin (1860–1940). *A Son of the Middle Border*. 1917.

Garland, Hamlin (1860–1940). *Prairie Songs.* 1893.

Garland, Hamlin (1860–1940). *Cavanagh: Forest Ranger Sunset Edition.* 1910.

Garland, Hamlin (1860–1940). *Main Traveled Roads.* 1899.

Garland, Hamlin (1860–1940). *Other Main Travelled Roads.* 1910.

Garrison, E. E. *The Roosevelt Doctrine.* 1904.

Gary, Alice. *Nellie's Stumbling Block.* 1870.

Gaskell, Mrs. *Collection of British Authors: Wives and Daughters,* vol. 1. 1866.

Gatty, H. K. F. *Aunt Judy's Christmas Volume for 1875.* 1875.

Gatty, H. K. F. (Editor). *Aunt Judy's Christmas Volume for 1878.* 1878.

Gatty, Mrs. Alfred (Editor). *Aunt Judy's Christmas Volume for Young People.* 1870.

Gautier, Leon. *La Chanson de Roland.* 1876.

Gautier, Leon. *La Chanson de Roland.* 1872.

Gay, Sydney. *Howard James Madison* (American Statesmen Series), vol. 12. 1898.

Gay, Sydney. *Howard James Madison* / American Statesmen. 1884.

G.C., The. *Practical Dinners with Plain Directions for Their Preparation.* 1887.

Gedder, Patrick, and John Arthur Thomson (1861–1933). *Evolution.* 1911.

Geil, William Edgar (1865–1925). *The Great Wall of China.* 1909.

General William Walker. *The War in Nicaragua.* 1860.

Generalftabe, Troken. *1806 Das Preubifche Dfizierforps und die Unterfuchung der Krieg Sereigniffe.* 1906.

Gentleman with a Duster. *The Mirrors of Downing Street.* 1921.

Gentry, Thomas G. *Nests and Eggs of Birds of the United States.* 1882.

George, Andrew J. *Wordsworth's Complete Poetical Works.* 1904.

George, R. I. *The King's Book of Quebec* (2-vol. set). 1911.

George, W. L. *The Second Blooming.* 1915.

Gerard, W. James. *Face to Face with Kaiserism.* 1918.

Gibbon, Edward (1737–1794). *Gibson's Roman Empire.* 1862.

Gibbon, Edward (1737–1794). *The Decline and Fall of the Roman Empire,* vol. 2. 1912.

Gibbon, Edward (1737–1794). *Gibbon's Roman Empire,* vol. 6 (*The History of the Decline and Fall of the Roman Empire*). 1838.

Gibson, Hugh (Editor). *The Ciano Diaries: 1939–1943.* 1946.

Gibson, H. Henry. *American Forest Trees.* 1913.

Gibson, Hugh. *A Journal from Our Legation in Belgium.* 1917.

Gibson, Hugh. *Belgium.* 1939.

Gilder, Richard Watson. *Letters of Richard Watson Gilder.* 1916.

Giles, Herbert A. *Gems of Chinese Literature.* 1922.

Giles, Herbert A. *A History of Chinese Literature.* 1901.

Gillmore, Parker. *Prairie and Forest.* 1881.

Gilman, Bradley. *Roosevelt the Happy Warrior.* 1921.

Gilman, Daniel C. *James Monroe* (American Statesmen Series), vol. 14. 1898.

Gilman, Daniel C. *James Monroe* / American Statesmen. 1885.

Gilmore, Parker. *Travel, War, and Shipwreck.* 1880.

Giustiniano, Agostino. *Giustiniano Storia Di Genova.* 1537.

Glasgow, Ellen. *The Deliverance*. 1904.

Glaspell, Susan. *The Glory of the Conquered: The Story of a Great Love*. 1909.

Gleason, Arthur, and Helen Hayes Gleason, with Theodore Roosevelt (Introduction). *Golden Lads*. 1916.

Gleaves, V. Admiral Albert. *A History of the Transport Service*. 1921.

Goethals, Gen. George Washington (1858–1928). *The Panama Canal*. September 23, 1911.

Goethe, Johann Wolfgang (1749–1832). *Goethe's Wilhelm Meister*. 1851.

Goethe, Johann Wolfgang (1749–1832). *Faust* (in German). 1873.

Gogol, NikolaiVasilyevich (1809–1852). *Taras Bulba*. 1915.

Goldman, Edward A. *North American Fauna #31, Revision of the Woodrats of the Genus Neotoma 1910*. 1918.

Goldman, Edward A. *North American Fauna #41, Grizzly and Big Brown Bears (Ursus)*. 1918.

Goldsmith. *A League to Enforce Peace*. N.d.

Goldsmith, Oliver (1728–1774). *Goldsmith's Works: The Works of Oliver Goldsmith*, 4 vols. 1854.

Goodwin, Philo A. *Biography of Andrew Jackson*. 1833.

Goose, Edmund W. *English Odes*. 1909.

Gorce, Pierre De La. *The History of the Second Empire Francaise* (7-vol. Set). 1904.

Gordon, Duff, Lady. *Letters from Egypt*. 1904.

Gordon, George Byron. *Rambles in Old London*. 1924.

Gordon-Cumming, Roualyn. *Five Years of a Hunter's Life in the Far Interior of South Africa*, vols. 1–2. 1850.

Gorman, Herbert. *The Incredible Marquis*. 1929.

Gounouilhou, Editeur Paris 1916. *Histoire Illustree de la Guerre de 1914*. 1916.

Gracie, Archibald. *The Truth about Chickamauga*. 1911.

Graham, G., and R. B. Cunningham. *Father of Archangel of Scotland*. 1896.

Graham, George Edward. *Schley and Santiago*. 1902.

Graham, Stephen. *A Private in the Guards*. 1919.

Grahame, Kenneth (1859–1932). *The Golden Age*. 1900.

Grahame, Kenneth (1859–1932). *The Wind in the Willows*. 1908.

Grahame, Kenneth (1859–1932). *The Golden Age*. 1904.

Grahame, Kenneth (1859–1932). *Dream Days*. 1904.

Grant, the Major Madison. *Hank*. 1937.

Grant, Ulysses Simpson (1822–1885). *Personal Memoirs of U.S. Grant*, 2 vols. 1885.

Gray, Asa (1810–1888). *Gray's New Lessons and Manual of Botany*. 1872.

Gray, David. *The American Army in France 1917–1919*. 1920.

Gray, David. *Mr. Carteret*. 1910.

Gray, Elizabeth Janet. "Anthology with Comments." 1942.

Grebenc, Lucile. *The Time of Change*. 1938.

Green, Alice Stopford. *The Making of Ireland and Its Undoing 1200–1600*. 1909.

Greenaway, Catherine (1846–1901). *A Day in A Child's Life*. N.d.

Greenaway, Catherine (1846–1901). *The April Baby's Book of Tunes.* 1927.

Greenaway, Catherine (1846–1901). *Kate Greenaway's Birthday Book for Children.* N.d.

Greene, F. V. *Army Life in Russia.* 1881.

Greene, Francis Vinton (1850–1921). *The Mississippi: Campaigns of the Civil War.* 1882.

Greene, Francis Vinton (1850–1921). *The Russian Army and Its Campaigns in Turkey 1877–1878.* 1879.

Greene, Francis Vinton (1850–1921). *General Greene.* 1893.

Greene, Francis Vinton (1850–1921). *The Revolutionary War and the Military Policy of the United States,* vol. 1. 1911.

Greenough, James Bradstreet. *Words and Their Ways in English Speech.* 1901.

Gregg, Josiah. *Commerce of the Prairies: Journal of a Santa Fe Trader* (2-vol. set). 1844.

Gregorovius, Ferdinand. *Rome in the Middle Ages,* vol. 1. 1900.

Gregorovius, Ferdinand. *Rome in the Middle Ages,* vol. 2. 1902.

Gregorovius, Ferdinand. *Rome in the Middle Ages,* vol. 3. 1903.

Gregorovius, Ferdinand. *Rome in the Middle Ages,* vol. 4, Part 1. 1896.

Gregorovius, Ferdinand. *Rome in the Middle Ages,* vol. 4, Part 2. 1905.

Gregorovius, Ferdinand. *Rome in the Middle Ages,* vol. 6, Part 1. 1906.

Gregorovius, Ferdinand. *Rome in the Middle Ages,* vol. 6, Part 2. 1906.

Gregorovius, Ferdinand. *Rome in the Middle Ages,* vol. 7, Part 1. 1900

Gregorovius, Ferdinand. *Rome in the Middle Ages,* vol. 7, Part 2. 1900

Gregorovius, Ferdinand. *Rome in the Middle Ages,* vol. 8, Part 1. 1902.

Gregorovius, Ferdinand. *Rome in the Middle Ages,* vol. 8, Part 2. 1902.

Gregory, Eliot. *Worldly Ways and Byways.* 1899.

Gregory, Eliot. *The Ways of Men.* 1899.

Gregory, Isabella Augusta, Lady (Nee Persse) (1852–1932). *Irish Folk History Plays* (1st series, tragedies; 2nd series, tragi-comedies). 1912.

Gregory, Isabella Augusta, Lady (Nee Persse) (1852–1932). *Our Irish Theatre (A Chapter of Autobiography).* 1913.

Gregory, Isabella Augusta, Lady (Nee Persse) (1852–1932). *The Kiltartan History Book.* 1909.

Gregory, Isabella Augusta, Lady (Nee Persse) (1852–1932). *The Image: A Play in Three Acts.* 1910.

Gregory, J. W. *The Great Rift Valley.* 1896.

Gregory, William K. *The Orders of Mammals.* 1910.

Grenfell, Wilfred T. *Down North on the Labrador.* 1911.

Gribayedoff, Valerian. *The French Invasion of Ireland in '98.* 1890.

Gribble, Francis Henry (1862–1946). *Rousseau and the Women He Loved.* 1908.

Grimm, Jakob (1785–1863) and Wilhelm Grimm (1786–1859). *Kinder Und Hausmarch.* 1885.

Grimm, Jakob (1785–1863), Wilhelm Grimm (1786–1859), and Hans Christian Andersen (1805–1875). *German Popular Tales,* vol. 3. c. 1865.

Grinnell, George Bird. *Brief History of the Boone and Crockett Club*. 1910.

Grinnell, George Bird. *The Fighting Cheyennes*. 1915.

Grinnell, George Bird. *American Duck Shooting*. 1901.

Grinnell, George Bird (1849–1938), and Theodore Roosevelt (Editors). *American Big Game Hunting*. 1901.

Grinnell, George Bird, and Theodore Roosevelt (Editors). *Roosevelt's Works, Trail and Campfire*. 1914.

Grinnell, George Bird, and Theodore Roosevelt (Editors). *Hunting in Many Lands: The Book of the Boone and Crockett Club*. 1914.

Griscom, Lloyd C. *Diplomatically Speaking*. 1940.

Griswold, Gray, F. *Observations on a Salmon River*. 1921.

Grivel, Jean Baptiste, Baron (1778–1869). *Memoires du Vice-Admiral Baron Grivel*. 1914.

Grondys, L. H. *The Germans in Belgium: Experiences of a Neutral*. 1916.

Grotius, Hugo (1583–1645). *Grotius on the Freedom of the Seas*. 1916.

Grudger, W. E. *Natural History Notes on Some Beaufort (N.C.) Fishes*. 1913.

Guedalla, Philip (1889–1944). *Wellington*. 1931.

Guernsey, Lucy Ellen. *Tabby and Her Travels or the Holiday Adventures of a Kitten*. 1867.

Guest, Edgar A. *Poems of Patriotism*. 1927.

Guillaume, Albert. *Le Tennis a Travers Les Ages*. Unknown.

Gwynn, Stephen. *The Letters and Friendships of Sir Cecil Spring Rice*. 1929.

H. H. *Bits of Talk for Young Folk*. 1876.

Hagedorn, Hermann (1882–1964). *The Magnate / William Boyce Thompson and His Time* (1869– 1930). 1935.

Hagedorn, Hermann (1882–1964). *The Rough Riders: A Romance*. 1927.

Hagedorn, Hermann (1882–1964). *A Troop of the Guard*. 1919.

Hagedorn, Hermann (1882–1964). *Leonard Wood*. 1931.

Hagedorn, Hermann (1882–1964). *The Bomb That Fell on America*. 1946.

Hagedorn, Hermann (1882–1964). *Ladders through the Blue: A Book of Lyrics*. 1925.

Hagedorn, Hermann (1882–1964). *Theodore Roosevelt: A Biographical Sketch*. 1919.

Hagedorn, Hermann (1882–1964). *The Boys' Life of Theodore Roosevelt*. 1918.

Hagedorn, Hermann (1882–1964). *Roosevelt: Prophet of Unity*. 1924.

Hagedorn, Hermann (1882–1964). *Roosevelt in the Badlands*. 1921.

Hagner, Alexander B. *A Personal Narrative of the Acquaintance of My Father and Myself with Each of the Presidents of the United States*. 1913.

Hagner, Alexander B. (1826–1915). *History and Reminiscences of St. Johns Church, Washington D.C.* 1906.

Hahnel, Lieut. Ludwig Von. *Discovery by Count Teleki of Lakes Rudolf and Stefanie*. 1894.

Haiden, Max. *Die Jagd in Bildern*. 1903 (Inscription).

Hale, Annie Riley. *Excerpts from Rooseveltian Fact and Fable*. 1908.

Hale, Annie Riley. *Roosveltian Fact and Fable*. 1908.

Hale, Edward Everett (1822–1909). *The Man Without a Country*. 1902.

Hale, Lucretia P. *The Last of the Peterkins*. 1903.

Hale, William Bayard. *A Week in the White House*. 1908

Halifax, John. *Poems*. 1860.

Hall, Charles Frances. *Arctic Researches and Life among the Esqimaux*. 1865.

Hall, Eliza Calvert. *Aunt Jane of Kentucky*. 1907.

Hall, Eliza Calvert. *The Land of Long Ago*. 1910.

Hall, Eliza Calvert. *A Book of Hand-woven Coverlets*. 1912.

Hall, James (1811–1898). *Natural History of New York Part 6, Paleontology*, vol. 1. 1847.

Hall, James (1811–1898). *Natural History of New York Part 6, Paleontology*, vol. 2. 1852.

Hall, James (1811–1898). *Natural History of New York Part 4, Geology*. 1843.

Hall, S. C. *Ireland; Its Scenery, Character, Etc.* (3-vol. set). 1911.

Hall, S. C. (Editor). *The Book of British Ballads*. 1844.

Hallistec, N. *North American Fauna #32 A Systemic Synopsis of the Muskrats*. 1911.

Halt, L. H., and A. W. Chilton. *European History 1862–1914*. 1917.

Hamerton, Gilbert, Philip. *The Intellectual Life*. 1915.

Hamerton, Philip Gilbert. *The Intellectual Life*. 1899.

Hamerton, Philip Gilbert. *Human Intercourse*. 1894.

Hamilton, Alexander (1757–1804) and Alexander Hamilton (1757–1804). *Works of Alexander Hamilton 9 the Federalist*. 1886.

Hamilton, Alexander (1757–1804), and Henry Cabot Lodge (1850–1924). *The Works of A. Hamilton, Taxation and Finance*, vol. 2. 1886.

Hamilton, Alexander (1757–1804), and Henry Cabot Lodge (1850–1924). *The Works of A. Hamilton Commerce Foreign Relations*, vol. 3. 1885.

Hamilton, Alexander (1757–1804), and Henry Cabot Lodge (1850–1924). *The Works of A. Hamilton Foreign Relations*, vol. 4. 1886.

Hamilton, Alexander (1757–1804), and Henry Cabot Lodge (1850–1924). *The Works of A. Hamilton Foreign Relations Whiskey Rebellion*, vol. 5. 1886.

Hamilton, Alexander (1757–1804), and Henry Cabot Lodge (1850–1924). *The Works of A. Hamilton Military Papers Reynolds Pamphlet Misc.*, vol. 6. 1886.

Hamilton, Alexander (1757–1804), and Henry Cabot Lodge (1850–1924). *The Works of A. Hamilton Misc. Papers (Cont) Private Correspondence*, vol. 7. 1886.

Hamilton, Alexander (1757–1804), and Henry Cabot Lodge (1850–1924). *The Works of Alexander Hamilton*, vol. 1, *The Revolution—The Constitution*. 1885.

Hamilton, Alexander (1757–1804), and Henry Cabot Lodge (1850–1924). *Works of Alexander Hamilton 8 Private Correspondence Indices*. 1886

Hamilton, Angus. *Afghanistan* (Oriental Series), vol. 18. 1910.

Hamilton, Angus. *Korea* (Oriental Series), *Its History; Its People; and Its Commerce*, vol. 13. 1910.

Hamilton, Cicely. *Marriage as a Trade*. 1909.

Hamilton, Dr. Alexander. *Hamilton's Itinerarium; A Narrative of a Journey*. 1907.

Hamilton, General Sir Ian. *Compulsory Service*. 1910.

Hamilton, General Sir Ian. *A Staff Officer's Scrap Book*. 1906.

Hamilton, W. T. *My Sixty Years on the Plains*. 1905.

Hamley, General Sir Edward. *The War in the Crimea*. 1890.

Hamlin, Augustus C. *The Battle of Chancellorsville, Jackson's Attack*. 1896.

Hammond, C. S. *The New Reference Atlas of the World*. 1935.

Hammond, Jabez D. *Political History of New York*, vol. 2. 1842.

Hanotaux, Gabriel. *Artilleurs Faisant Fonctionner 675*. 1916.

Harben, Will N. *Northern Georgia Sketches*. 1900.

Harcourt, Edward Vernon. *Maderia*. 1851.

Hardlicka, Ales. *Early Man in South America*. 1912.

Hare, Augustus J. C. *The Life and Letters of Baroness Bunsen* (2 vol. in 1 book). 1926.

Hare, Augustus J. C. *The Story of My Life*, vol.1, vol. 2. 1896.

Hare, Augustus, J. C. *Walks in London*. 1880.

Hare, James. *Photographic Record of the Russo-Japanese War*. 1905.

Harlan, Richard, M.D. (1796–1843). *Fauna Americana: A Description of the Mammiferous Animals*. 1825.

Harraden, Beatrice. *Interplay*. 1908.

Harris, Ada Van Stone. *Poems by Grades Primary*. 1907.

Harris, Capt. Cornwallis. *Harris's Game and Wild Animals of Southern Africa*. 1840.

Harris, Frank. *A Mad Love: The Strange Story of a Musician*. 1920.

Harris, Joel Chandler (1848–1908). *Mingo and Other Sketches in Black and White*. 1884.

Harris, Joel Chandler (1848–1908). *Uncle Remus and Brer Rabbit*. 1906.

Harris, Julia Collier. *Joel Chandler Harris / Julia Collier Harris*. 1918.

Harrison, Burton, Mrs. *The Old-Fashioned Fairy Book*. 1920.

Harrison, Frederic. *National and Social Problems*. 1908.

Harrison, Frederic. *Annals of an Old Manor-House*. 1893.

Harrison, Henry Sydnor. *Queed*. 1911.

Harrison, Henry Sydnor. *Captivating Mary Carstairs*. 1914.

Hart, Albert Bushnell. *Salmon Portland Chase*. American Statesmen. 1889.

Hart, Albert Bushnell. *The Monroe Doctrine: An Interpretation*. 1916.

Hart, Albert Bushnell (1854–1943). *Salmon Portland Chase*. American Statesmen. 1899.

Hart, Albert Bushnell (1854–1943). *The American Nation: A History. National Ideals Historically Traced*. 1901.

Hart, Albert Bushnell, and Herbert Ronald Ferleger. *Theodore Roosevelt Cyclopedia*. 1941.

Hart, Henry H. *Garden of Peonies*. 1938.

Hart, Henry H. *The Hundred Names*. 1933.

Hart, Henry H. *A Chinese Market*. 1931.

Harte, Francis Bret (1836–1902). *Poems*. 1871

Harte, Francis Bret (1836–1902). *The Complete Works of Bret Harte*, vols. 1–2, and 4. 1890.

Harte, Francis Bret (1836–1902), and Catherine Greenaway (1846–1901). *The Queen of the Pirate Isle*. 1887.

Harting, James Edmund. *Essays on Sport and Natural History*. 1883.

Hartley, C. Gasquoine. *The Truth about Woman*. 1914.

Harvard Club of NY. *Roll of Honor 1941–1945*. 1947.

Haseman, John D. *Annals of the New York Academy of Sciences*, vol. 22, *Some Factors of Geographical Distribution in South America*. 1912.

Haskell, Frank Aretas. *The Battle of Gettysburg*. 1910.

Hatch, P. L., Dr. *Notes on the Birds of Minnesota*. 1892.

Haven, Catherine Elizabeth. *Diary of a Little Girl in Old New York*. 1920.

Haweis, H. R. *Pet or Pastimes and Penalties*. Unknown.

Hawks, Francis L., D.D. LLD. *United States Japan Expedition by Commodore Perry: Narrative of the Expedition of An American Squadron to the China Seas and Japan Performed in the Years 1852, 1853 and 1858 under the Command of Commodore M.C. Perry United States Navy* (3 vol.). 1856.

Hawthorne, Julian. *The Lock and Key Library / The Most Interesting Stories of All Nations*. 1915

Hawthorne, Nathaniel (1804–1864). *Hawthorne's Works / Blithedale Romance*. 1880.

Hawthorne, Nathaniel (1804–1864). *The Dolliver Romance, Septimius Felton*. 1890.

Hawthorne, Nathaniel (1804–1864). *Doctor Grimshawe's Secret*. 1890.

Hawthorne, Nathaniel (1804–1864). *French and Italian Notebooks*. 1890.

Hawthorne, Nathaniel (1804–1864). *American Notebooks*. 1889.

Hawthorne, Nathaniel (1804–1864). *Sketches, Etc. Life – Index*. 1888.

Hawthorne, Nathaniel (1804–1864). *The Marble Faun or the Romance of Monte Beni*. 1890.

Hawthorne, Nathaniel (1804–1864). *Twice-Told Tales*. 1889.

Hawthorne, Nathaniel (1804–1864). *Mosses from An Old Manse*. 1889.

Hawthorne, Nathaniel (1804–1864). *The House of the Seven Gables and the Snow Image and Other Twice-Told Tales*. 1890.

Hawthorne, Nathaniel (1804–1864). *A Wonder-Book Tanglewood Tales and Grandfather's Chair*. 1890.

Hawthorne, Nathaniel (1804–1864). *Scarlet Letter and Blithedale Romance*. 1888.

Hawthorne, Nathaniel (1804–1864). *Our Old Home and English Notebooks*. 1888.

Hawthorne, Nathaniel (1804–1864). *Trans-Formations*. 1860.

Hay, Helen. *The Rose of Dawn: A Tale of the South Sea*. 1901.

Hay, Hon. John. *In Praise of Oma*. 1800.

Hay, Ian. *Scally*. 1914.

Hay, Ian. *The First Hundred Thousand 'K1.'* 1916.

Hay, Ian. *All in It "K (1)" Carries On*. 1917.

Hay, Ian. *The First Hundred Thousand*. 1916.

Hay, Ian, and Graham Cootes. *A Safety Match*. 1911.

Hay, John. *Castilian Days*. 1903.

Hay, John. *Commemoration of the Battle of Harlem Plains on Its 100th Anniversary by the NY Historical Society, Oration by John Hay*. 1876.

Hay, John. *Ballads*. 1885—Ad.

Hay, John. *Letters and Diaries of John Hay* (3-vol. set). 1908.

Hay, John. *The Complete Poetical Works of John Hay*. 1916.

Hay, John (1838–1905), and John Nicolay (1832–1901). *Abraham Lincoln: Complete Works*, vol.1–2. 1902.

Hay, John (Editor). *Complete Works of Abraham Lincoln*, 12 vols. 1894.

Hay, John, and Elihu Root. *The Republican Party*. 1904.

Hayden, F. V. *US Geological Survey of the Territories*, vol. 11. 1877.

Hayden, F. V. *North American Rodentia*. 1877.

Hayes, Dr. I. I. *The Open Polar Sea: A Voyage of Discovery towards the North Pole in the Schooner "United States."* 1867.

Hayes, Isaac I. *An Arctic Boat Journey / In Autumn of 1854*. 1867.

Hayes, Martha Summer. *Vanished Arizona*. 1908.

Hayne, Paul. *Hamilton in the Sixties and the Seventies*. 1882.

Haynes, William, and Joseph Leroy Harrison. *Camp Fire Verse*. 1917.

Hays, Matilda M. *Fadette, A Domestic Story* (from the French). 1851.

Headley, J. T. *The Adirondack Or Life in the Woods*. 1849.

Healy, James C. *Foc's'le and Glory-Hole / A Study of the Merchant Seaman and His Occupation*. 1936.

Hearn, Lafcadio (1850–1904). *Youma*. 1890.

Hearne, Samuel. *Hearne's Journey: From Prince of Wales Fort in Hudson's Bay to the Northern Ocean*. 1795.

Hedgecock, S. E. *The Marsh Arab Haji Rikkan*. 1928.

Hedin, Sven Anders (1865–1952). *Trans-Himalaya Discoveries and Adventures in Tibet*, vol. 1. 1910.

Hedin, Sven Anders (1865–1952). *Trans-Himalaya*, vol. 2. 1910.

Hedin, Sven Anders (1865–1952). *Overland to India*, vol. 1. 1910.

Hedin, Sven Anders (1865–1952). *Overland to India*, vol. 2. 1910.

Hegg, E. A. (Illustrator). *Souvenir of Alaska and Yukon Territory*. 1900.

Heigall, Arthur E. P. B. *The Treasury of Ancient Egypt*. 1911.

Heine, Heinrich (1797–1856). *Travel Pictures and the Romantic School*. 1901.

Heismann, Martin. *How to Attract and Protect Wild Birds*. 1908.

Henderson, Colonel G. F. R. *The Science of War*. 1913.

Henderson, G. F. R. *Stonewall Jackson and the American Civil War*, vols. 1–2. 1900.

Henderson, George. *Lady Nairne and Her Songs*. 1906.

Henderson, John B. *The Cruise of the Tomas Barrera*. 1916.

Hendrick, Burton J. *Life and Letters of Walter H. Page*, vol. 1–3. 1925.

Henry, John, and James Parker. *Plain Sermons of the Book of Common Prayer*. 1856.

Henshaw, Sarah Edwards. *Rhymes and Jingles*. 1892.

Henty, G. A. *The Young Carthaginian*. c. 1890–1900.

Henty, G. A. *Redskin and Cowboy*. 1896

Henty, G. A. *Beric the Briton*. 1902.

Herber, Right Rev. Reginald. *Narrative of a Journey through the Upper Provinces of India*, vol. 1–2. 1828.

Herbert, George (1593–1633). *The English Poems of George Herbert*. 1888.

Herbert, Henry William. *The Horse of America*, vol. 1–2. 1857.

Herbert, Henry William. *Frank Forester's Field Sports*. 1848.

Hercell, H. Arthur. *North American Fauna #36 US Dept of Agriculture Revision of the American Harvest Mice*. 1914.

Herford, Oliver. *The Rubaiyat of a Persian Kitten*. 1904—Ad.

Herford, Oliver. *The Astonishing Tale of a Pen and Ink Puppet*. 1907.

Herford, Beatrice, and Oliver Herford. *Monologues*. 1908.

Herndon, William Lewis, and Hardner Gibbons. *Exploration of the Valley of the Amazon* (in 2 vols.). 1853.

Herodotus (5th Century B.C.). *Herodotus*. 1897.

Heron, Robert Esq. *Junius*, vols. 1–2. 1804.

Herr, Charlotte, B. *How Punky Dunk Helped Old Prince*. 1913.

Herrick, Francis Hobart (1858–1940). *Nests and Nest-Building in Birds: In Three Parts*. 1911.

Herrick, John P. *Founding a Country Newspaper Fifty Years Ago*. 1938.

Hervey, Harry. *Caravans by Night*. 1922.

Hervey, James. *Theron and Aspasi; or, A Series of Dialogues*, vol. 1. 1760.

Hewins, Caroline M. *A Mid-Century Child and Her Books*. 1926.

Heymel, Alfred Walter. *Heymel–Gesammelte Gedichte*. 1914.

Heyward, Dubose (1885–1940). *Jasbo Brown*. 1931.

Hichens, Robert. *The Paradine Case*. 1933.

Higginson, Thomas Wentworth. *Part of a Man's Life*. 1905.

Hildreth, Richard. *The History of the United States*. 1856.

Hill, Adams Sherman. *The Foundations of Rhetoric*. 1896.

Hill, Percy A. *Old Manila*. 1928.

Hillern, Wilhelmine. *Hoher Als Die Kirche*. 1892.

Hilliard, W. *Letters of Earl of Chatham to His Nephew Thomas Pitt, Esq*. 1805.

Hind, Lewis C. *Augustus Saint Gaudens*. 1908.

Hinshaw, David. *The Home Front*. 1943.

Hittell, Theodore H. *The Adventures of James Capen Adams*. 1911.

Hobbes, John Oliver. *The Flute of Pan*. 1905.

Hobson, Elizabeth C. *Recollections of a Happy Life*. 1914.

Hobson, Ruth A. *The Daisy or Cautionary Stories in Verse / Great Grandmother's Book*. N.d.

Hodgkin, Thomas. *Italy and Her Invaders*, vol. 1–3. 1880.

Hodgkin, Thomas. *Italy and Her Invaders*, 535–553. 1885.

Hohenlohe-Schillingsfuerst, Prince Chlodwig of (1819–1901). *Memoirs of Prince Chlodwig of Hohenlohe-Schillingsfuerst*. 1906.

Holbein, J. *La Danse Des Morts a Basle*. Unknown.

Holbrook, John Edwards (1794–1871). *North American Herpetology*. 1836.

Holder, Charles Frederick. *Big Game at Sea*. 1908.

Holland, Leicester B. *The Garden Bluebook*. 1915.

Holls, Frederick William. *Correspondence between Ralph Waldo Emerson and Herman Grimm*. 1903.

Holmes, Bettie Fleischmann. *Log of the Laura in Polar Seas*. 1907.

Holmes, Oliver Wendell (1809–1894). *The Poet at the Breakfast Table*. N.d.

Holmes, Oliver Wendell (1809–1894). *The Professor at the Breakfast Table*. N.d.

Holmes, Oliver Wendell (1809–1894). *Poems*. 1848.

Holmes, Oliver Wendell (1809–1894). *The Poet at the Breakfast Table: His Talks with His Fellow Boarders and the Reader*. 1878.

Holmes, Oliver Wendell (1809–1894). *The Autocrat of the Breakfast Table: Every Man His Own Boswell*. 1877.

Holmes, Oliver Wendell (1809–1894). *Holmes' Poetical Works*. 1892.

Holmes, Oliver Wendell (1809–1894). *The Professor at the Breakfast Table: With the Story of Iris*. 1877.

Holmes, Oliver Wendell (1809–1894). *Over the Teacups*. 1891.

Holmes, Oliver Wendell (1809–1894). *Elsie Venner: A Romance of Destiny*, vols. 1 and 2. 1861.

Holmes, Oliver Wendell (1809–1894). *The Autocrat of the Breakfast Table*. 1858.

Holmes, Oliver Wendell (1809–1894). *Oliver Wendell Holmes: Life and Letters*. 1896.

Holmes, Oliver Wendell (1841–1935) (Supreme Court Justice). *Speeches of Oliver Wendell Holmes*. 1900.

Holmes, Prescott. *Young People's History of the War with Spain*. 1900.

Holst, Dr. H. Von. *John C. Calhoun / American Statesmen*. 1884.

Holst, Dr. H. Von (1841–1904). *John C. Calhoun*. American Statesmen. 1899.

Holst, Dr. H. Von (1841–1904). *Constitutional and Political History of the United States* (3-vol. set: 1750–1832; 1828–1846;1846–1850). 1877.

Holt, L. Emmett, M.D. *The Care and Feeding of Children*. 1914.

Homer. *Munford's Homer Iliad*. 1846.

Homer (8th Century B.C.). *The Iliad of Homer* (2-vol. set). 1898.

Hood, Thomas. *The Plea of the Midsummer Fairies*. 1827.

Hood, Thomas. *Hood's Choice Works*. 1852.

Hood, Thomas (1799–1845). *The Loves of Tom Tucker and Little Bo-Peep; A Rhyming Rigamarole*. 1863.

Hood, Thomas (1799–1845). *Petsetilla's Posy: A Fairy Tale*. 1870.

Hooker, Margaret Huntington. *Ye Gentlewoman's Housewifery*. 1896.

Hooker, Thomas. *A Survey of the Summer of Church-Discipline*. 1648.

Hooker, Thomas (1586?–1647). *The Poor Doubting Christian Drawn to Christ*. 1743.

Hopkinson, Arthur W. *Pastor's Progress*. 1943.

Hornaday, William Temple (1854–1937). *Wild Life Conservation*. 1914.

Horsbrugh, Major Boyd. *The Game Birds and Water Fowl of South Africa*. 1912.

Hosie, Alexander. *Manchuria (Oriental Series): Its People, Resources and Recent History*, vol. 14. 1910.

Hosmer, James K. *Samuel Adams* (American Statesmen Series), vol. 2. 1898.

Hosmer, Margaret. *Little Rosie Stories / Little Rosie in the Country.* 1869.

Hough, Emerson. *54–40 Or Fight.* 1909.

House, Edward J. *A Hunter's Camp-Fires.* 1909.

Houssaye, Henry. *1815 Waterloo.* 1900.

How, Louis (1873–1947). *A Hidden Well.* 1916.

Howard, Henry. *Poems of Henry Howard, Earl of Surrey.* 1831.

Howard, W. Stanton (Introduction). *Catalogue of Collection of Foreign and American Paintings Owned by George A. Hearn.* 1908.

Howard, Montague. *Old London Silver: Its History, Its Makers, Its Marks.* 1903.

Howard, O. O. Brig. Gen. U.S.A. *Joseph His Pursuit and Capture.* 1881.

Howe, Bruce. *"Dear Ancients" Letters of Bruce Howe.* N.d.

Howe, M. A. Dewolfe. *George Von Lengerke Meyer (His Life and Public Services).* 1919.

Howell, H. Arthur. *North American Fauna #36 Revision of the American Harvest Mice.* 1914.

Howell, H. Arthur. *North American Fauna #44 Revision of the American Flying Squirrels.* 1918.

Howell, H. Arthur. *North American Fauna #43 the Rice Rats of North America.* 1918.

Howell, H. Arthur. *North America Fauna #26, Revision of the Skunks of the Genus Spilogale.* 1906.

Howells, W. D. *Italian Journeys.* 1867.

Howells, William Dean. *A Boy's Town.* 1890.

Howitt, Mary. *Mary Howitt's Tales of English Life.* 1881.

Howitt, Mary (1799–1888). *Who Shall Be Greatest?* 1841.

Hoyle, Edmond. *Hoyle's Games Autograph Edition.* 1913.

Hrdlicka, Ales (1869–1943). *Bureau of American Ethnology, Bulletin 33, Skeletal Remains.* 1907.

Hrdlicka, Ales (1869–1943). *The Natives of Khargo Oasis, Egypt.* 1912.

Huard, Frances Wilson. *My Home in the Field of Honor.* 1916.

Hubbard, Charles D. *An Old New England Village.* 1947.

Hubbard, Lucius L. *Woods and Lakes of Maine Illustrated.* 1884.

Hudson, W. H. *Far Away and Long Ago: A History of My Early Life.* 1918.

Hudson, William C. *Random Recollections of an Old Political Reporter.* 1911.

Hudson, William Henry (1841–1922). *Tales of the Pampas.* 1906.

Hudson, William Henry (1841–1922). *The Purple Land.* 1911.

Hudson, William Henry (1841–1922). *The Naturalist in La Plata.* 1892.

Hueffer, Ford Madox. *Between St. Dennis and St. George, A Sketch of Three Civilizations.* 1915.

Hueffer, Oliver Madox. *Some of the English: A Study Towards a Study.* 1930.

Hugessen, Knatchbull E. *A Hit and a Miss.* 1893.

Hughes, Charles. *Shakespeare's Europe*. 1903.

Hughes, M. Vivian. *A London Child of the Seventies*. 1934.

Hugo, Victor. *Les Orientales*. 1845.

Hugo, Victor. *Les Voix Interieures: Les Rayous Et Les Ombres*. 1850.

Hugo, Victor (1802–1885). *Notre-Dame De Paris*, vols. 1–2. 1841.

Hugo, Victor (1802–1885). *V. Hugo*. 1836.

Hugo, Victor (1802–1885). *V. Hugo*. 1838.

Huidekoper, Frederic Louis. *The Military Unpreparedness of the United States*. 1915.

Hume, David. *History of England*, vol. 6. 1796.

Hume, David. *The History of England from the Invasion of Julius Caesar to the Revolution in 1688 in Thirteen Volumes*, vol. 9. 1793.

Humfreville, Capt. J. Lee. *Twenty Years among Our Hostile Indians*. 1903.

Humphreys, Andrew. *Campaigns of the Civil War: The Virginia Campaign of 1864 and 1865*. 1883.

Humphris, Edith. *At Cheltenham Spa / Or Georgians in a Georgia Town*. 1928.

Humphris, Edith, and Douglas Sladen. *Adam Lindsay Gordon*. 1912.

Hunt, Gaillard. *John C. Calhoun*. 1908.

Hunt, Howard. *East of Farewell*. 1942.

Hunt, Leigh. *A Book for A Corner*. 1852.

Hunt, Leigh. *Essays by Leigh Hunt–Indicator–The Seer*. 1840.

Hunt, Leigh (James Henry Leigh Hunt) (1784–1859). *Stories from the Italian Poets*. 1853.

Hunter, George Leland. *Tapestries: Their Origin, History and Renaissance*. 1912.

Huntington, Dwight W. *Brush, Sedge, and Stubble*. 1898.

Huntington, Dwight W. *Our Feathered Game*. 1903.

Hurter, Julius Sr. *Herpetology of Missouri*. 1911.

Hutchins, Charles L. *The Church Hymnal*. 1905.

Hutchins, Charles, D. D. *The Church Hymnal*. 1914.

Huxley, Leonard. *The Life and Letters of Thomas Henry Huxley* (in 2 vols.). 1901.

Huxley, Thomas Henry (1825–1895). *Science and Education—Essays*. 1914.

Huxley, Thomas Henry (1825–1895). *Method and Results Essays*. 1911.

Huxley, Thomas Henry (1825–1895). *Darwinian Essays*. 1912.

Huxley, Thomas Henry (1825–1895). *Science and Hebrew Tradition—Essays*. 1914.

Huxley, Thomas Henry (1825–1895). *Science and Christian Tradition—Essays*. 1913.

Huxley, Thomas Henry (1825–1895). *Hume with Helps to the Study of Berkeley Essays*. 1914.

Huxley, Thomas Henry (1825–1895). *Man's Place in Nature*. 1894.

Huxley, Thomas Henry (1825–1895). *Discourses Biological and Geological Essays*. 1909.

Huxley, Thomas Henry (1825–1895). *Evolution and Ethics and Other Essays*. 1914.

Hyde, Douglas. *The Love Songs of Connacht*. 1904.

Hyde, Thomas W. *Following the Greek Cross or Memories of 6th Army Corps*. 1894.

Hyde, William Dewitt. *From Epicurius to Christ*. 1905.

Hyde, William Dewitt. *Jesus' Way*. 1903.

Ilchester, the Earl of (Editor). *The Journal of the Hon. Henry Edward Fox*. 1923.

Imlay, Gilbert. *A Topographical Description of the Western Territory 1797*. 1797.

Ingelow, Jean. *Stories Told to a Child*. 1891.

Ingelow, Jean. *Poems*. 1863.

Ingersoll, Ernest. *Alaskan Bird-Life*. 1914.

Ingersoll, Ernest. *The Wit of the Wild*. 1907—Ad.

Ingoldsby, Thomas. *The Ingoldsby Legends First Series*. 1843.

Ingoldsby, Thomas (Pseudonym for Richard Barham [1788–1845]). *The Ingoldsby Legend; Or, Mirth and Marvels*, vols. 1–2. 1870.

Ingoldsby, Thomas (Pseudonym for Richard Barham [1788–1845]). *Witches Frolic*. 1888.

Irving, Pierre M. *Memorial Edition Washington Irving*. 1883.

Irving, Washington (1783–1859). *The Life of George Washington* (5 vols.). 1883.

Irving, Washington (1783–1859). *Alhambra*. 1865.

Irving, Washington (1783–1859). *Tales of a Traveller*. 1865.

Irving, Washington (1783–1859). *Astoria or Ancedotes of an Enterprise beyond the Rocky Mountains*. 1868.

Irving, Washington (1783–1859). *Spanish Papers*. 1868.

Irving, Washington (1783–1859). *Conquest of Granada*. 1850.

Irving, Washington (1783–1859). *The Adventures of Captain Bonneville, USA*. 1868.

Irving, Washington (1783–1859). *Bracebridge Hall*. 1868.

Irving, Washington (1783–1859). *The Crayon Miscellany*. 1853.

Irving, Washington. *Letters to Kermit from Theodore Roosevelt*. 1946.

Irving, Washington (1783–1859). *A History of New York from the Beginning of the World to the End of the Dutch Dynasty*. Unknown.

Irving, Washington (1783–1859). *Oliver Goldsmith*. 1864.

Irving, Washington (1783–1859). *Sketch Book*. Unknown.

Irving, Washington (1783–1859). *Salmagundi*. Unknown.

Irving, Washington (1783–1859). *The Life and Voyages of Christopher Columbus*, vol. 1–3. 1868.

Irving, Washington (1783–1859). *Mahomet and His Successors* (vols. 1–2). Unknown.

Irving, Washington (1783–1859). *Irving's Works: Life and Letters of Washington Irving*, vols. 2 and 3. 1869.

Irving, Washington (1783–1859). *Irving's Works*, vols. 1–14 (Each Book Has Additional Specific Title Name). 1851.

Irving, Washington (1783–1859). *Life of Washington*. 1855.

Irving, Washington (1783–1859). *Life of George Washington*, vols. 1–5. 1873.

Jackson, Hartley H. T. *The Land Vertebrates of Ridgeway Bog, Wisconsin*. 1914.

Jackson, Hartley H. T. *North American Fauna #35, A Review of the American Moles*. 1915.

Jackson, Thomas (1824–1863), and Mary Anna Jackson. *Memoirs of Stonewall Jackson*. 1895.

Jacobsen, J. P. *Marie Grubb*. 1917.

Jaenicken, Frederick H. *The Book of the Presidents of the United States*. 1924.

James, F. L. *The Wild Tribes of the Soudan*. 1883.

James, H. *Fugitives from Justice (Verses and Reverses)*. 1912.

James, Hartwell. *Altemus' Young People's Library Heroes of the United States Navy / Their Life History*. 1899.

James, Henry. *English Hours*. 1905.

James, Philip. *A Butler's Recipe Book*. 1935.

James, William. *Full and Correct Account of the Military Occurrences of the Late War (of 1812)*. 1818.

James, William. *Naval Occurences of the Late War Between Great Britain and the USA*. 1817.

Jamison, V. C. *Lady Jane*. 1891.

Janvier, Thomas A. *Color Studies*. 1885.

Janvier, Thomas Allibone (1849–1913). *The Passing of Thomas and Other Stories*. 1901.

Jardine, Sir William. *Humming Birds*. 1836.

Jefferson, Thomas (1743–1826). *Notes on the State of Virginia*. 1794.

Jefferson, Thomas (1743–1826). *The Life and Morals of Jesus of Nazareth: Extracted Textually from the Gospels in Greek, Latin, French, and English*. 1904.

Jeffery, Edward, and Son. *Essay on Hunting*. 1820.

Jeffries, Richard. *The Amateur Poacher*. 1881.

Jenkin, H. C. Fleeming. *Mrs. Siddons As Lady Macbeth*. 1915.

Jensen, Marguerite Edith. *War Documents and Addresses Illinois in The World War*, vol. 6. 1923.

Jessopp, Augustus, D. D. *England's Peasantry and Other Essays*. 1914.

Jewett, Sarah O. *Play Days*. 1898.

Job, Herbert K. *The Sport of Bird Study*. 1908.

Job, Herbert K. *Wild Wings*. 1905.

Job, Herbert K. *Among the Waterfowl*. 1902.

Job, Herbert K. *Propagation of Wild Birds*. 1915.

Johns, Thomas, Translator. *Memoirs of John Lord De Joinville*, vol. 1 and 2—One vol. 1807.

Johnson, Alvin J., and Son (Publisher). *Johnson's Universal Cyclopedia*, vols. 1–8. 1893.

Johnson, Corinne. *I Want a Garden*. 1940.

Johnson, James Weldon. *Fifty Years and Other Poems*. 1917.

Johnson, James Weldon. *God's Trombones (Seven Negro Sermons in Verse)*. 1927.

Johnson, William Samuel. *Prayer for Peace*. 1915.

Johnston, Joseph E., and edited by Bradley Johnson. *Memoirs of E. Johnston*. 1891.

Johnston, Mary. *The Fortunes of Garin*. 1915.

Johnston, Mary. *Prisoners of Hope*. 1899.

Johnston, R. M. *Bull Run Its Strategy and Tactics*. 1913.

Johnston, Sir Harry Hamilton (1858–1927). *George Grenfell and the Congo*. 1908.

Johnston, Sir Harry Hamilton (1858–1927). *Pioneers in Tropical America*. 1914.

Johnston, Sir Harry Hamilton (1858–1927). *Liberia; Republic of Liberia, the Love of Liberty Brought Us Here*. 1906.

Johnston, Sir Harry Hamilton (1858–1927). *Britain across the Seas; A History and Description of the British Empire in Africa*. N.d.

Johnston, Sir Harry Hamilton (1858–1927). *The Uganda Protectorate* (2-vol. set). 1902.

Johnston, Sir Harry Hamilton (1858–1927). *British Mammals*. 1903.

Johnston, Stoddard, J. *First Exploration of Kentucky Dr Thomas Walkies' Journal*. 1898.

Johnston, William Preston. *The Life of Gen. Albert Sidney Johnston*. 1878.

Johonnot, James. *Book of Cats and Dogs and Other Friends, for Little Folks (National Historic Series)*. 1884.

Jones, Mary Cadwalder. *Lantern Slides*. 1937.

Jones, Thomas S., Jr. *The Voice in the Silence*. 1925.

Jones, Thomas S., Jr. *Sonnets of the Cross*. N.d.

Jones, Thomas S., Jr. *Sonnets of the Saints* (Pamphlet). 1925.

Jonson, Ben / Alden, Ed. *Bartholomew Fair*. 1904.

Jordan, David Starr. *Manual of the Vertebrates*. 1880.

Josephus, Flavius (37 A.D.–100). *The Works of Flavius Josephus*. 1843.

Jowett, Benjamin (1817–1893). *The Politics of Aristotle*, vols. 1 and 2. 1885.

Jowett, Benjamin (1817–1893). *Thucydides Translated into English*. 1900.

Juncos, Manuel Fernandez and Musica De Braul. *Canciones Escolares*, vols. 1 and 2. 1925.

Junius. *The Letters of Junius*. 1807.

Jusserand, J. J. *Piers. Plowman*. 1894.

Jusserand, J. J. *Historie Literaire du Peuple Anglais*. 1904.

Jusserand, J. J. *The School for Ambassadors and Other Essays*. 1924.

Jusserand, J. J. *A French Ambassador at the Court of Charles the Second*. 1902.

Jusserand, J. J. *Jacques Ier D'ecosse Fut-Il Poete Etude sur L'authenticite Due "Cahier du Roi."* 1897.

Jusserand, J. J. *With Americans of Past and Present Days*. 1916.

Jusserand, Jean Jules (1855–1932). *What to Expect of Shakespeare, the British Academy's First Annual Shakespeare Lecture*. 1911.

Jusserand, Jean Jules (1855–1932). *Piers Plowman, the Work of One or Five*. 1909.

Jusserand, Jean Jules (1855–1932). *Les Sports et Jeux D'exercise dans L'ancienne France*. 1901.

Kadich, Dr. Hanas Maria Von. *Der Graue Wolf Nordamerikas*. 1901.

Kamata, Shigekichi. *A Study* (in Japanese Text) *of Great Personalities, A Record of Roosevelt's Quotes and Actions*. 1907.

Kane, Elisha Kent. *The U.S. Grinnell Expedition in Search of Sir John Franklin*. 1854.

Kane, Elisha Kent. *Arctic Explorations Illustrated*. 1868.

Kane, Elisha Kent MD, USN. *Arctic Explorations: The 2nd Grinnell Expedition in Search of Sir John Franklin 1853, '54, '55* (2 vols.). 1856.

Kaneko, Kentaro. *Mosume Sets Yo; Or, Woman's Sacrifice.* 1905.

Kangesberg, Henry. *Addresses at the Republican National Convention, 1904.* 1904.

Karten. *Studien Zur Ruiezacifchichte Undtabofck V.* 1870.

Kavanagh, Julia. *Grace Lee.* 1855—Ad.

Kavanagh, Julia. *Adele.* 1858.

Kavanagh, Julia. *Silvia.* 1870.

Kearton, R. *Wild Nature's Ways.* 1904.

Keary, Charles F. *The Vikings of Christendom.* 1891.

Keast, Lord John. *At Home in the Wilderness.* 1876.

Keats, John (1795–1821). *The Complete Poetical Works and Letters of John Keats.* 1899.

Keeler, Charles. *Bird Notes Afield.* 1907.

Keightley, Thomas. *The Fairy Mythology (Romance and Superstition of Various Countries).* 1860.

Kellogg, Vernon L. *Darwinism Today, A Discussion of Present-Day Scientific Criticism of the Darwinian Selection Theories, Together with a Brief Account of the Principal Other Proposed Auxiliary and Alternative Theories of Species-Forming.* 1908.

Kelly, Myra. *Little Aliens.* 1910.

Kelly, Myra. *Little Citizens: The Humors of School Life.* 1904.

Kelly, R. Talbot. *Burma* (Oriental Series): *The Land and the People*, vol. 17. 1910.

Kemp-Welch, Alice. *The Chatelaine of Vergi.* 1903.

Kempis, Thomas. *Imitation of Christ.* 1875.

Kenly, John R. *Memoirs of a Maryland Volunteer: In the War with Mexico (1846–7–8).* 1873.

Kennan, George. *Campaigning in Cuba.* 1899.

Kennan, George Frost (1904–?). *Report of the International Commission of Inquiry into the Balkan Wars.* 1914.

Kennedy, John P. *Horse-Shoe Robinson.* 1866.

Kennedy, Philip Pendleton (1808–1864). *The Blackwater Chronicle.* 1853.

Kent, Louise Andrews. *Mrs. Appleyard's Year.* 1941.

Kerr, Water Montagu, C.E., F.R.G.S. (1814–1888). *The Far Interior.* 1886.

Keyser, Leander S. *Birds of the Rockies.* 1902.

Khayyam, Omar (?-1123) and Edward Fitzgerald (1809–1883) (Translated by). *Rubaiyat of Omar Khayyam.* 1907.

Khayyam, Omar (?-1123) and Edward Fitzgerald (1809–1883) (Translated by). *Rubaiyat of Omar Khayyam.* 1894.

Kidd, Benjamin. *Social Evolution.* 1894.

Killikelly, Sarah H. *Curious Questions.* 1886.

Kimber, Clara E. *The Story of the First Flag.* 1920.

King, Captain Charles. *Trails of a Staff Officer.* 1881.

King, Clarence. *Clarence King Memoirs: The Helmet of Membrino.* 1904.

Kingsley, Charles (1819–1875). *The Water Babies / A Fairy Tale for A Land Baby.* Unknown.

Kingsley, Charles (1819–1875). *The Roman and the Teuton.* 1864.

Kingsley, Charles (1819–1875). *Charles Kingsley's Poems.* 1872.

Kingsley, Charles (1819–1875). *Poems – vol. 1 / Poems – vol. 2.* 1884—Ad.

Kingsley, Charles (1819–1875). *Prose Idylls.* 1907.

Kingsley, Charles (1819–1875). *At Last.* 1913.

Kingsley, Martin. *The Magic of Monarchy.* 1937.

Kingston, William H. G. (1814–1880). *Washed Ashore on the Tower of Stormount Bay.* 1868.

Kinkead, Thomas L. *A Catechism of Christian Doctrine.* 1901.

Kipling, J. L. *The Second Jungle Book.* 1908.

Kipling, Rudyard. *Vampire and Other Verses.* 1899–1900

Kipling, Rudyard (1865–1936). *Captains Courageous.* 1905.

Kipling, Rudyard (1865–1936). *The Way That He Took the Outsider.* 1904.

Kipling, Rudyard (1865–1936). *The Five Nations.* 1903.

Kipling, Rudyard (1865–1936). *Rewards and Fairies.* 1910.

Kipling, Rudyard (1865–1936). *Puck of Pook's Hill.* 1906.

Kipling, Rudyard (1865–1936). *Stalky and Company.* 1908.

Kipling, Rudyard (1865–1936). *Soldiers Three, The Story of the Gadsbys.* 1909.

Kipling, Rudyard (1865–1936). *Wee Willie Winkie.* 1908.

Kipling, Rudyard (1865–1936). *Kim.* 1902.

Kipling, Rudyard (1865–1936). *Traffics and Discoveries.* 1904.

Kipling, Rudyard (1865–1936). *Plain Tales from the Hills.* 1907.

Kipling, Rudyard (1865–1936). *From Sea to Sea and Other Sketches,* vol. 1–2. 1909.

Kipling, Rudyard (1865–1936). *Just So Stories for Little Children.* 1908.

Kipling, Rudyard (1865–1936). *The Seven Seas.* 1908.

Kipling, Rudyard (1865–1936). *Barrack-Room Ballads.* 1908.

Kipling, Rudyard (1865–1936). *The Day's Work.* 1909.

Kipling, Rudyard (1865–1936). *Actions and Reactions.* 1909.

Kipling, Rudyard (1865–1936). *Life's Handicap.* 1908.

Kipling, Rudyard (1865–1936). *Many Inventions.* 1908.

Kipling, Rudyard (1865–1936). *Captains Courageous.* 1908.

Kipling, Rudyard (1865–1936). *Departmental Ditties and Other Verses.* 1909.

Kipling, Rudyard (1865–1936), and Wolcott Balestier. *The Naulahka.* 1908.

Kipling, Rudyard (1865–1936), W. H. Drake, and J. L. Kipling. *The Jungle Book.* 1908.

Kirkland, Caroline Matilda Stansbury (1801–1864). *The School Girl's Garland.* 1864.

Klein, Felix. *Au Pays De La Vie Intense.* 1904.

Klein, L'abbe Felix. *La Guerre Vue D'une Ambulance.* 1915.

Klemm, L. R. (Editor). *Poesie for Haus und Schule.* 1879.

Klumpke, Anna (1856–1942). *Rosa Bonheur.* 1909.

Knatchbull-Hugessen, E. H. *Higgledy-Piggledy.* 1876.

Knight, E. F. *Turkey (Oriental Series): The Awakening of Turkey—the Turkish Revolution*, vol. 21. 1910.

Knight, Edward Frederick (1852–1925). *The Cruise of the Falcon*. 1886.

Knight, Edward Frederick (1852–1925). *The Falcon on the Baltic*. 1889.

Knight, Ora Willis. *Birds of Maine*. 1908.

Knight, Sarah Kemble (1666–1727). *The Private Journal of Sarah Kemble Knight*. 1901.

Knish, Anne, and Emanuel Morgan. *Spectra*. 1916.

Knox, A. E. *Autumns on the Spey*. 1872.

Knox, Cleone. *The Diary of a Young Lady of Fashion in the Year 1764–1765*. 1927.

Koerner, Theodor. *Koerner's Sammtliche Werke*. 1847.

Kraitsir, Charles. *The Poles in the United States of America*. 1837.

Kullnick, Max. *Kullnick Vom Reitersmann Zum Prasidenten*. 1908.

La Gorce, Pierre De (1846–1934). *The History of the Second Republique Francaise* (2-vol. set). 1904.

La Graviere, Jurien De. *Guerres Maritimes* (2 vols.). 1881.

L'abbe Gaultier. *Lectures Graduees Pour Le Enfants De Premier Age*. 1786.

Lacroix, Paul. *Vie Militaire Et Religieuse au Moyen Age et de L'epoque de la Renaissance*. 1873.

Lady, A. *Nothing to Do: An Accompaniment to "Nothing to Wear."* 1857.

Lagerlof, Selma (1858–1940). *Invisible Links*. 1899.

Lagerlof, Selma (1858–1940). *The Story of Gosta Berling*. 1899.

Laigle, Mathilde. *Le Livre des Trois Vertus de Christine de Pisan and Son Milieu Historique et Littéraire*. 1912.

Laing, Janet. *Before the Wind*. 1918.

Laking, Guy Francis. *The Furniture of Windsor Castle*. 1905.

Laking, Guy Francis. *The Armoury of Windsor Castle*. 1906.

Laking, Guy Francis. *Sèvres Porcelain of Buckingham Palace and Windsor Castle*. 1907.

Lamartine, M. De. *Lamartine: Premiers Meditations Poetiques la Mort de Socrate par M De Lamartine*. 1848.

Lamartine, M. De. *Lamartine: Nouvelles Meditations Poetiques le Dernier Chant du Pelerinage D'harold Chant Du Sacre*. 1845.

Lamartine, M. De. *Lamartine: Harmonies Poetiques et Religieuses (Tome 3)*. 1847.

Lamb, Charles (1775–1834). *The Works of Charles Lamb*, vols. 1–5. 1877.

Lamb, Charles (1775–1834). *The Letters of Charles Lamb*. 1905.

Lamb, Charles (1775–1834). *The Letters of Charles Lamb*, vol. 1. 1905.

Lamb, Charles (1775–1834) and Mary (1764–1847). *Tales from Shakespeare*. 1909.

Lamb, Harold. *The Crusades / Iron Men and Saints*. 1930.

Lamont, James. *Seasons with the Sea-Horses*. 1861.

Lampton, William J. *The Trolley Car and the Lady*. 1908.

Landor, Walter Savage (1775–1864). *Classical Conversations*. 1901.

Lane, Charles. *Mrs. Leicester's School and Other Writings*. 1893.

Lang, A. (Translator). *Theocritus Bion Moschus*. 1892.

Lang, Andrew. *Ballads and Verses Vain*. 1884.

Lang, Herbert. *Famous Ivory Treasures of a Negro King*. 1918.

Lang, Lincoln, A. *Ranching with Roosevelt*. 1926—Ad.

Lange, Algot. *In the Amazon Jungle*. 1912.

Langlois, H., General. *Enseignements de Deux Guerres Resentes*. Unknown.

Langworthy, Ashel. *Biography of Colonel Richard M. Johnson*. 1833.

Lankester, Ray. *From an Easy Chair*. 1901.

Lankester, Ray, Sir. *Science from an Easy Chair*. 1910.

Lapauze, Henri. *Hommage des Artistes et des Ecrivains Francais aux Etats-Unis d'Amérique*. 1915.

Lapsley, Arthur Brooks. *The Works of Abraham Lincoln*, vols. 1–7, 1832–1865. 1905.

Larin-Kyost. *A Short Story and a Poem*. 1932.

Larson, Marcellus Laurence (Translator). *The King's Mirror*. 1917.

Larzini, Luigi Von. *Musden*. 1906.

Latour, A. Lacarriere. *Historical Memoir of the War in West Florida and Louisiana 1814–15*. 1816.

Lauzanne, Stephane. *Fighting France*. 1918.

Law, Judge. *Colonial History of Vincennes*. 1858.

Lawless, Emily. *With the Wild Geese*. 1902.

Lawrence, William. *Memories of a Happy Life*. 1926.

Lawrence, William. *Henry Cabot Lodge: A Biographical Sketch*. 1925.

Lazell, Frederick John. *Some Winter Days in Iowa*. 1907.

Le Gallienne, Richard. *Prose Fancies*. 1896.

Lea, Henry Charles. *A History of the Inquisition of the Middle Ages* (3 vols.). 1888.

Lea, Homer. *The Valor of Ignorance*. 1909.

Lear, H. L. Sidney. *Pearls*. 1881.

Leary, John J., Jr. *Talks with TR*. 1920.

Lecky, William Edward Hartpole (1836–1903). *History of England of the Eighteenth Century*, vols. 1–8. 1888 / 1890.

Lecky, William Edward Hartpole (1836–1903). *History of European Morals: From Augustus to Charlemagne* (vol. 1 and 2). 1883.

Lecky, William Edward Hartpole (1836–1903). *The Map of Life*. 1900.

Lecky, William Edward Hartpole (1836–1903). *Leaders of Public Opinion in Ireland*. 1871.

Leclerc, Marc. *Honorably Discharged*. 1932.

Le Couteulx De Canteleu, Jean Baptiste. *La Chasse Du Loup*. 1861.

Lee, Alfred. *Memoir of Benjamin Lee* (Addressed to His Grandchildren by His Grandson). N.d.

Lee, Alva. *America Swings to the Left*. 1933.

Lee, General Robert E. *Recollections and Letters of General Robert E. Lee*. 1904.

Lee, Henry. *Lee's Memoirs* (2-vol. set). 1812.

Lee, James W. *"Uncle Remus," Joel Chandler Harris as Seen and Remembered by a Few of His Friends*. 1908.

Lee, Mrs. R. *Anecdotes of the Habits and Instincts of Animals*. 1852.

Lee, Viscount of Fareham. *A Good Innings and a Great Partnership*. 1939.

Legouve, Ernest. *Legouve Soixante Ans De Souvenirs*. N.d.

Leonard, Martia. *O All Ye Green Things*. 1947.

Leonard, William Ellery. *Gilgamesh (Epic of Old Babylonia)*. 1934.

Leonard, Zenas, and F. W. Wagner (Editor). *The Narrative of Zenas Leonard (Adventure of Zenas Leonard)*. 1904.

Leroux, Ernest. *Revue D' Ethnographie et de Sociologie*. 1913.

Leroux, Gaston. *Le Fauteuil Hante*. 1911.

Leroux, Gaston. *The Perfume of the Lady in Black*. 1909.

Leroux, Gaston (1868–1927). *Le Fils De Trois Peres (Hardigras) Roman Provencal*. 1926.

Leroy-Beaulieu, Anatole (1842–1912). *The Empire of the Tsars and of the Russians* (3-vol. set). 1902.

Leseur, Elizabeth. *A Wife's Story / The Journal of Elizabeth Leseur with an Introduction by Her Husband*. 1933.

Lesley, Susan I. *Recollections of My Mother*. 1889.

Leti, Gregorio. *Het Leven Van Oliver Cromwell* (2-vol. set). 1706.

Letts, W. M. *Halloween and Poems of the War*. 1916.

Leupp, Francis E. Hornby. *Walks about Washington*. 1915.

Leupp, Francis E. *The Man Roosevelt; A Portrait Sketch*. 1904.

Lewis, Wm. Draper, Ph.D. *Life of Theodore Roosevelt*. 1919.

Ligenmann, Carl H. *Memoirs of the Carnegie Museum: The Cheirodontinae*, vol. 7, no. 1. Unknown.

Lindsey, Ben B., and Harvey J. O'Higgins. *The Beast*. 1910.

Line Officer, A. *The Campaign of Fredericksburg*. 1886.

Linesman. *The Mechanism of War*. 1902.

Linnaean, Carolus (1707–1778). *Systema Naturae*. 1788.

Linton, J. W. *Rare Poems of the Sixteenth and Seventeenth Centuries*. 1883.

Linton, W. J., and R. H. Stoddard. *Ballads and Romances*. 1883.

Lipsius, Justus. *Outline of the History of Libraries: In the 17th and 18th Centuries*. 1907.

Livingstone, R. W. (Editor). *The Pageant of Greece*. 1923.

Livius, Titus (Livy) (59 B.C.–17 A.D.). *The History of Rome (On Spine: Livy's History)* vols. 1–4. 1892.

Lloyd, A. *Imperial Songs / Poems by T. M. the Emperor and Empress of Japan*. 1904.

Lloyd, L. *The Birds and Wild Fowl of Sweden and Norway*. 1867.

Loch, G. M. *The Growth of Modern Nations*. 1907.

Locke, John (1632–1704). *An Essay concerning Human Understanding*. 1748.

Locke, William J. *Septimus*. 1908.

Locker, Frederick. *London Rhymes*. 1893.

Lockwood, Sarah M. *Antiques*. 1926.

Lodge, George Cabot. *Poems and Dramas*, vols. 1–2. 1911.

Lodge, George Cabot. *The Soul's Inheritance*. 1909.

Lodge, Henry Cabot (1850–1924). *Preface to the History of Nations*. 1904.

Lodge, Henry Cabot (1850–1924). *Daniel Webster*. American Statesmen. 1899.

Lodge, Henry Cabot (1850–1924). *The Story of the Revolution* (2 vols). 1898.

Lodge, Henry Cabot (1850–1924). *Speeches and Addresses 1884–1909*. 1909.

Lodge, Henry Cabot (1850–1924). *Speeches*. 1892.

Lodge, Henry Cabot (1850–1924). *Early Memories*. 1913.

Lodge, Henry Cabot (1850–1924). *Anna Cabot Mills Lodge*. 1918.

Lodge, Henry Cabot (1850–1924). *George Washington* (American Statesmen Series), vol. 4. 1898.

Lodge, Henry Cabot (1850–1924). *Alexander Hamilton* (American Statesmen), vol. 7. 1898.

Lodge, Henry Cabot (1850–1924). *Two Addresses (Commencement)*. 1915.

Lodge, Henry Cabot (1850–1924). *War Addresses 1915–1917*. 1917.

Lodge, Henry Cabot (1850–1924). *Address by the Hon. Henry Cabot Lodge on the Occasion of the One Hundredth Anniversary of the Birth of Abraham Lincoln*. 1909.

Lodge, Henry Cabot (1850–1924). *One Hundred Years of Peace*. 1913.

Lodge, Henry Cabot (1850–1924). *Frontier Town and Other Essays*. 1906.

Lodge, Henry Cabot (1850–1924). *Theodore Roosevelt*. 1919.

Lodge, Henry Cabot (1850–1924). *A Short History of the English Colonies in America*. 1886.

Lodge, Henry Cabot (1850–1924). *The Pilgrims of Plymouth*. 1921.

Lodge, Henry Cabot (1850–1924). *Boston – Historic Towns Series*. 1891.

Lodge, Henry Cabot (1850–1924). *Daniel Webster* / American Statesmen. 1885.

Lodge, Henry Cabot (1850–1924). *George Washington / I* / American Statesmen. 1889.

Lodge, Henry Cabot (1850–1924). *George Washington / II* / American Statesmen. 1889.

Lodge, Henry Cabot (1850–1924). *Alexander Hamilton* / American Statesmen. 1884.

Lodge, Henry Cabot (1850–1924) and Theodore Roosevelt. *Roosevelt's Works, Hero Tales*. 1918.

Lodge, Henry Cabot. *Many Memorial Addresses Delivered on the House and Senate Floors by Henry Cabot Lodge*. 1925.

Loening, C. Grover. *Military Aeroplanes*. 1918.

Lofting, Hugh (1886–1948). *The Story of Doctor Dolittle*. 1920.

Lomax, John Avery (1867–1948). *Cowboy Songs*. 1910.

Lombard, Nathan G. *The Trumpeter's Manual*. 1910.

Lombroso, Gina. *The Soul of Woman*. 1925.

Longfellow, Henry Wadsworth (1807–1882). *Hyperion: A Romance*. 1877.

Longfellow, Henry Wadsworth (1807–1882). *The Song of Hiawatha*. 1891.

Longfellow, Henry Wadsworth (1807–1882). *Prose Works*, vols. 1–2. 1897.

Longfellow, Henry Wadsworth (1807–1882). *Poetical Works*, vols. 1, 2, 4, 5, 6, and 8. 1900.

Longfellow, Henry Wadsworth (1807–1882). *Tales of a Wayside Inn*. 1864.

Longworth, Alice. *Crowded Hours*. 1933.

Lonnberg, Einar. *Methodus Avium Sveticarum*. 1907.

Lonnberg, Einar. *Carl Von Linni und die Lehre von Den Wirbeitieren*. 1909.

Lonnberg, Einar. *Einar Lonnberg Fauna Och Flora Huft 1901*. 1909.

Looker, Earle. *The White House Gang*. 1929.

L'opprimee. *L'enseigment De L'heure*. 1925.

Loring, J. Alden. *African Adventure Stories*. 1914.

Loringhoven, Frentag V. Frhr. *Krieg and Politik in Der Neuzeit*. 1911.

Lossing, Benson J. *The Pictorial Field Book of the War of 1812 (Or Pen and Pencil Illustrations by Pen and Pencil of the History, Biography, Scenery, Relics, and Traditions of the Last War for American Independence)*. 1869.

Lothrop, Stoddard (1883–1950). *The New World of Islam*. 1921.

Lothrop, Stoddard (1883–1950). *The Revolt against Civilization*. 1922.

Lothrop, Thornton Kirkland. *William H. Seward*. American Statesmen. 1899.

Loundes, Belloc, Mrs. *Good Old Anna*. 1915.

Lounsbury, T. R. *History of the English Language* (2-vol. set). 1894.

Lounsbury, Thomas R. *Yale Book of American Verse*. 1912.

Lounsbury, Thomas R. *Studies in Chaucer*. 1892.

Lounsbury, Thomas R. *The Early Literary Career of Robert Browning: Four Lectures*. 1911.

Lowell, Abbott Lawrence (1856–1943). *The Government of England*. 1908.

Lowell, Abbott Lawrence (1856–1943). *Governments and Parties in Continental Europe* (2 vols.). 1896.

Lowell, Edward J. *The Hessians and Other German Auxiliaries of Great Britain in the Revolution War*. 1884.

Lowell, James Russell (1819–1891). *Lowell's Complete Peotical Works*. 1890.

Lowell, James Russell (1819–1891). *The Complete Works of James Russell Lowell "Cabinet Edition."* 1899.

Lowell, James Russell (1819–1891). *Latest Literary Essays and Addresses of James Russell Lowell*. 1892.

Lowell, James Russell (1819–1891). *My Study Windows*. 1884.

Lowell, James Russell (1819–1891). *Fireside Travels*. 1883.

Lowell, James Russell (1819–1891). *Poetical Works*. 1884.

Lowell, James Russell (1819–1891). *Among My Books*. 1884.

Lowell, James Russell (1819–1891). *The Old English Dramatists*. 1892.

Lowell, James Russell (1819–1891). *Democracy and Other Addresses*. 1887.

Lownsbury, Thomas R. *American Men of Letters: James Fenimore Cooper*. 1883.

Lucas, Bernard. *Conversations with Christ: A Biographical Study*. 1907.

Lucas, E. V. *At the Shrine of St. Charles*. 1934.

Lucas, E. V. *Four and Twenty Toilers*. Unknown.

Ludwig Salvator, Archduke of Austria (1847–1915). *Versuch Einer Geschichte Von Parga*. 1908.

Ludwig, Archduke. *Bismarck*. 1927.

Lull, Richard S. *The Evolution of Earth*. 1918.

Lull, Richard S. *The Evolution of the Elephant*. 1909.

Lydekker, Richard (1849–1915). *A Geographical History of Mammals* (2-vol. set). 1896.

Lyell, Charles, Sir. *Principles of Geology*. 1859.

Lynch, Major Charles. *American National Red Cross Text Book on First Aid and Relief Columns*. 1908.

Lyon, Laurence. *The Pomp of Power*. 1922.

Lyon, Lilian Bowes. *The Poems of Lilian Bowes Lyon*. 1948.

Lyon-Caen, Charles. *Notice sur la Vic et les Travaux de M. Theodore Roosevelt (1858–1919)*. 1921.

Lyon-Caen, M. Charles. M. *Theodore Roosevelt (1858–1919)*. 1921.

Mabbott, T., and F. Pleadwell. *The Life and Works of Edward Coote Pinkney*. 1926.

Mabie, Hamilton W. *My Study Fire*. 1899.

Mac Gillewisy, William. *Naturalists Library VII Mammalia*. 1838.

Macaulay, Thomas Babington (1800–1859). *The History of England from the Accession of James II* (4-vol. set). 1849.

Macaulay, Thomas Babington (1800–1859). *Lays of Ancient Rome*. 1876.

Macaulay, Thomas Babington (1800–1859). *Macaulay's Miscellaneous Works*. 1880.

Macdonagh, Thomas. *Literature in Ireland*. 1916.

Macgahan, J. A. *Campaigning on the Oxus and the Fall of Khiva*. 1876.

Macgrath, Harold. *Half A Rogue*. 1906.

Mackail, J. W. *Lectures on Greek Poetry*. 1910.

Mackay, Helen. *Accidentals*. 1915.

Mackenzie, Alexander Slidell. *Mackenzie's Voyage (The Fur Trade 1789–1793)*, 2 vols. 1802.

Mackenzie, Alexander Slidell. *The Life of Paul Jones* (2-vol. set). 1845.

Macleish, Archibald. *New Found Land / Fourteen Poems*. 1930.

Macleish, Archibald. *In Honor of a Man and Ideal . . . Three Talks on Freedom*. December 02, 1941.

Macpherson, Geraldine. *Memoirs of the Life of Anna Jameson*. 1878.

Macpherson, H. B. *The Home Life of a Golden Eagle*. 1910.

Macrae, Alexander. *Deer Stalking*. 1880.

Madeira, Percy Child (1862–?). *Hunting in British East Africa*. 1909.

Madelin, Louis. *The French Revolution*. 1916.

Maeterlinck, Maurice. *Our Friend the Dog*. 1905.

Magnusson, Eirikr, and William M. Morris. *The Volsunga Saga*. 1906.

Magruder, Allan B. *John Marshall* (American Statesmen Series), vol. 10. 1898.

Magruder, Allan B. *John Marshall* / American Statesman. 1885.

Mahaffy, (Sir) John Pentland (1839–1919). *Greek Life and Thought*. 1887.

Mahaffy, (Sir) John Pentland (1839–1919). *Story of the Nations Alexander's Empire*. 1887.

Mahaffy, (Sir) John Pentland (1839–1919). *Rambles and Studies in Greece*. 1887.

Mahaffy, (Sir) John Pentland (1839–1919). *The Greek World under Roman Sway.* 1890.

Mahaffy, (Sir) John Pentland (1839–1919). *Problems in Greek History.* 1892.

Mahaffy, (Sir) John Pentland (1839–1919). *The Empire of the Ptolemies.* 1895

Mahan, Capt. Alfred Thayer (1840–1914). *The Gulf and Inland Waters: The Navy in the Civil War.* 1883.

Mahan, Capt. Alfred Thayer (1840–1914). *The Life of Nelson.* 1897.

Mahan, Capt. Alfred Thayer (1840–1914). *Admiral Farragut.* 1892.

Mahan, Capt. Alfred Thayer (1840–1914). *America's Interest in International Conditions.* 1910.

Mahan, Capt. Alfred Thayer (1840–1914). *The Influence of Sea Power upon the French Revolution and Empire* (Set of 2). 1892.

Mahan, Capt. Alfred Thayer (1840–1914). *The Interest of America in Sea Power Present and Future.* 1897.

Mahoney, Francis (1804–1866), and Daniel Maclise (1806–1870). *Prout's Reliques,* vol. 1 (A); *Prout's Reliques,* vol. 2 (B). 1836.

Major Bowes. *Verses I Like.* 1937.

Malleson, Col. G. B. *The Indian Mutiny.* 1891.

Malleson, Col. G. B. *Ambushes and Surprises.* 1885.

Malory, Sir Thomas. *Norroena / Anglo-Saxon Tales / Arthurian Legends.* 1906.

Malot, Hector. *Sans Famille.* 1902.

Maltby, Isaac. *The Elements of War.* 1811.

Malthus, Thomas Robert. *Malthus on Population: An Essay in the Principle of Population; Or A View of Its Past and Present Effects on Human Happiness,* vols. 1 and 2. 1807.

Manning, J. A. *Maximes De Napoleon.* 1913.

Manzoni, Alessandro. *I Promessi Sposi.* 1908.

Manzoni, Alessandro. *Manzoni's the Betrothel.* 1908.

Manzoni, Alessandro. *The Betrothed.* 1876.

Marbot, General Baron De. *Memoires of General Baron De Marbot* (3-vol. set). 1891.

Marbot, General Baron De, and John W. Thomason. *Adventures of General Marbot.* 1935.

Marcosson, Isaac F. *An African Adventure.* 1921.

Mark, Matthew, Luke, John. *New Testament.* 1858.

Marley, John. *The Life of Gladstone: The Life of William Ewart Gladstone 1809–1859* (3-vol. set). 1903.

Marlitt, E. *The Second Wife.* 1887.

Marryat, Captain Frederick (1792–1848). *The Settlers in Canada.* 1875.

Marshall, Archibald. *The Old Order Changeth.* 1918.

Marshall, Archibald. *Watermeads: A Novel.* 1920.

Marshall, Archibald. *The Greatest of These.* 1919.

Marshall, Archibald. *Richard Baldock.* 1920.

Marshall, Archibald. *Abington Abbey.* 1920.

Marshall, Archibald. *The Eldest Son: Being the Second Book in the Chronicles of the Clintons.* 1920.

Marshall, Archibald. *The Squire's Daughter: Being the First Book in the Chronicles of the Clintons.* 1920.

Marshall, Archibald. *The Honour of the Clintons: Being the Third Book in the Chronicles of the Clintons.* 1920.

Marshall, Archibald. *The Old Order Changeth: Being the Fourth Book in the Chronicles of the Clintons.* 1920.

Marshall, Archibald. *The Clintons and Others: Being the Fifth Book in the Chronicles of the Clintons.* 1920.

Marshall, John. *The Life of George Washington.* 1804.

Marshall, John. *The Life of George Washington* (6 vol. set, vols.1,2,3). 1804.

Martin, Annie. *Home Life on An Ostrich Farm.* 1891.

Martin, Ben. *Mr. Smith and Mr. Schmidt / A Story in Pictures.* 1940.

Martin, Edward Sandford. *The Luxury of Children and Some Other Luxuries.* 1904.

Martindale, Thomas. *Sport Indeed.* 1901.

Martineau, Harriet. *The Crofton Boys.* 1868.

Martinez, Albert B. *Baedeker De La Republique Argentine.* 1913.

Martyr, Peter. *De Nuovo Orbe; Or the Historie of the West Indies.* 1612.

Marvel, J. K. *Reveries of a Bachelor or a Book of the Heart.* 1852.

Marzials, Theo. *Pan Pipes (A Book of Old Songs).* 1885.

Masefield, John (1878–1967). *The Tragedy of Nan and Other Plays.* 1912.

Masefield, John (1878–1967). *The Daffodil Fields.* 1916.

Masefield, John (1878–1967). *The Everlasting Mercy.* 1914.

Masefield, John (1878–1967). *The Daffodil Fields.* 1913.

Masefield, John (1878–1967). *The Story of a Round-House.* 1914.

Masefield, John (1878–1967). *Gallipoli.* 1917.

Mason, A. E. W. *The Courtship of Morrice Buckler.* 1901.

Mason, A. E. W. *The Four Corners of the World.* 1918

Mason, Gregory. *Silver Cities of Yucatan.* 1927

Mason, Richard. *The Gentleman's New Pocket Farrier, the Horse.* 1825

Maspero, G. *Histoire Ancienne des Peuples de L'orient.* 1905

Massinger, Philip. *The Dramatic Works of Philip Massinger.* 1761.

Masson, Frederic. *Aventures de Guerre 1792–1809.* N.d.

Mather, William Williams (1804–1859). *Natural History of New York Part IV Geology.* 1842.

Matthews, J. Brander. (1852–1929). *Molière: His Life and Works.* 1916.

Matthews, J. Brander. (1852–1929). *Americanisms and Briticisms.* 1892.

Matthews, J. Brander. (1852–1929). *Aspects of Fiction and Other Ventures in Criticism.* 1896.

Matthews, J. Brander. (1852–1929). *Shakespeare As a Playwright.* 1913.

Matthews, J. Brander. (1852–1929). *The Economic Interpretation of Literary History.* 1911.

Matthews, J. Brander. (1852–1929). *Poems of American Patriotism.* 1882.

Matthews, J. Brander. (1852–1929). *The Bookshelf of Brander Matthews.* 1931.

Matthews, William Dennis (1875–?). *Climate and Evolution.* 1915.

Maugham, R. C. F. *Wild Game in Zambezia.* 1914.

Maurice, Maj-Gen Sir Fred. *Robert E. Lee the Soldier.* 1925.

Maury, General Dabney Herndon (1822–1900). *Recollections of a Virginian.* 1894.

Mavor, William. *The English Spelling Book.* 1885.

Maxwell, Sir Herbert. *The Life of Wellington: The Restoration of the Martial Power of Great Britain,* vols. 1 and 2. 1915.

May, Carrie. *Brownie Sanford.* 1884.

Mayer, Dr. Michael. *Das Fischereibush Kaiser Maximilians.* 1901.

Maynard, C. J. *The Birds of Florida (Part 1).* 1872.

Maynard, C. J. *The Birds of Florida (Part 2).* 1873.

Maynard, C. J. *The Birds of Florida (Part 3).* 1874.

Maynard, C. J. *The Birds of Florida (Part 4).* 1878

Maynard, C. J. *The Birds of Florida (Part 5).* 1878.

Maynard, C. J. *The Birds of Florida (Part 6).* 1878.

Maynard, C. J. *The Birds of Florida (Part 7).* 1878.

Maynard, C. J. *The Birds of Florida (Part 8).* 1878.

Maynard, C. J. *The Birds of Florida (Part 9).* 1878.

Mayo, Katherine. *Mother India.* 1927.

Mayo, William Starbuck, M.D. (1812–1895). *Kaloolah.* 1855.

McAtee, Waldo Lee (1883–1962). *Experimental Method of Testing the Efficiency of Warning and Crystal Coloration in Protecting Animals from Their Enemies.* 1912.

McCabe, Lida Rose. *Ardent Adrienne: The Life of Madame De Lafayette.* 1930.

McCall, Samuel W. *Thaddeus Stevens.* American Statesmen. 1899.

McCall, Samuel W. *Thaddeus Stevens /* American Statesmen. 1889.

McCalla, W. L. *Adventures in Texas Chiefly in the Spring and Summer of 1840.* 1841.

McCarthy, Justin. *A History of Our Own Times.* N.d.

McClellan, H. B., A. M. *The Life and Campaigns of Stuart's Cavalry.* 1885.

McClintock, H., James. *Arizona the Youngest State* (vols. 1 and 2). 1916.

McClintock, Walter. *The Old North Trail, Life, Legends and Religion of the Blackfeet Indians.* 1910.

McClure, C. H. *Early Opposition to Thomas Hart Benton.* 1916.

McCutcheon, George B. *The Roses in the Ring.* 1910.

McCutcheon, John Tinney (1870–1949). *Dawson '11 Fortune Hunter.* 1912.

McCutcheon, John Tinney (1870–1949). *The Mysterious Stranger and Other Cartoons.* 1905.

McCutcheon, John Tinney (1870–1949). *Cartoons by McCutcheon.* 1903.

McCutcheon, John Tinney (1870–1949). *TR in Cartoon.* 1910.

McFee, William. *Command.* 1922.

McGaffey, Ernest. *Outdoors.* 1907.

McGaffey, Ernest. *Poems of Gun and Rod.* 1892.

McGaffey, Ernest (1861). *New Hampshire Hills.* N.d.

McGaffey, Ernest (1861). *Poems of Gun and Rod.* 1892.

McKeever, Harriet B. *Little Red Cloak.* 1886.

McKeever, Harriet B. *Children with the Poets.* 1868.

McKinley, William. *McKinley Speeches and Addresses.* 1900.

McKinley, William. *Speeches and Addresses of William McKinley / From March 1, 1897 to May 20, 1900.* 1900.

McKinney, Lawrence. *People of Note.* 1940.

McLaughlin, Andrew C. *Lewis Cass.* American Statesmen. 1899.

McMaster, John Bach. *History of the People of the United States.* 1883.

Mearns, Edgar Alexander, M.D. (1856–1916). *Mammals of the Mexican Boundary of the United States (Part 1).* 1907.

Melnoth, William. *Letters of Pliny the Consul* (2-vol. set). 1805.

Melville, Herman (1819–1891). *Fifty Years Exile.* 1855.

Melville, Herman (1819–1891). *Omoo: A Narrative of Adventure in the South Seas,* 6th Edition. 1850.

Melville, Herman (1819–1891). *Moby Dick Or the White Whale (Everyman Library).* 1851.

Melville, Whyte. *Riding Recollections.* N.d.

Meredith, George. *Poems.* 1907.

Meredith, Owen. *Lucile.* 1892.

Meredith, Owen (1831–1891). *Poems by Owen Meredith* (3-vol. set). 1875.

Meredith, Owen (1831–1891). *Owen Meredith's Poems.* 1882.

Meredith, Owen (1831–1891). *Owen Meredith Poems: Lucile.* 1869.

Merlet, Gustave. *Choix De Poetes Du XIX Siecle.* 1917.

Merriam, C. Hart. *The Dawn of the World, Myths and Weird Tales Told by the Mewan Indians of CA.* 1910.

Merriam, C. Hart. *North American Fauna #5, 1891 Results of A Biological Survey of South-Central Idaho.* 1891.

Merriam, C. Hart. *North American Fauna #10 Copy 1 Review of Shrews.* 1895.

Merriam, C. Hart. *North American Fauna #10 Copy 2 Review of Shrews.* 1895.

Merriam, C. Hart. *North American Fauna #11 Synopsis of the Weasels.* 1896.

Merriam, C. Hart. *North American Fauna #11 Synopsis of the Weasels of North America.* 1896.

Merriam, C. Hart., Dr. *North American Fauna #12 Copy 2 Genera and Subgenera of Vobst Trimmings.* 1896.

Merriam, C. Hart. *North American Fauna #16 Results of Bial Survey of Mt Shasta.* 1899.

Merriam, C. Hart. *North American Fauna #41, Grizzly and Big Brown Bears.* 1918.

Merriam, C. Hart., Dr. *North American Fauna #17 Copy 1 Review of American Voles.* 1900.

Merriam, C. Hart., Dr. *North American Fauna #20 Review of the Skunks.* 1901.

Merriam, C. Hart., Dr. *North American Fauna #8. Monographic Revision of the Pocket Gophers Family Geomyidae.* 1895.

Merriam, Clinton Hart. *Mammals of the Adirondack Region.* 1884.

Merriam, Dr. C. Hart. *North American Fauna #1 Revision of the North American Pocket Mill.* 1889.

Merriam, Dr. C. Hart. *North American Fauna #2 Descriptions of 14 New Species and 1 New Genus of North American Mammals.* 1889.

Merriam, Dr. C. Hart. *North American Fauna #3 (Results of Biological Survey of San Francisco).* 1890.

Merriam, Florence A. *Birds through an Opera Glass.* 1889.

Merriam, John C. *Memoirs of the University of California,* vol.1, no.2, *The Fauna of Rancho La Brea Part II Canidae.* 1912.

Merrick, Leonard. *The Man Who Was Good.* 1923.

Merrill, A. Hyatt. *Isles of Spice and Palm.* 1915.

Merrill, William A. *Latin Hymns.* 1904.

Merriman, Henry Seton (1872–1903). *The Velvet Glove.* 1901.

Merriman, Henry Seton (1872–1903). *The Isle of Unrest.* 1900.

Mershon, W. B. *The Passenger Pigeon.* 1907.

Metcalfe, Charles Theophilus (1837–1892). *The Native Narratives of the Mutiny in Delhi.* 1898.

Mets, J. A. *Naval Heroes of Holland.* 1902.

Meyer, Cord, Jr. *Peace or Anarch.* 1947.

Meyer, Eduard. *Geschichte des Alterthums Vierter Band.* 1901.

Meyer, Eduard. *Geschichte des Alterthums Funfter Band.* 1902.

Meyer, Eduard. *Geschichte des Alterthums.* 1901.

Meyer, Hon. George, and Charles Stewart. *Official Records of the Union and Confederate Navies in the War of the Rebellion* (series 1, vol. 24). 1911.

Meynell, Wilfred (1852–1948). *Aunt Sarah and the War: A Tale of Transformations.* 1916.

Meyneng, Mayette. *The Broken Arc.* 1944.

Mikszath, Kalman. *St. Peter's Umbrella.* 1900.

Milburn, John George. *John George Milton, Jr.—A Memoir.* 1938.

Miller, Francis T. (Editor). *The Photographic History of the Civil War* (#7 of 10 vol. set) *Prisons and Hospitals.* 1911.

Miller, Gerrit S., Jr. *North American Fauna #12 Genera and Subgenera of Voles and Lemmings.* 1896.

Miller, Gerrit S., Jr. *North American Fauna #13 Rev. North American Bats of the Family Vespertilionide.* 1897.

Miller, Hugh. *The Cruise of the Betsey.* 1858.

Miller, J. W. *The A-B-C of National Defense.* 1915.

Miller, James. *Little Charlotte's Home in Murmah.* 1867.

Miller, Leo E. *In the Wilds of South America.* 1918.

Miller, Olive Thorne. *The Children's Book of Birds.* 1901.

Miller, Olive Thorne. *Upon the Tree-Tops.* 1897—Ad.

Miller, Roman J. *Around the World with the Battleships.* 1909.

Miller, Theodore. *Theodore W. Miller: Rough Rider (His Diary as a Soldier Together with His Life Story).* 1899.

Miller, Theodore W. *Rough Riders.* 1899.

Miller, Thomas. *Little Blue Hood.* 1864.

Miller, William. *The Modern Ship of Fools.* 1807.

Millet, F. D. *A Capillary Crime and Other Stories.* 1892.

Millis, Walter. *The Martial Spirit: A Study of Our War with Spain.* 1931.

Mills, William Wirt. *The Roosevelt Administration: Book of Photographs Compliments of Frank A. Ferris.* 1904.

Milner, J. *Key of Heaven or A Manual of Prayer.* c. 1910.

Milton, John. *L'allegro, Il Penseroso, Comus, and Lycidas.* 1900.

Milton, John. *Lycidas.* 1903.

Milton, John (1608–1674). *Paradise Lost.* 1846.

Minot, Henry Davis (1859–1890). *Land and Game Birds of New England: With Descriptions of the Birds, Their Nests and Eggs, Their Habits and Notes.* 1877.

Miss Mulock. *Little Sunshine's Holiday.* N.d.

Mistral, Frederic (1830–1914). *Memoirs of Mistral.* 1907.

Mistral, Frederic (1830–1914). *Mireille.* 1884.

Mistral, Frederic (1830–1914). *Mireille.* 1891.

Mitchell, Mason. *Birds of Samoa.* 1909.

Mitchell, S. Weir. *Hugh Wynne, Free Quaker*, vol. 2. 1896.

Mitford, A. B. *Tales of Old Japan* vols. 1–2. 1871.

Mittag, Johann Gottfried. *Leben Und Thaten Gustav Adolphs.* 1740.

Mittell, Phillip. *Violin Classics*, vol. 1. 1898.

Moddie, Mrs. *Roughing It in the Bush, Part II.* July 15,1852.

Mohammed. *The Koran.* N.d.

Mohomed, Mirza, and Cecil Spring Rice. *The Story of Valeh and Hadijeh.* 1903.

Molière (1622–1673). *Deuvres Completes de Molière.* 1884.

Mommsen, Theodore. *The History of Rome.* 1911.

Mommsen, Theodore. *The History of Rome*, vols. 1–4. Unknown.

Monk, William Henry. *Hymns, Ancient and Modern.* 1861.

Montagu, Mary Wortley. *The Letters and Works of Mary Wortley Montagu Volume CLXIX of the Collection of Ancient and Modern British Novels and Romances.* 1837.

Montgomery, G. W. *Narrative of A Journey to Guatemala in Central America in 1858.* 1839.

Moon, Frederick Franklin. *The Book of Forestry.* 1916.

Moon, Frederick Franklin, and Nelson Courtlandt Brown. *Elements of Forestry.* 1914.

Moore, Charles. *Wakefield / Birthplace of George Washington.* 1932.

Moore, Charles. *The Family Life of George Washington.* 1926.

Moore, Charles. *Daniel H. Burnham: Architect, Planner of Cities.* 1921.

Moore, Charles. *The Life and Times of Charles Follen McKim.* 1929.

Moore, Charles. *Washington Past and Present.* 1929.

Moore, Charles (Compiler). *Lincoln's Gettysburg Address and Second Inaugural.* 1927.

Moore, Clement Clarke (1779–1863). *A Visit from Saint Nicholas*. 1862.

Moore, Frank. *Songs of the Soldiers*. 1864.

Moore, Frank. *Personal and Political Ballads*. 1864.

Moore, Frank (Editor). *Lyrics of Loyalty*. 1864.

Moore, N. Hudson. *The Lace Book*. 1904.

Moore, Thomas. *The Life of Oliver Cromwell: Lord Protector of the Commonwealth*. 1741.

Moore, Thomas. *The Works of Lord Byron*, vols. 1–4. 1876.

Moore, Thomas. *The Life of the Right Honourable Richard Brinsley Sheridan* (2-vol. set). 1827.

Morehead, James T. *An Address in Commemoration of the First Settlement of Kentucky*. 1841.

Morgan, Lewis H. *The American Beaver and His Works*. 1868.

Morgan, Lewis H. *League of the Ho-De'-No-Sau-Nee or Iroquois* (vol. 2 of 2-vol. set). 1901.

Morin, Henry. *Mon Journal*. 1910.

Morley, John (1838–1923). *Critical Miscellanies*. 1904.

Morley, John (1838–1923). *Voltaire*. 1896.

Morley, John (1838–1923). *Burke*. 1902.

Morris, Beverley Robinson. *British Game Birds and Wildfowl*. N.d.

Morris, Charles. *The Life of Queen Victoria and the Story of Her Reign / A Beautiful Tribute to England's Greatest Queen in Her Domestic and Official Life: And, Also the Life of the New King, Edward VII*. 1901.

Morris, Earl H. *The Temple of the Warriors*. 1931.

Morris, William (1834–1896). *The Earthly Paradise* (3-vol. set). 1884.

Morris, William (1834–1896), and Eirikr Magnusson (1833–1913). *Howard the Halt*. 1891.

Morris, William O'Connor. *Hannibal, Soldier, Statesman, Patriot, and the Crisis of the Struggle between Carthage and Rome*. 1897.

Morris, William O'Connor. *Napoleon (Warrior and Ruler and Military Supremacy of Revolutionary France)*. 1893.

Morse, John T. *Abraham Lincoln*. American Statesmen. 1899.

Morse, John T. *Benjamin Franklin* (American Statesmen Series), vol. 1. 1898.

Morse, John T., Jr. *Thomas Jefferson*. American Statesmen. 1885.

Morse, John T., Jr. *John Adams* (American Statesmen), vol. 6. 1898.

Morse, John T., Jr. *Thomas Jefferson* (American Statesmen Series), vol. 11. 1898.

Morse, John T., Jr. *John Quincy Adams* (American Statesmen Series), vol. 15. 1898.

Morse, John T., Jr. *John Quincy Adams* / American Statesmen. 1884.

Morse, John T., Jr. *Abraham Lincoln* / American Statesmen. 1893.

Morse, John T., Jr. *Benjamin Franklin* / American Statesmen. 1891.

Morse, John T., Jr. *John Adams* / American Statesmen. 1885.

Morse, John T., Jr. *Abraham Lincoln* / American Statesmen, 2 vols. 1893.

Mortland, Samuel. *Twa Mouthfu's O' Naething*. 1917.

Mortley, John Lothrop. *History of the Netherlands 1584–1586*, 4 vols. 1879.
Mortley, John Lothrop. *The Rise of the Dutch Republic*, 3 vols. 1879.
Mortley, John Lothrop. *The Life and Death of John of Barneveld*, 2 vols. 1879.
Mowat, Robert Balmain. *Americans in England*. 1935.
Mowatt, Anna Cora. *Autobiography of an Actress: Or Eight Years on the Stage*. 1854.
Mowry, George E. *Theodore Roosevelt and the Progressive Party*. 1946.
Mozans, H. J., A.M., PhD. *Up the Orinoco and Down the Magdalena*. 1910.
Muffer, Theodor. *The Song of Roland*. 1906.
Muir, John. *A Thousand-Mile Walk to the Gulf*. 1916.
Muir, John. *Our National Parks*. 1901.
Muir, John. *The Mountains of California*. 1901.
Muir, John. *The Yosemite*. 1911.
Mullgardt, Louis C. *The Architecture and Landscape Gardening of the Exposition*. 1915.
Munn, Charles Allen. *Three Types of Washington Portraits*. 1908.
Munro, George. *The Waters of Hercules*. 1885.
Munro, H. A. J. (Editor). *Lucretius—Munro*. 1900.
Munroe, Kirk. *The Painted Desert*. 1897.
Munson, Edward Lyman. *The Principles of Sanitary Tactics*. 1911.
Murdoch, Walter. *Alfred Deakin: A Sketch*. 1923.
Murdock, Harold. *The Life and Death of Sir William Kirkaldy of Orange*. 1906.
Murphy, Arthur. *The Works of Cornelius Tacitus*. 1813.
Murray, Gilbert. *Euripides and His Age*. 1913.
Murray, Gilbert. *The Rise of the Greek Epic*. 1907.
Murray, Gilbert M.A., LL.D. (Translator). *Euripides*. 1902.
N. M. *A Chamber of Horrors with Profane Passages*. 1896.
Nansen, Fridtjof (Translated). *In Northern Mists: Arctic Explorations in Early Times*. 1911.
Napier, Major-General Sir William Francis Patrick (1785–1860). *History of the War in the Peninsula and in the South of France*. 1882.
Naslin, Victor, Mme. *Nouvelle Methode De Lecture*. N.d.
Nassau County YWCA. *Recipes from Historic Long Island*. 1940.
Nathan, Robert. *Selected Poems of Robert Nathan*. 1935.
Nathan, Robert. *Road of Ages*. 1935.
Native Georgian, A. *Georgia Scene*. 1859.
Nature Lovers Library. *Birds of America* (4-vol. set). 1917.
Naude, Gabriel. *Cardinal Mozarin's Library: Preceded by the Surrender of the Library (News from France)*. 1907.
Naumberg, Elsie M. B. *The Birds of Matto Grasso Brazil*. 1930.
Negri, Gaetano. *Julian the Apostate* (2-vol. set). 1905.
Nelson, Edward W. *The Eskimo about Bering Strait*. 1900.
Nelson, Edward W. *Report upon Natural History Collections Made in Alaska*. 1887.
Nelson, Edward W. *North American Fauna #29, The Rabbits of North America*. 1909.
Nelson, Edward W. *Wild Animals of North America*. 1918.

Nelson, Edward W., J. N. Rose, Mary L. Rathbun, and Leonhard Stejneger. *North American Fauna #14 Natural History of the Tres Marrias Island, Mexico*. 1899.

Nevins, Allan. *Henry White: Thirty Years of American Diplomacy*. 1930.

New York State Legislature. *State of New York in Memoriam: Theodore Roosevelt: Born October 27, 1858; Died January 6, 1919*. 1919.

Newberry, Harriet Barnes. *A Beautiful Life*. 1944.

Newman, John Henry Cardinal. *An Essay on the Development of Christian Doctrine*. 1888.

Newton, Thomas Wodehouse Legh, 2nd Baron (1857–?). *Lord Lyons, Lord Newton*, vol. 1. 1913.

Newton, Thomas Wodehouse Legh, 2nd Baron (1857–?). *Lord Lyons, Lord Newton*, vol. 2. 1913.

Newton, A. Edward. *A Magnificent Farce: and Other Diversions of a Book Collector*. 1921.

Newton, Lady. *Lyme Letters (1660– 1760)*. 1925.

Nichal, Compiled by Mrs. R. *Things Good and Wholesome*. 1907.

Nicolay, John, and John Hay. *Abraham Lincoln, A History* (in 10 vols.). 1890.

Nicolay, John G. *The Outbreak of the Rebellion: Campaigns of the Civil War*. 1881.

Nicoll, John Michael (1880–1925). *Three Voyages of a Naturalist*. 1908.

Nicoll, Maud Churchill. *Knitting and Sewing*. 1918.

Nicoll, W. Robertson. *The Key of the Blue Closet*. 1906.

Nicols, Arthur. *Zoological Notes*. 1883.

Nicolson, Harold. *Portrait of a Diplomatist*. 1930.

Nimrod. *Sporting by Nimrod*. 1838.

Ninck, Johannes. *Jesus A / S Charakter: Eine Unterfuchiing*. 1906.

Nohl, Louis. *Biographies of Musicians / Life of Wagner*. 1884.

Nolthenius, R. P. J. Tutein. *Theodore Roosevelt Deman Tier Tien Geboden*. 1904.

Norris, Frank. *The Octopus*. 1901.

North, Arthur Walbridge. *Camp and Camino in Lower California*. 1910.

North, Marianne. *Recollections of a Happy Life*, vol. 1. 1892.

Norton, Charles Eliot. *Letters of James Russell Lowell* (2-vol. set). 1894.

Nott, Charles Cooper. *The Seven Great Hymns of the Mediaeval Church*. 1868.

Oakley, Thorton. *Cecilia Beaux*. 1943.

Obata, Kyugoro. *An Interpretation of the Life of Viscount Shibusawa*. 1937.

Ober, Frederick A. *Camps in the Caribbees / Adventures in the Lesser Antilles*. 1880.

O'Donovan, Gerald. *Father Ralph*. 1913.

O'Donovan, Edmond. *The Merv Oasis*, vols. 1 and 2. 1883.

O'Donovan, Gerald. *Waiting*. 1915.

O'Hara, John Myers. *Manhattan by John Myers O'Hara*. 1915.

Ohlinger, Gustavus. *Their True Faith and Allegiance*. 1916.

O'Laughlin, John Callan. *From the Jungle through Europe with Roosevelt*. 1910.

Olcott, Francis Jenkins. *Good Stories for Great Holidays*. 1914.

Oldschool, Oliver. *Portfolio*. 1809.

Oliver, Ellinor McMillin. *A Memory.* N.d.

Oliver, F. S. *The Endless Adventure: 1710–1727,* vol. 1. 1930.

Oliver, F. S. *The Endless Adventure: 1727–1735,* vol. 2. 1931.

Oliver, F. S. *The Endless Adventure.* 1935.

Oliver, Frederick Scott. *Ordeal by Battle.* 1915.

Oliver, Frederick Scott. *Alexander Hamilton: An Essay on American Union.* 1920.

Oliver, Frederick Scott. *Alexander Hamilton: An Essay on American Union.* 1906.

Oliver, Frederick Scott. *Alexander Hamilton: An Essay on American Union.* 1907.

Oliver, Nola Nance. *Natchez.* 1940.

Olmsted, Frederick Law. *A Journey through Texas: Or A Saddle-Trip on the Southwestern Frontier.* 1860.

Oman, Charles. *Seven Roman Statesmen of the Later Republic.* 1906.

O'Neill, Moira. *Songs of the Glens of Antrim.* 1906.

Opie, Amelia Alderson (1769–1853). *Mrs. Opie's Works / Madeline.* 1827.

Opie, Amelia Alderson (1769–1853). *Mrs. Opie's Works / Simple Tales.* 1827.

Oppenheim, E. Phillips. *The Long Arm of Mannister.* 1914.

Optic, Oliver. *The Yankee Middy.* 1875.

Orczy, Baroness Emma (1865–1947). *Unravelled Knots.* 1926.

Ord, George (1781–1866). *Reprint of the North American Zoology by George Ord.* 1894.

O'Reilly, John Boyle. *Songs, Legends and Ballads.* 1878.

Origo, Iris. *Tribune of Rome: A Biography of Cola Di Rienzo.* 1938.

Origo, Iris. *Leopardi (A Biography).* 1935.

O'Ryan, John F. *The Modern Army in Action.* 1914.

Osborn, Henry Fairfield (1857–1935). *Our Plundered Planet.* 1940.

Osborn, Henry Fairfield (1857–1935). *Impressions of Great Naturalists.* 1924.

Osborn, Henry Fairfield (1857–1935). *The Causes of Extinction of Mammalia.* 1906.

Osborn, Henry Fairfield (1857–1935). *Evolution of the Mammalian Molar Teeth.* 1907.

Osborn, Henry Fairfield (1857–1935). *The Origin and Evolution of Life.* 1917.

Osborn, Henry Fairfield (1857–1935). *Men of the Old Stone Age.* 1915.

Osgood, Wilfred. *North America Fauna #30, Biological Investigations in Alaska and Yukon Territory 1909.* 1909.

Osgood, Wilfred H. *North American Fauna #24 A Biological Reconnaissance of the Base of the Alaska Peninsula.* 1904.

Osgood, Wilfred H. *North American Fauna #21 Natural History of Queen Charlotte Islands, British Columbia, Natural History of the Cook Inlet Region, Alaska.* 1901.

Osgood, Wilfred, George H. Parker, and A. Edward Preble. *The Fur Seals and Other Life of the Pribilof Islands / Alaska in 1914.* 1915.

O'Shaughnessy, Edith. *Viennese Medley.* 1932.

O'Shea, V. M. *The World Book from A to Blight,* vol. 1. 1918.

O'Shea, V. M. *The World Book from Blindness to Crow,* vol. 2. 1918.

O'Shea, V. M. *The World Book from Crow to Gloucester,* vol. 3. 1918.

O'Shea, V. M. *The World Book from Glove to Lemay,* vol. 4. 1918.

O'Shea, V. M. *The World Book from Lemberg to New Year*, vol. 5. 1918.

O'Shea, V. M. *The World Book from New York to Rice*, vol. 6. 1918.

O'Shea, V. M. *The World Book from Richard to Tides*, vol. 7. 1918.

O'Shea, V. M. *The World Book from Tie to Zwingli*, vol. 8. 1918.

Oswald, Felix. *Zoological Sketches*. 1883.

Overton, Jacqueline. *The Talented Mount Brothers*. 1942.

Owen, Mary Alicia. *Voodoo Tales*. 1893.

Oxenham, John. *Bees in Amber*. 1917.

Packard, A. S., Jr. *Guide to the Study of Insects*. 1876.

Packard, A. S., Jr. *The American Naturalist: A Popular Illustrated Magazine*, vol. 1. 1868.

Paflin, Roberta, and John F. Mckenna. *Lullaby Lyrics*. 1944.

Page, Thomas Nelson. *The Old Gentleman of the Black Stock*. 1900.

Page, Thomas Nelson (1853–1922). *In Old Virginia; Or Marse Chan and Other Stories*. 1888.

Paine, Albert Bigelow. *Thomas Nast: His Period and His Pictures*. 1904.

Palfrey, Winthrop, Francis. *Campaigns of the Civil War: The Antietam and Fredericksburg*. 1882.

Palmer Fredrick. *Clark of the Ohio: A Life of George Rogers Clark*. 1929.

Palmer, Frederick. *My Second Year of the War*. 1917.

Palmer, George Herbert (Translator). *The Odyssey of Homer*. 1891.

Pampaloni, Luigi. *Grilli Canterini Canzoni Populari Illustrate*. 1921.

Panin, Ivan Mikhailovich (1855–1942). *Aphorisms*. 1903.

Panin, Ivan Mikhailovich (1855–1942). *Thoughts*. 1886–1887.

Park, Mungo. *Travels in the Interior of Africa*. 1819.

Park, Mungo. *Travels 1795–1797*. 1816.

Parker, Capt. William Harwar. *Recollections of a Naval Officer*. 1883.

Parker, John H. *The Gatlings at Santiago: History of the Gatling Gun Detachment*. 1898.

Parkman, Francis (1823–1893). *Pioneers of France in the New World*. 1881.

Parkman, Francis (1823–1893). *The Old Regime in Canada: France and England in America, Part 4*. 1881.

Parkman, Francis (1823–1893). *The Oregon Trail*. 1881.

Parkman, Francis (1823–1893). *France and England in N. America Series: A Half Century of Conflict (Part Six)* (2-vol. set). 1892.

Parkman, Francis (1823–1893). *The Conspiracy of Pontiac and the Indian War after the Conquest of Canada* (2-vol. set). 1881.

Parkman, Francis (1823–1893). *Montcalm and Wolf* (2 vols.). 1884.

Parkman, Francis (1823–1893). *Jesuits in North America*. 1881.

Parkman, Francis (1823–1893). *La Salle and the Great West*. 1881.

Parkman, Francis (1823–1893). *Count Frontenac*. 1881.

Parks, Leighton. *Turnpikes and Dirt Roads*. 1927.

Parmel, Mary P. *A Short History of Russia*. 1900.

Parrish, Anne (1888–1957). *Floating Island*. 1930.

Parsons, Elsie Clews. *The Family: An Ethnographical and Historical Outline.* 1906.

Parsons, Mary Elizabeth. *The Wild Flowers of California.* 1907.

Pasha, Admiral Hobart. *Sketches from My Life.* 1886.

Paton, W. R. (Translator). *The Greek Anthology.* 1926.

Patten, William (Editor). *The Book of Sport.* 1901.

Patterson, Lt. Col. J. H. *The Man-Eaters of Tsave; and Other East African Adventures.* 1907.

Patterson, Lt. Col. J. H. *In the Grip of the Nyika.* 1909.

Paul, Herbert. *Men and Letters.* 1901.

Peabody, Francis G., and Robert Swain Peabody. *A New England Romance.* 1920.

Peabody, Josephine Preston (1874–1922). *The Harvest Moon.* 1916.

Peabody, Josephine Preston (1874–1922). *The Piper: A Play in Four Acts.* 1909.

Pearse, Padraic. *Collected Works of Padraic H. Pearse.* 1917.

Pearse, Padraic H. *Collected Works of Padraic H. Pearse.* 1918.

Pearson, Charles H. *National Life and Character: A Forecast.* 1893.

Pearson, Edmund Lester. *Theodore Roosevelt.* 1920.

Pearson, Edmund Lester (1880–1937). *Theodore Roosevelt: True Stories of Great Americans.* 1925.

Pearson, T. Gilbert. *The Bird Study Book.* 1917.

Peary, Robert E. *The North Pole.* 1910.

Pease, Sir Alfred E. *Rachel Gurney of the Grove.* N.d.

Peat, Frank Edwin. *Christmas Carols with the Christmas Story as Told by St. Luke and St. Matthew.* 1937.

Peck, Annie S. *The South American Tour; A Descriptive Guide.* 1916.

Peer, Frank Sherman. *Cross Country with Horse and Hound.* 1902.

Peet, Eric T. *Rough Stone Monuments and Their Builders.* 1912.

Pell, Herbert Claiborne. *L'exploration Portugaise et L'amerique du Nord.* 1939.

Pellew, George. *John Jay* (American Statesmen Series), vol. 9. 1898.

Pellew, George. *John Jay / American Statesmen.* 1891.

Penhallow, Samuel. *The History of the Wars of New England with the Eastern Indians, Or A Narrative of Their Continued Perfidy and Cruelty.* 1859.

Pepys, Samuel F.R.S. *Diary and Correspondence of Samuel Pepys, F. R. S.* 1855.

Percy, William Alexander. *Lanterns on the Levee.* 1941.

Perry, Frances M. *Famous Americans Series: A Life of Theodore Roosevelt.* 1903.

Perry, Frances M. *Four Great American Presidents / Garfield, McKinley, Cleveland, Roosevelt,* vol. 2. 1903.

Perry, Oliver Hazard. *Diary of Oliver Hazard Perry.* 1899.

Perry, Stella George Stern. *Melindy.* 1919.

Petherich, Mr. and Mrs. *Travels in Central Africa and Explorations of the Western Nile Tributaries,* vol. 1. 1869.

Petherick, Mr. and Mrs. *Travels in Central Africa,* vol. 2. 1869.

Petrie, W. M. Flinders. *The Revolution of Civilization.* 1911.

Pfeiffer, L. *Der Mentchentohn Verlag von Edwin Runge.* N.d.

Phebus, Gaston. *Livre de la Chasse* (in French). N.d.

Phelps, Elizabeth Stewart. *Gypsy Breynton*. April 1909.

Phelps, Elizabeth Stewart. *Beyond the Gates*. 1897.

Philippi, Charlotte. *Die Familie Schonberg-Cotta*. 1904.

Phillips, Arthur S. *My Wilderness Friends*. 1910.

Phillips, John C. *American Game Mammals and Birds. 1582–1925*. 1930.

Phillpotts, Eden. *The Joy of Youth*. 1913

Phister, Frederick. *Campaigns of the Civil War: Statistical Record of the Armies of the United States*. 1883.

Phoenix, John. *Phoenixiana: Or Sketches and Burlesques*. 1889.

Pickett, Albert James. *History of Alabama*. 1851.

Pierne, Gabriel. *The Children's Crusade: A Musical Legend in Four Parts: Vocal Score*. 1906.

Pierne, Gabriel. *Voyez Comme on Danse*. 1902.

Pike, Nicholas. *Sub-Tropical Rambles in the Land of the Aphanapteryx*. 1873.

Pike, Nicholas. *Sub-Tropical Rambles in the Land of the Aphanapteryx: Personal Experiences and Adventures in the Mauritus* (NY Edition). 1873.

Pike, Warburton Mayer (1861–1915). *The Barren Ground of Northern Canada*. 1892.

Pinchot, Gifford. *The Use of the National Forests*. 1907.

Pine, Johannes. *Horatius Pine*. 1733.

Platt, George W. *A History of the Republican Party*. 1904.

Playfair, Hugo. *Brother Jonathan: The Smartest Nation in All Creation* (3-vol. set). 1844.

Plutarch (46?–120? A.D.). *Plutarch's Works Miscellanies and Essays*. 1889.

Plympton, A. G. *The Mary Jane Papers / A Book for Young Girls*. 1884.

Poe, Edgar Allen (1809–1849). *The Works of Edgar Allen Poe / The Amontillado*. 1884.

Pollard, Josephine. *The Decorative Sisters*. 1881.

Pollen, Mrs. John Hungerford. *Seven Centuries of Lace*. 1908.

Polo, Marco. *The Travels of Marco Polo*. 1903.

Pond, George E. *The Shenandoah Valley: Campaigns of the Civil War*. 1883.

Poole, Ernest. *The Harbor*. 1915.

Pope, A., Jr. *Upland Game Birds of the United States*. 1878.

Popenol, Dorothy H. *Santiago de Los Cabelleros de Guatemalla*. 1933.

Porter, Captain David. *Porter's Journal: Journal of a Cruise Made to the Pacific Ocean 1812–1814*. 1815.

Potter, Beatrice. *Histoire de Pierre-Lapin*. 1921.

Pound, Ezra. *Ezra Pound: Selected Poems*. 1939.

Pound, Ezra (1885–). *Ezra Pound: His Metric and Poetry*. 1917.

Powell, Edward Alexander (1879–?). *Gentlemen Rovers*. 1913.

Powell-Cotton, Major P. H. G. *In Unknown Africa*. 1904.

Praed, Winthrop Mackworth. *Lillian and Other Poems*. 1852.

Praed, Winthrop Mackworth. *Praed's Poems*. 1909.

Preble, A. Edward. *North American Fauna #22 A Biological Investigation of the Hudson Bay Region.* 1902.

Prentiss, Elizabeth (1818–1878). *Little Lou's Sayings and Doings.* 1868.

Prentiss, Elizabeth (1818–1878). *The Flower of the Family: A Book for Girls.* 1868.

Prentiss, Elizabeth (1818–1878), and Edmund Evans (1826–1905). *Susy's Little Servants.* 1867.

Prentiss, Elizabeth (1818–1878), and Edmund Evans (1826–1905). *Susy's Six Teachers.* 1867.

Prentiss, Elizabeth (1818–1878), and Edmund Evans (1826–1905). *Susy's Six Birthdays.* 1869.

Prescott, William Hickling (1796–1859). *Prescott's Conquest of Peru,* vol. 2. 1847.

Prescott, William Hickling (1796–1859). *Prescott's Philip to Second,* vol. 1. 1855.

Prescott, William Hickling (1796–1859). *Philip the Second,* vol. 2. 1855.

Prescott, William Hickling (1796–1859). *History of the Conquest of Mexico* (3 vols.). 1846.

Prescott, William Hickling (1796–1859). *History of the Reign of Ferdinand and Isabella, the Catholic* (3-vol. set). 1845

Prescott, William Hickling (1796–1859). *Conquest of Peru,* vol. 1–2. 1850.

Prescott, William Hickling (1796–1859). *Philip the Second,* vol. 1. 1890.

Prescott, William Hickling (1796–1859). *Philip the Second,* vol. 2. 1890.

Prescott, William Hickling (1796–1859). *Philip the Second, King of Spain,* vol. 3. 1890.

Preston, Hayter. *Childhood Days (An Essay Suggested by the Etchings of Ms. E. Soper).* N.d.

Preston, Thomas (1834–1901). *A Sketch of Mrs. Elizabeth Russell.* 1888.

Prible, Edward A. *North American Fauna #27 A Biological Investigation of the Athabaska Mackenzie Region.* 1908.

Price, Rose Lambart, Sir, Bart. *A Summer on the Rockies.* 1898.

Prichard, H. Hesketh. *Through Trackless Labrador.* 1911.

Prichard-Agnetti, Mary. *Vicenza: The Home of "The Saint."* 1911.

Prideaux, John Selby. *Selby's British Ornithology.* 1833.

Prime, William C. *O Mother Dear Jerusalem, the Old Hymn, Its Origin and Genealogy.* 1867.

Primrose, Archibald Philip (Lord Roseberry) (1847–1929). *Lord Chatham: His Early Life and Connections.* 1910.

Pringle, Henry (1897–1958). *Theodore Roosevelt: A Biography.* 1931.

Proctor, Edna Dean. *The Song of the Ancient People.* 1893.

Progressive National Committee. *The Progressive Party and Its Record from January to July, 1916.* 1916.

Pry, Paul. *Oddities of London Life,* vol. 1. 1838.

Pryor, Roger A., Mrs. *The Mother of Washington and Her Times.* 1903.

Puleston, Capt. W. D., USN. *Mahan.* 1939.

Pulsifer, Harold Trowbridge. *Elegy for A House.* 1935.

Pulsifer, Harold Trowbridge. *Rowen a Collection of Verses.* 1937.

Pulsifer, Susan Nichols. *Fighting French Ballads*. 1943.

Punnett, R. C. *Mendelism*. 1909.

Purdon, K. F. *The Folk of Furry Farm*. 1914.

Putnam, Ruth. *Luxemburg and Her Neighbours*. 1918.

Pycraft, William Plane (1868–?). *The Infancy of Animals*. 1913.

Pycraft, William Plane (1868–?). *The Courtship of Animals*. 1913.

Pycraft, William Plane (1868–?). *A History of Birds*. 1910.

Pyle, Howard. *The Story of King Arthur*. 1903.

Pyle, Howard. *The Story of the Champions of the Round Table*. 1905.

Que Mando Escrevir-El Muy Al. *"Libro De La Monteria Que Mando Escrevir-El Muy Alt. Y Muy Podersos."* 1582.

Queen Anne. *A Proclamation of Queen Anne 1704: Ascertaining Foreign Coin Rates in America*. 1704.

Quiller-Couch, A. T. *The Delectable Duchy*. 1899.

Quisenberry, A. C. *Life and Times Hon. Humphrey Marshall*. 1892.

Radcliffe, A. G. *Schools and Masters of Painting*. 1903.

Radcliffe, C. R. E. *Big Game Shooting in Alaska*. 1904.

Raleigh, Walter, Sir. *Sir Walter Raleigh's History of the Reign of William the First*. 1693.

Ralph, Julian. *People We Pass*. 1896.

Ramach, S. *La Venus de Mile from Gazette des Beau Arts*. Unknown.

Ramsay, David. *The Life of George Washington*. 1807.

Rane, Frank W. *Massachusetts State Forester, Tenth Annual Report 1913, Public Document No. 73*. 1914.

Ransom, Fletcher C. *My Policies in Jungleland*. 1910.

Rathbune, Richard, and Charles D. Walcott. *Annual Report of the US National Museum, 1917*. 1918.

Rattray, Jeannette E. *Montauk: Three Centuries of Romance / Sport / Adventure*. 1938.

Ray, P. H. *Report of the International Polar Expedition to Point Barrow, Alaska*. 1885.

Rebsch, Moris. *Schiller's Liedvonder Glocke* (in German). 1849.

Redesdale, Algernon B. Freeman-Mitford, Baron (1837–1916). *Memories*. N.d.

Redpath, Henry A. (Editor), and Various Authors. *Holy Bible Cyclopedic Concordance*. N.d.

Reed, Charles. *The First Great Canadian; the Story of Pierre Le Moyne, Sieur D'berville*. 1910.

Reed, Sam Rockwell. *The Vicksburg Campaign 1862–1863*. 1882.

Rees, J. D. *India (Oriental Series): The Real India*, vol. 19. 1910.

Reeves, A. M. *The Finding of Wineland the Good (History of Icelandic Discovery of America)*. 1895.

Reformed Church. *Order of Worship*. 1901.

Reichenbach, Dr. U. B. *Naturgechichte Merichen und der Taugthiere*. 1855.

Reid, Christian. *The Land of the Sky: Or Adventures in Mountain By-Ways*. 1877.

Reid, Samuel C. *The Scouting Expeditions of McCullogh's Texas Rangers*. N.d.

Reid, Thomas Mayne. *Odd People*. 1884.

Reid, Whitelaw. *Abraham Lincoln.* 1910.

Remington, Frederic (1861–1909). *Pony Tracks.* 1895.

Remington, Frederic (1861–1909). *Crooked Trails.* 1898.

Remington, Frederic (1861–1909). *Book, Drawings by Frederic Remington.* 1897.

Remington, Frederic (1861–1909). *Book, Done in the Open.* 1902.

Remington, Frederic (1861–1909). *A Bunch of Buckskins-Eight Drawings in Pastel.* 1901.

Renault-Roulier, Gilbert (1904–1984). *Memoires D'un Agent Secret De La France Libre.* 1942.

Renshaw, Grahm. *Natural History Essays.* 1905.

Renshaw, Grahm. *More Natural History Essays.* 1905.

Renshaw, Grahm. *Final Natural History Essays.* 1907.

Reported by a Neighbor. *Judge West's Opinion.* 1908.

Repplier, Agnes. *Book, in Our Convent Days.* 1905.

Reprints of Tales and Stories. *Chatterbox.* Unknown.

Retsch, Moritz. *Umrisse Buerger's Balladen.* 1840.

Retsch, Moritz. *Umriffe Zu Schiller's Fridolin.* 1840.

Retsch, Moritz. Portfolio of Prints—Umrisee du Schillars *Kampf Mit Dem Drachen.* 1847.

Reynolds, Quentin (1902–1965). *A London Diary.* 1941.

Rhodes, Charles D. *History of the Cavalry of the Army of the Potomac.* 1900.

Rhodes, James Ford. *Lectures on the American Civil War Delivered at Oxford.* 1913.

Rhodes, James Ford. *History of the United States from the Compromise of 1850.* 1906.

Rice, Alice Caldwell Hegan (1870–1942). *Mrs. Wiggs of the Cabbage Patch.* 1903.

Rice, Alice Caldwell Hegan (1870–1942). *Lovey Mary.* 1903.

Rice, Cale Young. *Many Gods.* 1910.

Rice, Cecil Spring. *In Memoriam A.C.M.L.* 1918.

Rich, Walter H. *Feathered Game of the Northeast.* 1907.

Richards, Brintey. *The Songs of Wales: Royal Edition.* 1879.

Richards, Laura E. *Melody.* 1893.

Richards, Laura E. *Captain January.* 1892.

Richards, Laura E. (1850–1943). *The Hurdy-Gurdy.* 1902.

Richards, Mrs. Waldo. *High Tide: Songs of Joy and Vision from the Present-Day Poets of America and Great Britain.* 1916.

Richardson, Charles. *New Dictionary of the English Language L–Ske.* 1836.

Richardson, Charles. *New Dictionary of the English Language Skl–Z.* 1836.

Richardson, Charles. *New Dictionary of the English Language,* vol. 1 Part II E–K. 1863.

Richardson, Charles. *New Dictionary of the English Language.* 1863.

Richardson, James D. *A Compilation of the Messages and Papers of the Presidents* (Vol. 2–11 of 11 vols.). 1910.

Richardson, James. *A Compilation of the Messages and Papers of the Presidents 1789–1897.* 1897.

Richardson, John. *Fauna Boreali-Americana.* 1829.

Ridgeway, William. *Origin and Influence of the Thoroughbred Horse*. 1905.

Ridgeway, William. *The Early Age of Greece*. 1901.

Ridinger, Johann Elias. *Der Jagtbaren Thiere*. 1740.

Ridinger, Johann Elias. *Der Edlen Jagdbarkeit*. 1729.

Ridinger, Johann Elias. *Nach der Nature Entwurffene Vorstellungen*. 1750.

Riis, Jacob August (1849–1914). *Is There a Santa Claus?* 1904.

Riis, Jacob August (1849–1914). *Out of Mulberry Street*. 1898.

Riis, Jacob August (1849–1914). *The Making of an American*. 1901.

Riis, Jacob August (1849–1914). *Theodore Roosevelt the Citizen*. 1904.

Riis, Jacob August (1849–1914). *How the Other Half Lives: Studies among the Tenements of New York*. 1894.

Riley, James Whitcomb (1853?–1916). *Poems of Childhood*. 1940.

Riley, James Whitcomb (1853?–1916). *Child-Rhymes*. 1890.

Riley, James Whitcomb (1853?–1916). *The Complete Works of James Whitcombe Riley: Biographical Edition*, vols. 1–6. 1913.

Rinehart, Mary Roberts. *The Man in Lower Ten*. 1909.

Ripley, R. S. *The War with Mexico* (2-vol. set). 1849.

Riuigre, Henri. *La Marine Francaise sous Le Regne de Louis IV*. 1859.

Rives, George Lockhart. *The United States and Mexico 1821–1848* (2-vol. set). 1913.

Rizal, Dr., Jose. *An Eagle Flight: A Filipino Novel*. 1900.

Roberts, Lord of Kandahar. *Forty-One Years in India: From Subaltern to Commander-in-Chief*. 1897.

Robertson, W. Graham. *Life Was Worth Living*. 1931.

Robertson, William. *Robertson's Charles the Fifth*, vols. 1 and 2. 1890.

Robins, Elizabeth. *Time Is Whispering*. 1923.

Robinson, Corinne Roosevelt. *Out of Nymph-Poems*. 1930.

Robinson, Corinne Roosevelt. *Service and Sacrifice Poems*. 1919.

Robinson, Corinne Roosevelt. *The Call of Brotherhood and Other Poems*. 1912.

Robinson, Corinne Roosevelt. *One Woman to Another and Other Poems*. 1914.

Robinson, Edwin Arlington (1869–1935). *The Man Against the Sky*. 1916.

Robinson, Edwin Arlington (1869–1935). *Captain Craig / A Book of Poems*. 1915.

Robinson, Edwin Arlington (1869–1935). *Vanzorn / A Comedy in Three Acts*. 1914.

Robinson, Edwin Arlington (1869–1935). *Captain Craig: A Book of Poems*. 2nd Edition. 1903.

Robinson, Edwin Arlington (1869–1935). *Child of the Night: A Book of Poems*. 1897.

Robinson, H. M. *The Great Fur Land*. 1879.

Robinson, W. *English Flower Garden and Home Grounds*. 1911.

Rockhill, William Woodville. *The Journey of Friar William of Rubruck*. 1900.

Rockhill, William Woodville. *Diary of a Journey through Mongolia and Tibet in 1891–92*. 1894.

Rodd, Sir Rennell. *The Princes of Achaia and the Chronicles of Morea* (2-vol. set). 1907.

Rodd, Sir Rennell (1858–1941). *Love, Worship, and Death*. 1916.

Rodrigues, J. Barbosa. *Sertum Palmarum Brasiliensium*. 1903.

Rogers, Thorold. *The Industrial and Commercial History of England*. 1892.

Rogers, W. A. *America's Black and White Book*. 1917.

Roget, Peter Mark. *Roget's Thesaurus of English Words and Phrases*. 1909.

Rohde, Eleanour Sinclair. *Christmas*. N.d.

Romanes, J. G. *Romanes Lectures 1892–1900 Decennial Issue*. 1900.

Romig, Edgar Franklin. *The Tercentenary Year: Reformed Church in America*. 1929.

Roosevelt, Clinton. *The Science of Government Founded on Natural Law*. 1841.

Roosevelt, Edith Kermit. *The Story of Gertrude Tyler and Her Family 1660–1860*. 1928.

Roosevelt, Edith Kermit. *Cleared for Strange Ports*. 1927.

Roosevelt, Edith Kermit. *EKR's Account Book 1898–1918*. 1898–1918.

Roosevelt, Edith Kermit, and Richard Derby. *Cleared for Strange Ports*. 1924.

Roosevelt, Kermit. *Quentin Roosevelt: A Sketch with Letters*. 1921.

Roosevelt, Kermit. *War in the Garden of Eden*. 1919.

Roosevelt, Kermit. *The Long Trail*. 1921.

Roosevelt, Kermit, Richard Derby, Martha Bulloch Roosevelt, and Belle Willard Roosevelt. *Cleared for Strange Ports*. 1927.

Roosevelt, Kermit (Editor). *Quentin Roosevelt: A Sketch with Letters*. 1922.

Roosevelt, Nicholas. *The Philippines / A Treasure and A Problem*. 1933.

Roosevelt, Robert Barnwell. *The Game Birds of the Coasts and Lakes of the Northeastern States of America*. 1859.

Roosevelt, Robert Barnwell. *Superior Fishing; Or the Striped Bass, Trout and Black Bass of the Northern States*. 1865.

Roosevelt, Robert Barnwell. *The Game Fish of the North*. 1869.

Roosevelt, Theodore. *Fear God and Take Your Own Part*. 1916.

Roosevelt, Theodore. *Thomas H. Benton*. American Statesmen. 1899.

Roosevelt, Theodore. *Scribner's*. February 1910.

Roosevelt, Theodore. *The Roosevelt Book*. 1904.

Roosevelt, Theodore. *Outlook Editorials*. 1909.

Roosevelt, Theodore. *American Problems*. 1910.

Roosevelt, Theodore. *Collection of Articles by Theodore Roosevelt [From Scribner's]*. N.d.

Roosevelt, Theodore. *The Winning of the West*, vol. 1. 1889.

Roosevelt, Theodore. *Roosevelt: His Life Meaning and Messages*, vol. 1, vol. 3, vol. 4. 1919.

Roosevelt, Theodore. *My Life as a Naturalist, the American Museum Journal, May 1918*. 1918.

Roosevelt, Theodore. *Big Game Hunting*. 1899.

Roosevelt, Theodore. *Ranch Life and the Hunting Trail*. 1888.

Roosevelt, Theodore. *The Rough Riders*. 1899.

Roosevelt, Theodore. *Presidential Papers and State Papers*. 1910.

Roosevelt, Theodore. *The Works of Theodore Roosevelt (Hunting Trips of a Ranchman)*, vols. 1 and 2. 1906.

Roosevelt, Theodore. *The Works of Theodore Roosevelt, Thomas Hart Benton*, vol. 5. 1906.

Roosevelt, Theodore. *The Works of Theodore Roosevelt, The Winning of the West*, vols. 8–13. 1906.

Roosevelt, Theodore. *Nas Selvas Do Brasil.* 1943.

Roosevelt, Theodore. *The Foes of Our Own Household.* 1917.

Roosevelt, Theodore. *The Winning of the West*, vols. 1–6. 1903.

Roosevelt, Theodore. *Hunting Trips of a Ranchman*, vols. 1 and 2. 1902.

Roosevelt, Theodore. *The Naval War of 1812*, vols. 1 and 2. 1902.

Roosevelt, Theodore. *American Ideals*, vol. 2. 1903.

Roosevelt, Theodore. *Naval War of 1812.* 1883.

Roosevelt, Theodore. *The Winning of the West*, vols. 1–4. 1889.

Roosevelt, Theodore. *Theodore Roosevelt aus Meinem Leben.* 1914.

Roosevelt, Theodore. *Americanism and Preparedness.* 1917.

Roosevelt, Theodore. *African Game Trails.* 1909.

Roosevelt, Theodore. *A Book Lover's Holidays in the Open.* 1916.

Roosevelt, Theodore. *Roosevelt's Works Wilderness Hunter*, vols. 1 and 2. 1902.

Roosevelt, Theodore. *Roosevelt's Works Hunting Trips of a Ranchman*, vols. 1 and 2. 1902.

Roosevelt, Theodore. *Roosevelt's Works, Naval War of 1812*, vols. 1 and 2. 1902.

Roosevelt, Theodore. *Roosevelt's Works, the Brazilian Wilderness.* 1914.

Roosevelt, Theodore. *Roosevelt's Works, American and the World War.* 1918.

Roosevelt, Theodore. *Roosevelt's Works, an Autobiography.* 1913.

Roosevelt, Theodore. *Roosevelt's Works, American Ideals*, vols. 1 and 2. 1902.

Roosevelt, Theodore. *Roosevelt's Works, Gouverneur Morris.* 1916.

Roosevelt, Theodore. *Roosevelt's Works, History as Literature.* 1913.

Roosevelt, Theodore. *Roosevelt's Works, New York.* 1910.

Roosevelt, Theodore. *Roosevelt's Works, Oliver Cromwell.* 1917.

Roosevelt, Theodore. *Roosevelt's Works, Realizable Ideals.* 1912.

Roosevelt, Theodore. *Roosevelt's Works, The Strenuous Life.* 1911.

Roosevelt, Theodore. *Roosevelt's Works, The Rough Riders.* 1918.

Roosevelt, Theodore. *Roosevelt's Works, Thomas Hart Benton.* 1914.

Roosevelt, Theodore. *The Great Adventure.* 1918.

Roosevelt, Theodore. *The Winning of the West*, vol. 2. 1891.

Roosevelt, Theodore. *The Winning of the West*, vol. 3. 1894.

Roosevelt, Theodore. *The Winning of the West*, vol. 4. 1896.

Roosevelt, Theodore. *Through the Brazilian Wilderness.* 1922.

Roosevelt, Theodore. *A Book Lover's Holidays in the Open.* 1922.

Roosevelt, Theodore. *The Rough Riders.* 1922.

Roosevelt, Theodore. *The Foes of Our Household.* 1917.

Roosevelt, Theodore. *TR, An Autobiography.* 1913.

Roosevelt, Theodore. *The Winning of the West*, vol. 2. 1889.

Roosevelt, Theodore. *The Great Adventure, Subtitled Present-Day Studies in American Nationalism*. 1918.

Roosevelt, Theodore. *African Game Trails*. 1910.

Roosevelt, Theodore. *Administration—Civil Service*. 1900.

Roosevelt, Theodore. *The Naval Operations of the War Between Great Britain and the United States: The War of 1812*. 1901.

Roosevelt, Theodore. *Gouverneur Morris*. American Statesmen. 1888.

Roosevelt, Theodore. *Roosevelt's Writings*. 1922.

Roosevelt, Theodore. *The New Nationalism*. 1910.

Roosevelt, Theodore. *America and the World War*. 1915.

Roosevelt, Theodore. *Amerikanismus*. 1903.

Roosevelt, Theodore. *Roosevelt, The Strenuous Life*. 1910.

Roosevelt, Theodore. *Practical Politics – [Roosevelt]*. 1888.

Roosevelt, Theodore. *Addresses and Presidential Messages of Theodore Roosevelt 1902–1904*. 1904.

Roosevelt, Theodore. *African and European Addresses*. 1910.

Roosevelt, Theodore. *The Winning of the West*, vol. 6. 1907.

Roosevelt, Theodore. *National Strength and International Duty*. 1917.

Roosevelt, Theodore. *Applied Ethics*. 1910.

Roosevelt, Theodore. *Presidential Addresses and State Papers*. 1904.

Roosevelt, Theodore. *Hunting Trips of a Ranchman*. 1886.

Roosevelt, Theodore. *Theodore Roosevelt's Diaries of Boyhood and Youth*. 1928.

Roosevelt, Theodore. *History as Literature*. 1913.

Roosevelt, Theodore. *American Ideals and Other Essays*. 1897.

Roosevelt, Theodore. *Progressive Principles*. 1913.

Roosevelt, Theodore. *Jagdftreifzuge*. 1904.

Roosevelt, Theodore. *La Vie Intense*. N.d.

Roosevelt, Theodore. *Biological Analogies in History*. 1910.

Roosevelt, Theodore. *La Guerra Mundial*. 1915.

Roosevelt, Theodore. *A Vida Intensa*. 1909.

Roosevelt, Theodore. *El Deber De America Ante La Nueva Europa*. 1917.

Roosevelt, Theodore. *Die Rauhen Reiter*. 1906.

Roosevelt, Theodore. *California Addresses by President Roosevelt*. 1903.

Roosevelt, Theodore. *Americanism and Preparedness*. 1917.

Roosevelt, Theodore. *Biological Analogies in History*. 1910.

Roosevelt, Theodore. *Charter Day Address*. 1911.

Roosevelt, Theodore. *Le Citoyen D'une Republique*. 1910.

Roosevelt, Theodore. *Roosevelt's Works, Womanhood and Childhood*. 1912.

Roosevelt, Theodore. *Roosevelt's Works, Fear God and Take Your Own Part*. 1916.

Roosevelt, Theodore. *Roosevelt's Works, Winning of the West* [vol. 1 (A), vol. 2 (B), vol. 3 (C), vol. 4 (D)] Part One. 1900.

Roosevelt, Theodore. *Roosevelt's Works, Winning of the West* [vol. 1 (A), vol. 2 (B), vol. 3 (C), vol. 4 (D)] Part Two. 1900.

Roosevelt, Theodore. *Roosevelt's Works, African Game Trails.* 1910.

Roosevelt, Theodore. *Roosevelt's Works, African Game Animals,* vols. 1 and 2. 1914.

Roosevelt, Theodore. *Roosevelt's Works, Pastimes of An American Hunter.* 1908.

Roosevelt, Theodore. *Theodore Roosevelt.* 1919.

Roosevelt, Theodore. *The Great Adventure: Present-Day Studies in American Nationalism.* 1919.

Roosevelt, Theodore. *Invasion of the Crimea* (4 vols.). 1875.

Roosevelt, Theodore. *The Winning of the West,* vols. 1–4. 1889.

Roosevelt, Theodore. *Scribner's Magazine—March 1910 / Trekking through the Thirst to the Sotik / T. Roosevelt.* 1910.

Roosevelt, Theodore. *Scribner's Magazine:* April 1910, *Hunting in the Sotik.* 1910.

Roosevelt, Theodore. *Presidential Addresses and State Papers Nov. 15, 1907–Nov. 26, 1908,* vols. 1–7. 1910.

Roosevelt, Theodore. *Ritchie's Second Steps in Latin.* Unknown.

Roosevelt, Theodore. *The Strenuous Life.* 1903.

Roosevelt, Theodore. *Personal Memoirs of Theodore Roosevelt.* 1919.

Roosevelt, Theodore. *Through the Brazilian Wilderness.* 1914.

Roosevelt, Theodore. *The Winning of the West.* 1914.

Roosevelt, Theodore. *The Winning of the West.* 1903.

Roosevelt, Theodore. *TR Inaugural Address (March 4, 1905).* 1905.

Roosevelt, Theodore. *Special Message of the President of the United States concerning the Panama Canal.* 1906.

Roosevelt, Theodore. *Restoration of the White House: Message of the President of the U.S. Transmitting the Report of the Architect.* 1903.

Roosevelt, Theodore. *The Naval War of 1812.* 1882.

Roosevelt, Theodore. *Revealing and Concealing Coloration in Birds and Mammals.* August 23, 1911.

Roosevelt, Theodore. *Historic Towns; New York.* 1895.

Roosevelt, Theodore. *State of New York Public Papers of Theodore Roosevelt Governor.* 1900.

Roosevelt, Theodore. *Message of the President of the United States 1901 Fifty-Seventh Congress First Session.* 1901.

Roosevelt, Theodore. *Message of the President of the United States Communicated to the Two Houses of Congress at the Beginning of the Fifty-Eighth Congress.* 1904.

Roosevelt, Theodore. *Americanism in Religion.* 1908.

Roosevelt, Theodore. *Outlook Editorials.* 1909.

Roosevelt, Theodore. *Roosevelt vs. Newett: A Transcript of the Testimony Taken and Depositions Read at Marquette, Michigan.* 1914.

Roosevelt, Theodore. *The Progressive.* 1916.

Roosevelt, Theodore. *War Addresses 1917.* 1918.

Roosevelt, Theodore. *Theodore Roosevelt's Letters to His Children.* 1919.

Roosevelt, Theodore. *What the Japanese Stood for in the World War.* N.d.

Roosevelt, Theodore. *Why America Should Join the Allies.* N.d.

Roosevelt, Theodore. *Colonial Policies of the United States.* 1937.

Roosevelt, Theodore. *An Autobiography.* 1913.

Roosevelt, Theodore. *Big-Game Hunting in the Rockies and on the Great Plains Letters from Governors-Scrapbook.* 1899.

Roosevelt, Theodore. *Works of Theodore Roosevelt.* (24-vol. set). 1923–1925.

Roosevelt, Theodore. *Works of Theodore Roosevelt: The Wilderness Hunter / Outdoor Pastimes* vol. 2. 1926.

Roosevelt, Theodore. *Works of Theodore Roosevelt: The Winning of the West,* vol. 9. 1926.

Roosevelt, Theodore. *Works of Theodore Roosevelt: Hero Tales from American History / Oliver Cromwell / New York,* vol. 10. 1926.

Roosevelt, Theodore. *Works of Theodore Roosevelt: Literary Essays,* vol. 12. 1926.

Roosevelt, Theodore. *Works of Theodore Roosevelt: Campaigns and Controversies,* vol. 14. 1926.

Roosevelt, Theodore. *Works of Theodore Roosevelt: State Papers as Governors and President,* vol. 15. 1926.

Roosevelt, Theodore. *Works of Theodore Roosevelt: American Problems,* vol. 16. 1926.

Roosevelt, Theodore. *Works of Theodore Roosevelt: Social Justice and Popular Rule,* vol. 17. 1926.

Roosevelt, Theodore. *Works of Theodore Roosevelt: An Autobiography-Index,* vol. 20. 1926.

Roosevelt, Theodore. *Amerikanisme.* 1902.

Roosevelt, Theodore. *California Addresses.* Unknown.

Roosevelt, Theodore. *American Problems.* 1910.

Roosevelt, Theodore. *The Winning of the West Series (Parts 1–6) by TR.* 1900.

Roosevelt, Theodore. *Je Sais Tout Mes Chasses* (Paperback). 1906.

Roosevelt, Theodore. *Report of the Commission on Country Life.* 1911.

Roosevelt, Theodore. *Theodore Roosevelt: An Autobiography.* 1913.

Roosevelt, Theodore. *Campaigns and Controversies.* 1926.

Roosevelt, Theodore. *Roosevelt's Works, The Foes of Our Own Household.* 1917.

Roosevelt, Theodore. *Roosevelt's Works, Good Hunting.* 1907.

Roosevelt, Theodore. *Roosevelt's Works, National Strength and International Duty.* 1917.

Roosevelt, Theodore, and Ernest Hamlin Abbott. *Roosevelt's Works, The New Nationalism.* 1910.

Roosevelt, Theodore, and Joseph Bucklin Bishop (Editor). *Letters to His Children, Roosevelt.* 1919.

Roosevelt, Theodore, and Lewis Einstein. *A Prophecy of the War (1913–1914).* 1918.

Roosevelt, Theodore, and Henry Cabot Lodge (1850–1924). *Selections from the Correspondence of TR and Henry Cabot Lodge.* 1925.

Roosevelt, Theodore, and Henry Cabot Lodge (1850–1924). *Hero Tales from American History.* 1895.

Roosevelt, Theodore, and Frederic Remington (1861–1909). *Roosevelt's Works Ranch Life and the Hunting Trail.* 1918.

Roosevelt, Theodore, and Frederic Remington (1861–1909). *Ranch Life and the Hunting Trail.* 1899.

Roosevelt, Theodore, and Elihu Root. *Joseph Hodges Choate: Memorial Addresses.* 1918.

Roosevelt, Theodore, John S. Sargent (1856–1925), Booth Tarkington (1869–1946), et al. *For France (An Anthology).* 1917.

Roosevelt, Theodore, and S. T. Van Dyke, G. D. Elliot, and H. A. Stone. *Roosevelt's Works, the Deer Family.* 1903.

Roosevelt, Theodore. With an Introduction by Lawrence F. Abbott. *Roosevelt's Works, African and European Addresses.* 1918.

Roosevelt, Theodore. With an Introduction by Henry Cabot Lodge. *Roosevelt's Works, Addresses and Messages.* 1904.

Roosevelt, Theodore, Jr., and (Henry) Grantland Rice (1880–1954). *Taps: Selected Poems of the Great War.* 1932.

Roosevelt, Theodore, Jr., and Kermit Roosevelt. *East of the Sun and West of the Moon.* 1926.

Roosevelt, Theodore, Sr. *U.S. Allotment System: Report to the President of the U.S.* 1862.

Root, Elihu (1845–1937). *Men and Policies.* 1925.

Ropes, John Codman. *The Story of the Civil War (Part 1).* 1894.

Ropes, John Codman. *The Story of the Civil War, the Campaigns of 1862.* 1898.

Ropes, John Codman. *The Army under Pope: Campaigns of the Civil War.* 1881.

Ropes, John Codman. *The Campaign of Waterloo.* 1892.

Rose, George B. *Art and Archaeology.* September 1920.

Rosengarten, J. G. *The German Allied Troops in the North American War of Independence 1776–89.* 1893.

Rosenthal, E. *Peeps at Portugal: A Pocket Guide to the Sun Coast and Lisbon.* N.d.

Ross, Christian K. *Charlie Ross and the Kidnapped Child.* 1876.

Ross, Edward Alsworth. *Sin and Society: An Analysis of Latter-Day Iniquity.* 1907.

Rosser, Mrs. Thomas L. *Housekeeper's and Mothers' Manual.* 1895.

Rossetti, Christina Georgina (1830–1894). *Sing Song: A Nursery Rhyme Book.* 1893.

Rossetti, Dante Gabriel. *Poems (Spine: The Blessed Damozel and Other Poems).* 1882.

Rossetti, Dante Gabriel (1828–1882). *D. G. Rossetti's Collected Works*, vols. 1 and 2. 1886.

Rossetti, Dante Gabriel (1828–1882). *Pictures and Poems by Dante Gabriel Rossetti.* 1902.

Rossetti, Dante Gabriel (1828–1882). *Pictures and Poems.* 1899.

Rostand, Edmond. *Pour La Greece.* 1897.

Rostand, Edmond. *Les Musardises: Edition Nouvelle 1887–1893.* 1911.

Rostand, Edmond. *Chantecler*. 1910.

Rostand, Edmond. *La Samaritaine*. 1900.

Rostand, Edmond (1868–1918). *Discours De Reception a L'academe Francaise*. 1903.

Rostrand, Edmond. *L'illustration La Derniere Nuit de Don Juan*. 1921.

Rousseau, J. B. *Hommages Poetiques A La Fountains*. 1820.

Rouvier, Charles. *Histoire des Marins Francais sous La Republique*. 1789 / 1803.

Ruskin, John. *Sesames and Lilies / Two Lectures by John Ruskin*. 1904.

Ruskin, John. *Ruskin's Works*. 1856.

Russell, George W. *The Irish Home-Rule Convention*. 1917.

Russell, Osborne. *Journal of a Trapper*. 1914.

Ruxton, George Frederick. *Life in the Far West*. 1851.

Rydberg, Victor, Ph.D. *Teutonic Mythology*. 1906.

Ryder, Arthur. *Harvard Oriental Series, Lanman*, vol. 9, *The Little Clay Cart*. 1905.

Sadler, Michael. *Anthony Trollope: A Commentary*. 1927.

Sage, Dean, William C. Harris, H. M. Smith, and C. H. Townsend. *Salmon and Trout*. 1902.

Sagredo, Giovanni. *Memorie Istoriche de Monarchie Ottomani*. 1674.

Saintsbury, George. *The Later Nineteenth Century (Periods of European Literature)*. 1907.

Saintsbury, George. *A Short History of English Literature*. 1905.

Saintsbury, George. *History of English Prose Rhythm*. 1912.

Sakurai, Tadayoshi. *Human Bullets*. 1906.

Sala, George Augustus. *My Diary in America in the Midst of War* (2-vol. set). 1865.

Salani, Adriano. *Del Regno Delle Fate*. 1919.

Sale, Edith Tanis. *Manors of Virginia in Colonial Times*. 1909.

Salmon, Thomas. *Salmon's Grammar*. 1767.

Sanchez, Ramiro Guerra Y., Dr. *Historia Elemental De Cuba*. 1922.

Sandburg, Carl. *Abraham Lincoln: The Prairie Years*. 1926.

Sandys, Edwyn. *Upland Game Birds*. 1902.

Sargent, Epes. *What's to Be Done*. 1842.

Sargent, Helen Child, and George Lyman Kettredge (Editors). *Popular Ballads*. 1904.

Sargent, Herbert H. *The Campaign of Santiago De Cuba*, vols. 1–3. 1907.

Saroyan, William (1908–1981). *My Name Is Aram*. 1940.

Satterlee, Herbert L. *The Life of J. Pierpoint Morgan*. 1937.

Satterlee, Herbert L. *J. Pierpont Morgan: An Intimate Portrait*. 1939.

Sattler, Alb. (Editor). *La Danse des Morts a Bale (The Dance of Death)* N.d.

Saunders, George. *Builder and Blunderer: A Study of Emperor William's Character and Foreign Policy*. 1914.

Savin, Una. *The Little Gentleman in Green*. 1865.

Scammon, Charles Melville (1825–1911). *The Marine Mammals of the North-Western Coast of North America*. 1874.

Schaff, E., Dr. *Jagdtierkunde*. 1907.

Scharfer, Dr. Johann Wilhelm, Foreword by Dr. Schaefer. *Auswahl Deutscher Gedichte*. 1852.

Schauffler, Robert Haven. *The Joyful Heart*. 1914.

Schiller, Johann Christoph Friedrich Von (1759–1805). *Wallenstein*. N.d.

Schiller, Johann Christoph Friedrich Von (1759–1805). *Gedichte* (in German). N.d.

Schiller, Johann Christoph Friedrich Von (1759–1805). *Schiller's Werke*. 1877.

Schillings, C. B. *Mit Blitzlicht und Buchfe (With Flashlight and Rifle)*. 1905.

Schillings, Carl Georg (1865–1921). *Flashlights in the Jungle*. 1905.

Schillings, Don C. B. *Mit Blitzlicht Und Buchfe Im Zauber des Elelefcho*. 1910.

Schodler, Fredrich. *Brehm's Illufrirtes Thierleben*, vols. 1–3. 1870.

Schomburg, Arthur A. *Bibliographica Americana: Biographical Checklist of American Negro Poetry*, vol. 2. 1916.

Schomburgh, Hans. *Wild und Wilde in Herzen Afrikas*. 1910.

Schreyvogel, Charles. *My Bunkie and Others, Pictures of Western Frontier Life*. 1909.

Schurz, Carl (1829–1906). *Henry Clay*. American Statesmen. 1899.

Schurz, Carl (1829–1906). *Abraham Lincoln*. 1891.

Schurz, Carl (1829–1906). *Abraham Lincoln*. 1907.

Schurz, Carl (1829–1906). *Henry Clay (I)* / American Statesmen. 1887.

Schurz, Carl (1829–1906). *Life of Henry Clay*, vols. 1 and 2. American Statesmen.1887.

Schwatka, Frederick. *Nimrod in the North / Hunting and Fishing Adventures in the Arctic Regions*. 1885.

Sclater, Philip Lutley, and Thomas Oldfield. *The Book of Antelopes*, vols. 1–4. 1900.

Scollard, Clinton (1860–1932). *Let the Flag Wave, with Other Verses Written in War Time*. 1917.

Scott, Emmett (1873–1957. *Authorized Biography of Booker T. Washington*, School Edition. 1918.

Scott, Emmett (1873 1957), and Lyman Beecher Stowe (1880–1963). *Booker T. Washington, Builder of a Civilization*. 1916.

Scott, Frank Jesup. *Scott's Julius Caesar / Portraitures*. 1903.

Scott, James Brown. *Robert Bacon: Life and Letters*. 1923.

Scott, James Brown. *The Hague Conventions and Declarations of 1899 and 1907*. 1915.

Scott, James Brown. *A Survey of International Relations between United States and Germany 1914–1917*. 1917.

Scott, Lieut-General. *Memoirs of Lieut-General Scott, LL.D.*, vols. 1 and 2. 1864.

Scott, Robert F. *The Voyage of the Discovery*, vols. 1 and 2. 1907.

Scott, Sir Walter (1771–1832). *Waverly Novels*. 1879.

Scott, Sir Walter (1771–1832). *Kenilworth, Part 1 and 2* (Set of 2); *The Waverly Novels*, vols. 22 and 23. 1879.

Scott, Sir Walter (1771–1832). *The Pirate, Part 1 and 2* (Set of 2); *The Waverly Novels*, vols. 24 and 25. 1879.

Scott, Sir Walter (1771–1832). *Fortunes of Nigel; The Waverly Novels*, vol. 26. 1879.

Scott, Sir Walter (1771–1832) *Peveril of the Peak, Part 1, 2 and 3* (Set of 3); *The Waverly Novels*, vols. 28, 29, and 30. 1879.

Scott, Sir Walter (1771–1832). *Quentin Durward, Part 1 and 2* (Set of 2); *The Waverly Novels*, vols. 31 and 32. 1879.

Scott, Sir Walter (1771–1832). *St. Ronan's Well, Part 1 and 2* (Set of 2); *The Waverly Novels*, vols. 33 and 34. 1879.

Scott, Sir Walter (1771–1832). *Redgauntlet, Part 1 and 2* (Set of 2); *The Waverly Novels* vols. 34 and 35. 1879.

Scott, Sir Walter (1771–1832). *The Betrothed; The Waverly Novels*, vol. 37. 1879.

Scott, Sir Walter (1771–1832). *The Talisman; The Waverly Novels*, vol. 38. 1879.

Scott, Sir Walter (1771–1832). *Woodstock, Part 1 and 2* (Set of 2); *The Waverly Novels*, vols. 39 and 40. 1879.

Scott, Sir Walter (1771–1832). *Highland Widow; The Waverly Novels*, vol. 41. 1879.

Scott, Sir Walter (1771–1832). *Fair Maid of Perth, Part 1 and 2* (Set of 2); *The Waverly Novels*, vols. 42 and 43. 1879.

Scott, Sir Walter (1771–1832). *Anne of Geierstein, Part 1 and 2* (Set of 2); *The Waverly Novels*, vols. 44 and 45. 1879.

Scott, Sir Walter (1771–1832). *Count Robert of Paris, Part 1 and 2* (Set of 2); *The Waverly Novels*, vols. 46 and 47. 1879.

Scott, Sir Walter (1771–1832). *The Surgeon's Daughter and Castle Dangerous; The Waverly Novels*, vol. 48. 1879.

Scott, Sir Walter (1771–1832). *Waverley Novels—Abbotsford Edition—1 / Waverley —Guy Mannering.* 1851.

Scott, Sir Walter (1771–1832). *Waverley Novels—Abbotsford Edition—2 / the Antiquary—the Black Dwarf—Old Mortality.* 1851.

Scott, Sir Walter (1771–1832). *Waverley Novels—Abbotsford Edition—3 / Rob Roy— the Heart of Mid-Lothian.* 1851.

Scott, Sir Walter (1771–1832). *Waverley Novels—Abbotsford Edition—4 / Bride of Lammermoor—Legend of Montrose—Ivanhoe.* 1851.

Scott, Sir Walter (1771–1832). *Waverley Novels—the Abbotsford Edition—5 / the Monastery—the Abbot.* 1851.

Scott, Sir Walter (1771–1832). *Waverley Novels—the Abbotsford Edition—6 / Kenilworth—the Pirate.* 1851.

Scott, Sir Walter (1771–1832). *Waverley Novels—Abbostford Edition—7 / Fortunes of Nigel—Peveril of the Peak.* 1851.

Scott, Sir Walter (1771–1832). *Waverley Novels—Abbostford Edition—8 / Quentin Durward—St. Ronan's Well.* 1851.

Scott, Sir Walter (1771–1832). *Waverley Novels—Abbotsford Edition—9 / The Red Gauntlet—The Betrothed—The Talisman.* 1851.

Scott, Sir Walter (1771–1832). *Waverley Novels—Abbotsford Edition—10 / Woodstock—Chronicles.* 1851.

Scott, Sir Walter (1771–1832). *Waverley Novels—Abbotsford Edition—11 / Fair Maid of Perth—Anne of Geierstein.* 1851.

Scott, Sir Walter (1771–1832). *Waverley Novels—Abbotsford Edition—12 / Count Robt. of Paris—Castle Dangerous—Etc.—Index.* 1851.

Scott, Sir Walter (1771–1832). *The Waverly Novels,* vol. 2, *The Abbot.* 1886.

Scott, Sir Walter (1771–1832). *Tales of A Grandfather.* N.d.

Scotty, Frien, Yir. *Twa Mouthfu's O' Naething.* 1917.

Scrape, William. *Salmon Fishing in the Tweed.* 1854.

Scull, E. Marshall. *Hunting in the Arctic and Alaska.* 1914.

Sears, Anna Wentworth. *Two on a Tour in South America.* 1913.

Searson, John. *Mount Vernon; A Poem (The Home of George Washington in VA).* 1799.

Seawall, Molly Elliott. *The History of the Lady Betty Stair.* 1897.

Sedgwick, Jane Minot. *Sicilian Idyls and Other Verses.* 1898.

Seeley, John Robert. *Napoleon the First.* 1886.

Seidel, Paul. *Der Kaiser and Der Kunst.* 1907.

Seler, Edward. *Die Alten Ansiedelugen von Chacula',* vol. 1. 1901.

Selous, Frederick C. *A Hunter's Wanderings in Africa.* 1911.

Selous, Frederick C. *African Nature Notes–Reminiscences.* 1908.

Semonds, Frank H. *They Shall Not Pass.* 1916.

Service, Robert William (1874?–1958). *The Spell of the Yukon and Other Verses.* 1907.

Seton, Ernest Thompson (1860–1946). *The Trail of the Sandhill Stag.* 1900

Seton, Ernest Thompson (1860–1946). *Wild Animals I Have Known.* 1898.

Sewel, W. *A Large Dictionary English and Dutch.* 1735.

Seymour, E. L. D. *The Garden Encyclopedia.* 1936.

Shackelton, E. H. *The Heart of the Antarctic,* vols. 1 and 2. 1909.

Shackleton, E. H. *The Heart of the Antarctic, The Story of the British Antarctic Expedition 1907– 09.* 1909.

Shakespear, Emily. *The Tennyson Birthday Book.* 1878.

Shakespeare, William. *The Illustrated Shakespeare Birthday Book.* 1910.

Shakespeare, William (1564–1616). *Cariolanus.* 1901.

Shakespeare, William (1564–1616). *King Henry V: Part 2.* 1900.

Shakespeare, William (1564–1616). *The Taming of the Shrew.* 1901.

Shakespeare, William (1564–1616). *Timon of Athens.* 1901.

Shakespeare, William (1564–1616). *King John.* 1901.

Shakespeare, William (1564–1616). *Two Gentlemen of Verona.* 1901.

Shakespeare, William (1564–1616). *Rape of Lucreca.* 1901.

Shakespeare, William (1564–1616). *Troilus and Cressida.* 1901.

Shakespeare, William (1564–1616). *Titus Andronicus.* 1901.

Shakespeare, William (1564–1616). *Cymbeline.* 1901.

Shakespeare, William (1564–1616). *King Henry V.* 1900.

Shakespeare, William (1564–1616). *Timon of Athens.* 1905.

Shakespeare, William (1564–1616). *King Henry the V (2-vol. set).* 1905.

Shakespeare, William (1564–1616). *Shakespeare's Works VII.* 1878.

Shakespeare, William (1564–1616). *Shakespeare's Works XXI.* 1878.

Shakespeare, William (1564–1616). *Shakespeare's Works XII XIII*. 1878.

Shakespeare, William (1564–1616). *Shakespeare's Works XIV XV*. 1878.

Shakespeare, William (1564–1616). *The Works of William Shakespeare*. 1907.

Shakespeare, William (1564–1616). *Sonnets of Shakespeare*. 1905.

Shakespeare, William (1564–1616). *Venus and Adonis*. 1905.

Shakespeare, William (1564–1616). *Lucrece*. 1905.

Shakespeare, William (1564–1616). *The Passionate Pilgrim*. 1905.

Shakespeare, William (1564–1616). *Pericles*. 1905.

Shakespeare, William (1564–1616). *King Henry the VI* (3-vol. set). 1905.

Shakespeare, William (1564–1616). *King Henry V*. 1905.

Sharp, Dallas Lore (1870–1929). *The Face of the Fields*. 1911.

Sharp, Margery. *The Nutmeg Tree*. 1937.

Sharp, William. *The Silence of Amor Where the Forest Murmurs*. 1911.

Shaw, Albert. *The Annual Review of Reviews* (vol. 32). 1911.

Shaw, Albert. *A Cartoon History of Roosevelt's Career*. 1910.

Sheldon, Charles. *The Wilderness of the Upper Yukon*. 1919.

Shelford, Robert W. C. *A Naturalist in Borneo*. 1917.

Shelley, G. E. *Handbook to the Birds of Egypt*. 1872.

Shelley, Mary W. *Frankenstein: Or the Modern Prometheus*. 1882.

Shelley, Percy B. *Shelley's Works*. N.d.

Shepard, Edward M. *Martin Van Buren*. American Statesmen, vol. 25. 1899.

Shepard, Edward M. *Martin Van Buren* / American Statesmen. 1890.

Shepp, James W. *Shepp's World Fair Photographed*. 1893.

Sheridan, Philip Henry (1831–1888). *Personal Memoirs of P. H. Sheridan* (2 vols.). 1888.

Sheridan, Richard Brinsley (1751–1816). *The Works of the Late Richard Sheridan* (2-vol. set). 1821.

Sheridan, Richard Brinsley (1751–1816). *Sheridan's Comedies*. 1885.

Sherman, William Tecumseh (1820–1891). *Memoirs of Gen. W. T. Sherman*, 2 vols. 1875.

Shields, G. O. *Rustlings in the Rockies*. 1883.

Shields, G. O. *Cruisings in the Cascades and Other Adventures*. 1889.

Shillibeer, Lieut. J. *A Narrative of the Briton's Voyage to Pitcairn's Island*. 1817.

Shiras, George. *Hunting Wildlife with Camera and Flashlight*, vols. 1 and 2. 1935.

Shiras, Hon. George 3rd. *Hunting Wild Game with Camera and Flashlight*. 1906–1912.

Shirley, James. *The Constant Maid*. N.d.

Shore, Joseph, and John Stewart. *In Old St. James (Jamaica): A Book of Parish Chronicles*. 1911.

Shotwell, Walter G. *The Life of Charles Sumner*. 1910.

Shufeldt, R. W. *The Extermination of America's Bird Fauna*. 1914.

Siam, H. R. *The War of the Polish Succession*. 1902.

Sienkiewicz, Henryk (1846–1916). *On the Field of Glory*. 1906.

Sienkiewicz, Henryk (1846–1916). *The Knights of the Cross* (2-vol. set). 1900.

Sienkiewicz, Henryk (1846–1916). *The Deluge* (2-vol. set). 1919.

Sienkiewicz, Henryk (1846–1916). *Pan Michael.* 1893.

Sigourney, Mrs. L. H. *Mrs. Sigourney's Select Poems.* 1848.

Silous, Frederick Courteney. *Sport and Travel East and West.* 1900.

Simkhovitch, Vladimir. *Rome's Fall Reconsidered.* 1916.

Simkhovitch, Vladimir. *Marxism vs Socialism.* 1913.

Simonds, Frank H. *History of the World War*, vols. 1–2. 1917.

Simrock, Karl (Translator). *Das Nibelungenlied.* 1867.

Sinclair, May. *The Divine Fire.* 1905.

Sinclair, Upton. *The Jungle.* 1906.

Singer, Daniel J. *Big Game Fields of America North and South.* 1914.

Singleton, Esther. *The Story of the White House* (2 vols.). 1907.

Singmaster, Elsie. *A Boy at Gettysburg.* 1924.

Singmaster, Elsie (1879–1958). *Emmeline.* 1916.

Singmaster, Elsie (1879–1958). *Bred in the Bone and Other Stories.* 1925.

Sismondi, De, J. C. L. *Italian Republics (Being A View of the Origin Progress, and Fall of Italian Freedom.* N.d.

Sitgreaves, L. Captain. *Report of An Expedition—Zuni and Colorado Rivers.* 1854.

Skrine, Francis Henry. *Fontenoy and the War of the Austrian Succession.* 1906.

Slocum, Joshua. *Sailing Alone around the World.* 1900.

Smeeton, George. *Cromwelliana (Events in Which Oliver Cromwell Was Engaged 1642–1658).* 1810.

Smith, Adam. *Smith's Wealth of Nationals: Governeur Morris' Copy.* 1791.

Smith, Alexander. *Poems.* 1853.

Smith, Boyd E. *The Story of Noah's Ark.* 1905.

Smith, Emma L. *Emma L. Smiths' Journal Book 1850–51, Written at the Age of Six.* c. 1923.

Smith, Francis Hopkinson (1838–1915). *Old Fashioned Folks.* 1907.

Smith, G. C. Moore (Editor). *Autobiography of Sir Harry Smith.* 1903.

Smith, Horace, and James Smith. *Rejected Addresses on the New Theatrum Poetarum.* 1876.

Smith, Horace, and James Smith. *The Poetical Works of Horace Smith and James Smith.* 1857.

Smith, J. H., and S. M. M. Halsey. *Famous Old Receipts.* 1906.

Smith, James, and Horace Smith. *Rejected Addresses or the New Theatrum Poetarium.* 1873.

Smith, James, Col. *A Treatise on the Mode and Manner of Indian War.* 1812.

Smith, Louisa Hutchings. *Bermuda's "Oldest Inhabitants" / Tales of Plant Life.* 1934.

Smith, Marion Couthouy. *The Final Star.* 1918.

Smith, Nora Archibald. *Boys and Girls of Bookland.* 1923.

Smith, R. Bosworth. *Bird Life and Bird Lore.* 1909.

Smith, Rev. Alfred Charles. *The Attraction of the Nile and Its Banks*, vols. 1–2. 1868.

Smith, Rev. Sydney (1771–1845). *The Works of the Rev. Sydney Smith.* 1844.

Smith, Roland Cotton. *Preaching as A Fine Art.* 1922.

Smith, Theodore Clarke. *General Index to the Series.* American Statesmen. 1900.

Smith, Elizur Yale, Capt. *The Descendants of William Edwards*, vol. 1. Unknown.

Smith, Zachary F. *The Battle of New Orleans.* 1904.

Smyth, Piazzi C. *The Divine Plan of the Ages and Corroborative Testimony of the Great Pyramid.* 1886.

Snider, Susan Stratton, and Alan Alexander Milne (1882–1956). *Young America Wants to Help / They Have Grown Up.* 1941.

Snoilsky, Carl. *Svenska Bilder.* 1894.

Soane, Ely Bannister (1881–1923). *To Mesopotamia and Kurdistan in Disguise.* 1914.

Society of the Chagres. *Year Book 1915.* 1930.

Soley, James Russell. *The Blockade and the Cruisers: The Navy in the Civil War.* 1883.

Sollas, W. J. *Ancient Hunters.* 1915.

Somerville, Edith Anna Oenone (1858–1949), and Violet Florence Martin (1862–1915). *Irish Memories.* 1925.

Somerville, Edith Anna Oenone (1858–1949), and Violet Florence Martin (1862–1915). *Some Experiences of an Irish R.M.* 1905.

Sothern, Edward H. *The Melancholy Tale of "Me."* 1916.

Sowerby, Arthur. *Fur and Feather in North China.* 1914.

Sowerby, J. G., and Thomas Crane (1845–1915). *At Home.* 1934.

Speare, E. M. *The Pocket Book of Short Stories.* 1941.

Spears, John, and A. H. Clark. *A History of the Mississippi Valley.* 1903.

Spence, (James) Lewis Thomas Chalmers (1874–1955). *The Myths of North American Indians.* 1914.

Spencer, Edmund. *Prothalamion: Epipthalamion.* 1902.

Speranza, Florence (Editor). *The Diary of Gino Speranza, Italy 1915–1919* (2 vols.). 1941.

Speranza, Gino. *Verses.* 1943.

Speranzo, Gino. *Race or Nation.* 1925.

Spielman, M., and G. Layard. *Kate Greenaway.* 1905.

Spielman, M. A., and W. Jerrold. *Hugh Thomson.* 1931.

Spingarn, Joel (Elias) (1875–1939). *The New Hesperides.* 1911.

St. Benjamin. *The New Gospel of Peace According to St Benjamin.* 1863.

St. John, Charles. *Natural History and Sport in Moray.* 1882.

St. Mars, F. *On Nature's Trail.* 1912.

Stabler, John Herbert. *The Travels and Adventures of Don Francisco De Miranda (18th Century Diary).* 1931.

Stace, Machell. *Cromwelliana; A Chronological Detail of Events in Which Oliver Cromwell Was Engaged 1642–1658.* 1810.

Stahl, P. J. *Histoire de la Famille Chester.* N.d.

Stanley, Dorothy (Editor). *Autobiography of Henry M. Stanley.* 1909.

Stanley, Henry M. *Coomassie and Magdala (The Story of Two British Campaigns in Africa).* 1874.

Stanley, Sir Henry Morton (1841–1904). *In Darkest Africa*, vols. 1 and 2. 1891.

Stansbury, Howard. *Stansbury Expedition to the Great Salt Lake: Exploration and Survey of the Valley of the Great Salt Lake of Utah*. 1852.

Stanwood, Edward. *James G. Blaine*. 1905.

Stanwood, Edward. *John Sherman*. 1906.

Stark, Dame Freya (Madeline) (1893–1993). *The Southern Gates of Arabia a Journey in the Hadhramaut*. December 25, 1936.

Stassen, Harold E. *Where I Stand*. 1947.

Stedman, John W. *The Norwich Jubilee*. 1859.

Stedneger, Leonard, and Thomas Barbour. *A Check List of North American Amphibians and Reptiles*. 1917.

Steele, James. *Frontier Army Sketches*. 1883.

Stephen, Adeline Virginia (1882–1941) (Virginia Woolf). *The Common Reader: Second Series*. 1932.

Stephens, James. *The Crock of Gold*. 1914.

Stephens, James. *The Demi-Gods*. 1914.

Stephens, John L. *Incidents of Travel in Central America, Chiapas and Yucatan*. 1841.

Steuart, Mary D. *The Romance of the Paris Streets*. 1923.

Stevens, G. W. *With Kitchener to Khartum*. 1899.

Stevens, John Austin. *Albert Gallatin* (American Statesmen Series), vol. 13. 1898.

Stevens, John Austin. *Albert Gallatin* / American Statesmen. 1884.

Stevens, John L. *History of Gustavus Adolphus*. 1884.

Stevenson, Robert Louis (1850–1894). *The Works of Robert Louis Stevenson / Kidnapped*. Unknown.

Stevenson, Robert Louis (1850–1894). *Collection of British Authors*. 1888.

Stevenson, Robert Louis (1850–1894). *The Ebb-Tide by Robert Louis Stevenson and Lloyd Osbourne*. 1894.

Stevenson, W. B. *The Crusaders in the East*. 1907.

Stewart, Charles. *The Stars and Stripes from Washington to Wilson*. 1914.

Stewart, William M., and George Rothwell Brown (Editor). *Senator William M. Stewart of Nevada*. 1908.

Stiff, Edward. *The Texan Emigrant*. 1840.

Stirling-Maxwell, Sir William. *Don John of Austria*. 1883.

Stockton, Francis Richard (1834–1932). *The Late Mrs. Null*. 1886.

Stoddard, Henry Luther (1861–1947). *As I Knew Them: Presidents and Politics from Grant to Coolidge*. 1927.

Stoker, Bram. *Personal Reminiscences of Henry Irving* (2 vols.). 1906.

Stokes, I. N. Phelps. *New York Past and Present; Its History and Landmarks 1524–1939*. 1939.

Stokes, Olivia Egleston Phelps. *Letters and Memories of Susan and Anna Bartlett Warner*. 1925.

Stone, Witmer, and Cram, William Everett. *American Animals*. 1902.

Storey, Moorfield. *Charles Sumner*. American Statesmen. 1900.

Storms, G. *Anglo-Saxon Magic*. 1948.

Story, Joseph. *Exposition of the Constitution of the United States*. 1840.

Stowe, Harriet Beecher (1811–1896). *Queer Little People*. 1868.

Stowe, Harriet Beecher (1811–1896). *Uncle Tom's Cabin: Or Life Among the Lowly and A Bibliography of the Work*. 1892.

Stowe, Harriet Beecher (1811–1896). *The Minister's Wooing*. 1859.

Stowe, Harriet Beecher (1811–1896). *Agnes of Sorrento*. 1881.

Stowe, Harriet Beecher (1811–1896). *Uncle Tom's Cabin*. 1852.

Strachey, Amy. *St. Loe Strachey*. 1930.

Strachey, Lytton (1880–1932). *Queen Victoria*. 1921.

Straffen, Prof. Dr. Otto Zur. *Brehms Tierleben* (2-vol. set) (German Text). 1912.

Strakosch-Grassman, Gustave. *Der Einfall Der Mongolan in Mitteleuropa in Den Jahren 1244 und 1242*. 1893.

Straus, Oscar S. *Under Four Administrations: From Cleveland to Taft*. 1922.

Strauss, Yawcob (C. F. Adams). *Der Oak und der Vine*. 1902.

Street, Julian (1879–1947). *Book, American Adventures, Red Buckram Binding*. 1917.

Street, Julian (1879–1947). *The Most Interesting American*. 1915.

Street, Julian (1879–1947). *The Most Interesting American*. 1916.

Strickland, W. P. (Editor). *Autobiography of Peter Cartwright, the Backwoods Preacher*. 1856.

Stuart, Ruth McEnery. *A Golden Wedding and Other Tales*. 1893.

Stuart, Ruth McEnery. *Holly and Pizen*. 1899.

Stuckburgh, Evelyn S., M.A. *The Histories of Polybius*. 1889.

Studer, Jacob H. *The Birds of North America*. 1903.

Sturdza, Prince Gregoire. *En Birmanie Saunenirs de Chasse et de Voyage*. 1909.

Sturgis, R. Clipson, Mrs. *Random Reflections of a Grandmother*. 1917.

Sturluson, Snorri (1179–1241). *The Prose Edda*. 1916.

Sturluson, Snorri (1179–1241). *Norrena / Anglo-Saxon Classics / The Heimskringla I–III*. 1906.

Sturluson, Snorri (1179–1241). *The Saga Library: The Heimskringla*. 1893–1905.

Suard, Par M. *Lettres De Mme De Sevigne* (in French). 1846.

Suckly, George, and J. G. Cooper. *The Natural History of Washington Territory and Oregon with Much Relating to Minnesota, Nebraska, Kansas, Utah and California between the 36th and 49th Parallels of Latitude Being Those Parts of the Final Reports on the Survey of the Northern Pacific Railroad Route Relating to the Natural History of the Regions Explored, with Full Catalogues and Descriptions of Plants and Animals Collected*. 1860.

Sudworth, George B. *Forest Atlas: Geographic Distribution of North American Trees, Part I: Pines*. 1913.

Sullivan, Mark. *The Education of an American*. 1938.

Sullivan, Mark. *Our Times, The Turn of the Century 1900–1904 (The United States 1900–1925)*. 1926.

Sullivan, William. *The Political Class Book*. 1831.

Sully, Duc De (1560–1641). *Memoires Des Sages et Royalles Oeconomies D'estat, Domestiques, Politiques, Et Militaires De Henry Le Grand.* N.d.

Sumner, William Graham (1840–1910). *Andrew Jackson* / American Statesmen. 1884.

Sumner, William Graham (1840–1910). *Andrew Jackson* (American Statesmen Series), vol. 17. 1898.

Supreme Court, Apellate Div. *William Barnes against Theodore Roosevelt.* 1917.

Surtees, R. Mr. *Sponge's Sporting Tour.* 1852.

Sutherland, Alexander, M.A. *The Origin and Growth of the Moral Instinct.* 1898.

Sutherland, Harvey. *The Book of Bugs.* 1902.

Suydam, Rev. J. Howard. *Hendrick Rycken: The Progenitor of the Suydam Family in America 1663.* 1898.

Swen, Earl Gregg (Editor). *Letters on the Condition of Kentucky in 1825.* 1825.

Swift, Jonathan. *The Poetical Works of Jonathan Swift,* vol. 1. 1833.

Swinburne, Algernon Charles (1837–1900). *Atalante in Calydon.* 1877.

Swinburne, Algernon Charles (1837–1900). *Songs before Sunrise.* 1903.

Swinburne, Algernon Charles (1837–1900). *Tristram of Lyonesse and Other Poems.* 1882.

Swinburne, Algernon Charles (1837–1900). *Laus Veneris (And Other Poems and Ballads).* 1882.

Swinburne, Algernon Charles (1837–1900). *Atalanta in Calydon.* 1897.

Swinton, William. *The Life and Campaigns of Stuart's Cavalry.* 1867.

Szehlender, Alalbert. *Kaiserhusaren / Bei Custazza.* ca. 1910.

Tacitus, Cornelius (55?–117? A.D.). *Cornelii Taciti Opera Minora.* 1904.

Taillandier, Saint Rene. *Maurice De Saxe* (in French). 1865.

Taimate, Aril. *Tahiti.* 1901.

Tarleton, Lt. Col. *A History of the Campaigns of 1780 and 1781 (In Southern Provinces of N. America).* 1787.

Tarrant, Margaret Winifred. *Margaret Tarrant's Christmas Garland.* 1942.

Tasso, Torquato (1544–1595). *Jerusalem Delivered* (2 vols.). 1865.

Taunay, Alfred D'escragnolle (1843–1899). *La Retraite De Laguna.* 1871.

Tautphoeus, Baronessa. *At Odds.* 1863.

Taylor, Ann and Jane Taylor. *Little Ann: A Book and Other Poems.* c. 1883.

Taylor, Fitch W. *A Voyage Round the World.* 1848.

Taylor, Hannis. *Cicero: A Sketch of His Life and Works.* 1916.

Taylor, Henry. *Philip Van Artevelde.* 1863.

Taylor, Henry. *Deliverance.* 1915.

Taylor, Henry Osborn. *The Mediaeval Mind.* 1911.

Taylor, Jeremy, D.D. (1613–1667). *The Great Exemplar of Sanctity and Holy Life.* 1649.

Taylor, Theodore. *Thackeray.* 1864.

Taylor, Walter P. *Aplodontia Humboldtiana, A New Mountain Beaver.* 1916.

Taylor, Walter P., Dr. *The Museum of Natural History and the Conservation of Game*, vol. 9. 1915.

Tejeiro, Lt. Jose Muller y. *Battles and Capitulation of Santiago De Cuba* (2-vol. set) (translated from Spanish). 1898.

Temperley, H. W. V. *Life of Canning*. 1905.

Thackeray, Lance. *The Light Side of Egypt*. 1908.

Thackeray, William Makepeace (1811–1863). *Thackerayana Notes and Anecdotes*. 1875.

Thackeray, William Makepeace (1811–1863). *Ballads*. 1856.

Thackeray, William Makepeace (1811–1863). *The Great Hoggarty Diamond, Memoirs of C. J. Yellowplush and Burlesques*. 1878.

Thackeray, William Makepeace (1811–1863). *Thackeray's Works: Christmas Books*. 1878.

Thackeray, William Makepeace (1811–1863). *Adventures of Philip*. 1878.

Thackeray, William Makepeace (1811–1863). *The Virginians*. 1878.

Thackeray, William Makepeace (1811–1863). *The Newcomes*. 1878.

Thackeray, William Makepeace (1811–1863). *Roundabout Papers, the Four Georges and the English Humourist*. 1878.

Thackeray, William Makepeace (1811–1863). *Catherine, Lovel the Widower, Denis Duval, Ballad*. 1878.

Thackeray, William Makepeace (1811–1863). *Thackeray's Works: Henry Esmond, Barry Lyndon*. 1878.

Thackeray, William Makepeace (1811–1863). *The History of Pendennis*. 1878.

Thackeray, William Makepeace (1811–1863). *The Book of Snobs: Sketches of Life and Character*. 1878.

Thackeray, William Makepeace (1811–1863). *Thackeray's Works—Paris and Irish Sketchbooks, Cornhill to Grand Cairo*. 1878.

Thackeray, William Makepeace (1811–1863). *Vanity Fair*, vol. 1. 1878.

Thanet, Octave. *Otto the Knight (And Other Trans-Mississippi Stories)*. 1891.

Thanet, Octave. *The Man of the Hour*. 1905.

Thanet, Octave. *By Inheritance*. 1910.

Thanet, Octave (Pseudonym for Alice French [1850–1934]). *Was It the Good Bear?* 1904.

Thaxter, Celia. *Poems*. 1877.

Thayer, Gerald H. *Concealing Coloration in the Animal Kingdom*. 1909.

Thayer, James Bradley, LLD. (1831–1902). *Thayer Legal Essays*. 1908.

Thayer, William Roscoe. *Germany vs. Civilization*. 1916.

Thayer, William Roscoe. *Out of Their Own Mouths*. 1917.

Thayer, William Roscoe. *The Life of John Hay*. 1915.

Thayer, William Roscoe. *Life of Theodore Roosevelt*. 1919.

Thayer, William Roscoe. *Theodore Roosevelt*. 1919.

Thayer, William Roscoe. *The Life and Letters of John Jay*, vols. 1 and 2. 1916.

Thetherall, Elizabeth. *The Wide, Wide World*. 1852.

Thiers, M. A. *History of the French Revolution*, vols. 1–3. 1840.

Thiers, M. A. *History of the Consulate and the Empire of France under Napoleon.* 1849—Ad.

Thiers, M. A., and Forbes D. Campbell (Translator). *Thiers History of the Consulate and Empire*, vol. 2. 1849.

Thirlwall, Right Rev. Connop. *History of Greece*, vol. 2. 1845.

Thomas, Addison C. *Roosevelt among the People*. 1910.

Thomas, Bertram. *Alarms and Excursions in Arabia*. 1931.

Thomas, Bertram (1892–1950). *Arabia Felix: Across the Empty Quarter of Arabia.* 1932.

Thomas, Lowell. *Raiders of the Deep*. 1928.

Thomas, William S. *Hunting Big Game with Gun and with Kodak*. 1906.

Thompson, Charles Willis. *Presidents I've Known and Two Near Presidents*. 1929.

Thompson, Darcy W. (1860–1948). *Fun and Earnest or Rhyme with Reason*. 1865.

Thompson, Eben. *Quatrains of Omar Khayyam*. 1906.

Thompson, Henry Yates. *A Lecture on Some English Illuminated Manuscripts*. 1902.

Thompson, Maurice. *My Winter Garden*. 1900.

Thompson, Maurice. *Byways and Bird Notes*. 1885.

Thompson, P. A. *Siam (Oriental Series): An Account of the Country and Its People*, vol. 16. 1910.

Thomson, James. *The Seasons*. 1785.

Thorndike, Edward L. *Animal Intelligence: Experimental Studies*. 1911.

Thorndike, Rachel Sherman (Editor). *The Sherman Letters: Correspondence between General and Senator Sherman from 1837–1891*. 1894.

Thurston, E. Temple. *The Antagonists*. 1912.

Thwaites, Reuben Gold. *Story of the Black Hawk War*. 1892.

Thwaites, Reuben Gold (Editor). *Original Journals of the Lewis and Clark Expedition 1804–1806* (14 vols. and 1 Atlas). 1905.

Thwaites, Reubon Gold, and Louise Phelps Kellogg (Editor). *Documentary History of Dunmoxe's War 1774*. 1905.

Tiffany, Louis C. *The Artwork of Louis C. Tiffany*. 1914.

Tocqueville, Alexis De (1805–1859). *Democracy in America*. 1843.

Tolstoy, Alexei. *Moscow Art Theater Plays*. 1922.

Tomlinson, H. M. *Tide Marks*. 1924.

Tomlyn, Alfred W. *Our Scottish Songs*. Unknown.

Topelius, Zacharias (1818–1898). *The Surgeon's Stories* (6 vols). 1899.

Torrey, Bradford. *Birds in the Bush*. 1891—Ad.

Torrey, John (1796–1873). *Natural History of New York*, Part 2: Botany, vol. 1. 1843.

Tourqueneff / Tolstoi. *Les Reliques Vivantes / Les Cosaques* (in French). 1886.

Towne, Charles Hanson. *Autumn Loiterers*. 1917.

Towne, Charles Hanson, and Corinne Roosevelt Robinson (Introduction). *Roosevelt as the Poets Saw Him*. 1923.

Townsend, Charles Haskins (1859–1944). *Chameleons of the Sea*. 1910.

Townsend, Charles W. *Captain Cartwright and His Labrador Journal.* 1911.

Townsend, Charles W. *A Labrador Spring.* 1910.

Tracy, Gilbert A. *Uncollected Letters of Abraham Lincoln.* 1917.

Tracy, Louis. *One Wonderful Night.* 1922.

Trafton, Gilbert. *Methods of Attracting Birds.* 1910.

Travers, P. L. *Moscow Excursion.* 1934.

Trent, William P. *Southern Statesmen of the Old Regime.* 1897.

Trevelyan, George Macauley (1876–1962). *England under Queen Anne: The Peace and the Protestant Succession.* 1934.

Trevelyan, George Macauley (1876–1962). *The Life of John Bright.* 1913.

Trevelyan, George Macauley (1876–1962). *Clio, A Muse and Other Essays.* 1913.

Trevelyan, George Macauley (1876–1962). *Grey of Fallodon.* 1937.

Trevelyan, George Macauley (1876–1962). *The Marginal Notes of Lord Macaulay.* 1907.

Trevelyan, George Macauley (1876–1962). *Garibaldi's Defence of the Roman Republic.* 1907.

Trevelyan, George Macauley (1876–1962). *Garibaldi and the Thousand.* 1907.

Trevelyan, Sir George Otto (1838–1928). *Macaulay's Life and Letters* (vol. 1 of 2-vol. set). 1875.

Trevelyan, Sir George Otto (1838–1928). *The American Revolution 1766–1776,* Part 1. 1899.

Trevelyan, Sir George Otto (1838–1928). *Cawnpore.* 1899.

Trevelyan, Sir George Otto (1838–1928). *Interludes in Verse and Prose.* 1905.

Trevelyan, Sir George Otto (1838–1928). *The Early History of Charles James Fox.* 1881.

Trevelyan, Sir George Otto (1838–1928). *George the Third and Charles Fox.* 1914.

Trevor-Battye, A. *Ice-Bound on Kolgrier (A Chapter in the Exploration of Arctic Europe).* 1895.

Trites, W. B. *Barbara Gwynne.* 1913.

Trobriand, General Regis De. *Quatre Ans de Campagnes a L'armee du Potomac.* 1874.

Trollope, Anthony. *The West Indies and the Spanish Main.* 1860.

Trollope, Anthony. *The Vicar of Bullhampton.* c. 1924.

Trotter, W. *Instincts of the Herd in Peace and War.* N.d.

Troude, O. *Batailles Navales de la France,* vols. 1–4. 1867.

Turczynowicz, Laura De Gozdawa. *When the Prussians Came to Poland.* 1916.

Turner, George K. *The Taskmasters.* 1902.

Turner, John Hastings. *Simple Souls.* 1918.

Turner, Mrs. Elizabeth. *The Cowslip, / Or More Cautionary Stories in Verse.* 1811.

Turner-Turner, J. *The Giant Fish of Florida.* 1902.

Tuthill, Mrs. L. C. *Edith the Backwoods Girl.* 1865.

Twain, Mark (Samuel Clemens) (1835–1910). *The Innocents Abroad or the Pilgrims Progress.* 1881.

Twain, Mark (Samuel Clemens) (1835–1910). *Life on the Mississippi,* vol. 1. 1883.

Twain, Mark (Samuel Clemens) (1835–1910). *Following the Equator*. 1897.

Twining, Thomas. *Travels in America 100 Years Ago*. 1893.

Tyau, Min-Ch'ien T. Z. *Two Years of Nationalist China*. 1930.

Tyler, Daniel. *Daniel Tyler*. 1853.

Tyler, Lyon Gardiner. *The Cradle of the Republic*. 1906.

Tyler, Moses. *Patrick Henry* / American Statesmen. 1888.

Tyler, Moses Cait. *Patrick Henry* (American Statesmen Series), vol. 3. 1898.

Tyrwhitt-Wilson, Gerald Hugh, Baron Berners (1883–1950). *The Distant Prospect*. 1945.

Uhsen, H. Erdmann. *Der Romisch-Orientalisch-Deutschen Kayser Merckwurdiges Leben und Thaten*. 1716.

Unknown. *Genova Storia-Arte, Ai Delegati Della Conferenza Internazionale*. 1922.

Unknown. *Bible Picture Book*. N.d.

Unknown. *The Charm: A Book for Boys and Girls* (3 vols). 1854.

Unknown. *St Winifred's: Or the World of School*. 1863.

Unknown. *The Life of Lady Russell*. 1799.

Unknown. *Earth's Many Voices*. N.d.

Unknown. *The Gayworthys: A Story of Threads and Thrums*. 1865.

Unknown. *A Sister's Bye-Hours*. 1872.

Unknown. *Martha's Hooks and Eyes*. 1860.

Unknown. *Little Mother*. 1873.

Unknown. *The Sunny Side: Or the Country Minister's Wife*. 1851.

Unknown. *The Poor Rich Man and the Rich Poor Man*. 1836.

Unknown. *A Treasury of Pleasure Books for Young People*. N.d.

Unknown. *Il Cavalier Bambino*. c. 1896.

Unknown. *Lettere di Jacopo Novaro Ai Suoi Genitori*. 1931.

Unknown. *Reception de M. Jules Cambon, Le 20 Novembre 1919, Academie Francaise*. 1919.

Unknown. *Biblia Sacra Quadrilingvia Novt Testamenti Graeci*. 1736.

Unknown. *Littell's Living Age* (2-vol. set). 1853.

Unknown. *Simple Rhymes for Happy Times*. N.d.

Unknown. *Notes on the Harvard Tercentenary*. 1936.

Unknown. *The Hymnal*. 1892.

Unknown. *The Hymnal*. 1916.

Unknown. *Red and White Roses*. N.d.

Unknown. *The Heir of Redclyffe*, vol. 1. 1853.

Unknown. *The Girls Own Annual*, vol. 3. 1883.

Unknown. *The Marne Battlefields* (1914). 1917.

Unknown. *Original Poems*. 1868.

Unknown. *The Next Five Years, An Essay in Political Agreement*. 1935.

Unknown. *Edinburgh Review* (multiple volumes).

Unknown. *Consecration of the Theodore Roosevelt Window at Temple Keneseth Israel* (Series 33 #1). 1919.

Unknown. *The North British Review, American Edition* (multiple volumes).

Unknown. *Westminster Review* (multiple volumes).

Unknown. *Blackwood's Magazine* (multiple volumes).

Unknown. *North American Big Game*. 1939.

Unknown. *Heartease Or the Brother's Wife*. 1855.

Unknown. *Catholic's Pocket Manual*. c. 1905.

Unknown. *Japanese Book*. 1929.

Unknown. *Marriage and Inheritance*. 1835.

Unknown. *Roger Wolcott: Public Services in Memory of Roger Wolcott*. 1901.

Unknown. *The New Jerusalem: A Hymn of the Olden Time*. 1852.

Unknown. *Picture of Washington and Its Vicinity for 1848*. 1848.

Unknown. *The Book-Lovers Almanac for 1897*. 1896.

Unknown. *The Modern Home Cook Book and Family Physician*. 1892.

Unknown. *Oeuvres de J. Racine, De L' Academie Francoise*, vol. 1. 1770.

Unknown. *Oeuvres de J. Racine*, vol. 2. 1770.

Unknown. *Oeuvres de J. Racine*, vol. 3. 1773.

Unknown. *Misiones y Cataratas Del Iguazu* (Photographs). N.d.

Unknown. *Almanach De Gotha* (in French): *Annual Genealogical, Political and Statistical 1909*. 1909.

Unknown. *Vigor's Letters*. N.d.

Unknown. *Modern British Poetry*. 1925.

Unknown. *Original Poems*. 1868.

Unknown. *The Bay Psalm Book*. N.d. (Reprinted from 1640).

Unknown. *The New Netherland Register*, vol. 1, January 1911, no. 1. 1911.

Unknown. *The Arabian Night's Entertainment*. N.d.

Unknown. *Reliques of Ancient English Poetry*, vols. 1–3. 1875.

Unknown. *American Association for Labor Legislation, 3rd Annual Meeting, Labor and the Courts*. 1910.

Unknown. *Canal Record Sept 1 1909 to Aug 24 1910*, vol. 3. 1910.

Unknown. *Littell's Living Age* (multiple volumes).

Unknown. *Liberty China and Queen's Ware*. 1924.

Unknown. *Archives do Museo Nacional do Rio De Janeiro*, vol. 20, 1917. 1917.

Unknown. *Tactical Question No. 11, Discuss Handling of Fleet 1st, Superior 2nd, Inferior*. N.d.

Unknown. *Collectors Club Philatelist*, vol. 8 (July 1929 #3). 1929.

Unknown. *The Meriden Bird Club 2nd Report*. 1912.

Unknown. *The American Museum Journal*, vol. 18, May 1918, no.5. 1918.

Unknown. *Eighth Report, The Commission of Fine Arts*. 1920.

Unknown. *Hammond's Large Scale War Map of the Western Front*. 1917.

Unknown. *A Colloquy on the Necessity of Clergy in Government*. N.d.

Unknown. *Timehri: The Journal of the Royal Agricultural and Commercial Society of British Guiana*, vol. 4., War vol. 1917.

Unknown. *Pictures from Forest and Stream*. 1901.

Unknown. *Twenty-Two Years Work of the Hampton Normal and Agricultural Institute*. 1893.

Unknown. *Psalmen Gezangen En Geestekyke Liederen*. N.d.

Unknown. *Yearbook Society of the Chagres 1914*. 1914.

Unknown. *US Naval Institute Proceedings*, vol. 36, No. 1, 1910, Whole No. 133. 1910.

Unknown. *Friends of France, the Field Service of the American Ambulance Described by Its Members*. 1916.

Unknown. *The Progressive Party, Its Record from January to July, 1916*. 1916.

Unknown. *Transactions of the Linnaean Society of New York*, vol. 1. 1882.

Unknown. *Hymnal*. 1920.

Unknown. *Journal of the East Africa and Uganda Natural History Society*. 1914.

Unknown. *Winterage Auf Ithaka*. 1905.

Unknown. *Sommertage Ouf Ithaka*. 1903.

Unknown. *State of New York Forest, Fish and Game Commission Report 1900*. 1901.

Unknown. *State of New York Forest, Fish and Game Commission, Eighth and Ninth Reports, 1902–1903*. 1902, 1903.

Unknown. *Harvard College, Class of 1880, the Eleventh Report*. 1941.

Unknown. *Tenth Report U.S. Civil Service Commission July 1892–June 1893*. 1894.

Unknown. *U.S. Naval Institute Proceedings*, vol. 40, no. 4, 1914. 1914.

Unknown. *Timehri; the Journal of the Royal Agricultural and Commercial Society of British Guiana*, vol. 5. 1918.

Unknown. *The Cabinet of Natural History and American Rural Sports*, vol. 2. 1833.

Unknown. *The Cabinet of Natural History and American Rural Sports*, vol. 3. 1833.

Unknown. *The Cabinet of Natural History*, vol. 1. 1833.

Unknown. *Hymnal of the Reformed Church in the United States*. N.d.

Unknown. *From the Ladies of Central M.E. Church, Bridgetown, NJ*. 1908.

Unknown. *The Hymnal of the Reformed Church in the United States*. 1892.

Unknown. *A New Book of Sports*. 1885.

Unknown. *Tales from Blackwood*, vol. 12. 1903.

Unknown. *Book of Common Prayer*. 1892.

Unknown. *Die Nibelunge* (in German). 1904.

Unknown. *The Green Box of Monsieur de Sartine Found at Mademoiselle Du*. 1916.

Unknown. *The Child's Own Book and Treasury of Interesting Stories*. 1869.

Unknown. *Fidgetty Skeert*. 1859.

Unknown. *The Roosevelt Quarterly*, vols. 1–5. 1928.

Unknown. *Illustrated Inaugural History*. 1905.

Unknown. *Les Combattants Francais de la Guerre Armericain 1778–1783*. 1903.

Unknown. *Society of the Chagres*. 1913.

Unknown. *Studien zur Kriegsgelchichte und Taktik*. 1906.

Unknown. *Das Was Verschwindet: Trachten aus den Bergen und Inseln der Adria*. Unknown.

Unknown. *The Life of George Washington*. 1807.

Unknown. *Yacht-Reise in Den Syrten*. 1873–1874.

Unknown. *La Chancun de Willame*. 1903.

Unknown. *Shakespeares Comedies, Histories, and Tragedies*. N.d.

Unknown. *The Proceedings of the Convention of the New Hampshire Settlers*. 1917.

Unknown. *Royal Commission on the Decline of the Birth-Rate and on the Mortality of Infants*. 1904.

Unknown. *The Official and Pictorial Record of the Story of American Expansion*, vol. 2. 1904.

Unknown. *Soldier's Hand Book, U.S.A., Revised*. 1900.

Unknown. *Psalm Book*. 1904.

Unknown. *Ceremonials at the Funeral and Lying-in-State of His Late Majesty King Ed.* c. 1910.

Unknown. *The New York State Theodore Roosevelt Memorial*. 1936.

Unknown. *Manual of Handiwork*. c. 1915.

Unknown. *Long Island Favorites*. 1935.

Unknown. *Proceedings of the Conference on the Care of Dependent Children*. 1909.

Unknown. *Parga*. 1907.

Unknown. *Interborough Rapid Transit (The Subway) in New York*. 1904.

Unknown. *The Royal Collection of Paintings at Buckingham Palace and Windsor Castle*. 1905.

Unknown. *Guglielmo Ferrera*. 1902–1907.

Unknown. *Violin Classics*, vol. 3. 1875.

Unknown. *Four Sonnets of the Troubled Time*. 1915.

Unknown. *The Register of Brown's Hotel Washington DC*. 1847.

Unknown. *A Catalogue of the Pictures, etc. at 18 Kensington Palace Gardens London*. 1926.

Unknown. *Robin Red Breast*. N.d.

Unknown. *Charles Francis Adams*. 1900.

Unknown. *Samuel Adams*. 1900.

Unknown. *William H. Seward*. American Statesmen. 1897.

Unknown. *Old Fashioned Fairy Tales*. N.d.

Unknown. *The Round of the Year*. Nov. 1923.

Unknown. *Stories Merry Stories Wise*. 1828.

Unknown. *Beautiful Pearls of Catholic Truth*. 1897.

Unknown. *Baby World / New Edition*. N.d.

Unknown. *Mother's Little Rhyme Book*. c. 1914.

Unknown. *Official Louisiana Purchase Exposition*. 1904.

Unknown. *The Nation's Capital, Washington*. N.d.

Unknown. *Rhymes for the Nursery*. N.d.

Unknown. *Cinderella / Or the Little Glass Slipper 1903*. 1903.

Unknown. *History of the Department of State*. 1901.

Unknown. *Ali Baba and the Forty Thieves*. 1895.

Unknown. *The House That Jack Built*. 1895.

Unknown. *Family Genealogy*. c. 1870.

Unknown. *New York Album*. N.d.

Unknown. *Little Red Riding Hood*. 1895.

Unknown. *Prince Uno*. 1897.

Unknown. *Arctic Brotherhood*. May 23, 1903.

Unknown. *Collection of the Most Remarkable Monuments of the National Museum*, vol. 1. 1869.

Unknown. *Foreign Relations of the U.S. 1908*. 1912.

Unknown. *The Ark Quarterly Journal of Ornithology*. 1913.

Unknown. *Catalogue of the Hunting Trophies: American Exhibition, London 1887*. 1887.

Unknown. *Blackwood's Magazine (Jan.–June 1847)*. 1847.

Unknown. *Theodore Roosevelt, Senior: A Tribute* (Pamphlet). 1901.

Untermeyer, Louis (1885–1977). *Challenge*. 1914.

Untermeyer, Louis (1885–1977). *These Times*. 1917.

Upton, Brevet Major General Emory. *Military Policy of the United States*. 1904.

Utley, Henry M. *Michigan as a Province, Territory and State*, vol. 2–4. 1906.

Uuflage, Zehnte. *Diezels Niederlagd*. 1909.

Vacaresco, Helene (Collected by). *The Bard of Dimbovitza: Roumanian Folk Songs Collected from the Peasants*. 1891.

Vail, R. W. G. *Alice in Wonderland; A Christmas Gift to A Dear Child (The Manuscript)*. 1928.

Valery, Paul. *Discours de Reception de M. Le Marechal Petain a L'academie Francaise et Resonse*. 1931.

Van Doran, Carl. *Swift*. 1930.

Van Dyke, Henry. *Music and Other Poems*. 1905.

Van Luan, Henri. *French Literature*. 1877.

Vancouver, Capt. George. *Voyage of Discovery to the North Pacific Ocean and Round the World*. 3-vol. set. 1798.

Vandyke, Theodore S. *The Still Hunter*. 1883.

Vansittart, Rt. Hon. Lord. *Lessons of My Life*. 1943.

Vanuxem, Lardner (1792–1848). *Natural History of New York Geology Third District*. 1842.

Various. *The Presidents of the United States 1789–1914*. 1914.

Various. *British Essayists*. 1851.

Various. *The White House Gallery of Official Portraits of the Presidents*. 1901.

Various Artists. *Book of Early 1900's Sheet Music*. N.d.

Various Artists. *The Presidents: The White House Gallery of Official Portraits of the Presidents*. 1907.

Various Artists. *The World's Collection of Patriotic Songs and Airs of the Different Nations*. 1903.

Various Artists. *Summer Songs and Sketches*. N.d.

Various Artists. *Elegant Extracts Verse*. 1790.

Various Artists. *Christmas: An American Annual of Christmas Literature and Art*, vol. 17. 1947.

Various Artists. *Encyclopedia Britannica*, vol. 29 / Gla.–Jut. 1902.

Various Artists. *Encyclopedia Britannica*, vol. 30 / K–Mor. 1902.

Various Artists. *First Proof (Pages of Cartoons, Some of TR)*. c. 1905.

Various Artists. *Paintings in the Collection of Henry Clay Frick*. 1910.

Various Artists. *Encyclopedia Britannica*, vol. 32 / Pri-Sto. 10th Edition. 1902.

Various Artists. *New Testament Psalms*. Unknown.

Various Artists. *Encyclopedia Britannica*, vol. 34 / Maps. 1902.

Various Artists. *Encyclopedia Britannica*, vol. 35 / Index. 1902.

Various Artists. *London Quarterly Review*, vols. 65–66 (Dec 1839–Mar 1840). 1840.

Various Artists. *Music (Un Petit Rien Pour Le Piano)*. N.d.

Various Artists. *Half a Century of English History (Eng. Hist. in Cartoons from the Collection of Mr. Punch)*. 1884.

Various Artists. *Canti D'italia* (Bound) *Sheet Music*. N.d.

Various Artists. *French Musical Scores*. Pre 1854.

Various Artists. *Munseys Magazines*. 1918.

Various Authors. *The Holy Bible*. 1763.

Various Authors. *Holy Bible*. N.d.

Various Authors. *The Reading Circle 1917–1937*. c. 1937.

Various Authors. *The War of Democracy, The Allies Statement*. 1917.

Various Authors. *World Almanac and Encyclopedia*. 1903.

Various Authors. *The World's Great Classics, Oriental Literature*, vol. 2. 1899.

Various Authors. *Poems of Home Life*. 1874.

Various Authors. *The World's Almanac for 1879*. 1878.

Various Authors. *The Atlantic Monthly* (multiple volumes).

Various Authors. *The Book Lover's Almanac for the Year 1894*. 1894.

Various Authors. *The Book-Lovers Almanac for 1896*. 1896.

Various Authors. *Italian Masters*. 1940.

Various Authors. *The Capital of Our Country*. 1923.

Various Authors. *The Holy Bible*. 1777.

Various Authors. *The Holy Bible*. 1878.

Various Authors. *The Casquet*. 1829.

Various Authors. *Diseases of the Horse*. 1903.

Various Authors. *Bell's British Theatre*. 1780.

Various Authors. *London Society*. 1862.

Various Authors. *Ballads of the Fleet*. 1897—Ad.

Various Authors. *Encyclopedia Britannica*, vol. 25 / A-Aus. 1902.

Various Authors. *Encyclopedia Britannica*, vol. 27 / Chi-Eld. 1902.

Various Authors. *The American Museum Journal March 1914*, vol. 14, no. 3. 1914.

Various Authors. *Short Prayers: (Compiled by L. H. M. Soulsby)*. 1916.

Various Authors. *Roosevelt Wild Life Bulletin, Syracuse University Bulletin*, vol. 2, no. 4. 1925.

Various Authors. *The Condor: A Magazine of Western Ornithology*, vol. 16, no. 4. 1914.

Various Authors. *More Books: The Bulletin of the Boston Public Library*. 1931.

Various Authors. *Daughters of the American Revolution Magazine*, vol. 58, no. 9 Sept. 1924.

Various Authors. *The Holy Bible*. 1829.

Various Authors. *Common Prayer*. 1896.

Various Authors *Hymnal*. 1892.

Various Authors. *A: Hymnal / B: Common Prayer*. 1897.

Various Authors. *Encyclopedia Britannica Str–Zwo*, 10th Edition, vol. 33. 1902.

Various Authors. *Quarterly Review* (multiple volumes).

Various Authors. *The Spectator*. 1808.

Various Authors. *The New Testament – Translated Out of the Original Greek*. 1844.

Various Authors. *Harvard Lampoon* (multiple volumes).

Various Authors. *Forest and Stream* (multiple volumes).

Various Authors. *London Quarterly Review* (multiple volumes).

Various Authors. *Natural History of New York Part I Zoology*. 1842.

Various Authors. *State of New York, Fisheries Game and Forest Commission, Reports for 1895*. 1896.

Various Authors. *Taps*. 1932.

Various Authors. *Obituary Addresses on the Occasion of the Death of the Honorable Henry Clay*. 1852.

Various Authors. *The Architectural Record*. April 1903.

Various Authors. *Bulletin of the American Geographical Society*, vol. 46, no. 7. 1914.

Various Authors. *Encyclopedia Britannica*, vol. 26 / Aus–Chi. 1902.

Various Authors. *The War from This Side*. 1915.

Various Authors. *The War from This Side*, 2. 1916.

Various Authors. *Reports of Explorations and Surveys*, vol. 10. 1859.

Various Authors. *Encyclopedia Britannica*, vol. 28 / Fle–Gla. 1902.

Various Authors. *Encyclopedia Britannica*, vol. 31 / Mos–Pre. 1902. 1859.

Various Authors. *The Encyclopedia Britannica*, 9th Ed. 1877–1889.

Various Authors. *The Book of Common Prayer*. N.d.

Various Authors. *Campagne Del Principe Eugenio De Savoia* (20-vol. set). 1902.

Various Authors. *The Comprehensive Bible: Old and New Testament*. 1828.

Various Authors. *Holy Bible*. 1899.

Various Authors. *Annual Report of the Smithsonian Institution*. 1914.

Various Authors. *Proceedings of the Second Pan American Scientific Congress 1915–1916*. 1917.

Various Authors. *The Extinct Mammalian Fauna of Dakota and Nebraska Including an Account of Some Allied Forms from Other Localities Together with a Synopsis of the Mammalian Remains of North America*, vol. 7. 1869.

Various Authors. *King Albert's Book (A Tribute to the Belgian King and People)*. 1914.

Various Authors. *Holy Bible*. 1857.

Various Authors. *Inaugural Souvenir Book.* 1901.

Various Authors. *1901 Inaugural Souvenir.* 1901.

Various Authors. *In Memory of Brigadier General Theodore Roosevelt Jr.* 1944.

Various Authors. *Theodore Roosevelt Memorial Addresses Delivered before the Century Association.* February 2, 1919.

Various Authors. *A Decade of Progress in Eugenics: Scientific Papers of the 3rd International Congress of Eugenics.* 1934.

Various Authors. *New Webster Dictionary and Complete Vest Pocket Library.* c. 1894.

Various Authors. *Blackwood's Magazine,* Jan.–June 1865. 1865.

Various Authors. *The War from This Side: Editorials from the North American,* vol. 4. 1919.

Various Authors. *The Pocket Book of Verse.* 1940.

Various Authors. *Tales of Adventure by Sea and Land.* Unknown.

Various Authors. *Arctic Series of Publication.* N.d.

Vaulabelle, Achille De. *Campagn et Bataille de Waterloo.* 1845.

Vazov, Ivan Minchov (1850–1921). *Under the Yoke.* 1894.

Verdi, Giuseppi. *Il Trovatore.* 1857.

Verdy du Vernois, General J. von. *With the Royal Headquarters 1870–1871.* 1897.

Verne, Jules. *The Mysterious Island / The Secret of the Island.* 1876.

Verne, Jules. *Abandoned.* 1875.

Verner, Major Willoughly. *Rifle Brigade Chronicle.* 1893.

Vestal, Captain Samuel Curtis. *The Selection and Defense of Naval Bases.* 1910.

Villari, Luigi. *Russia* (Oriental Series), vol. 24. 1910.

Villari, Pasquale (1827–1917). *Barbarian Invasions of Italy.* 1902.

Vinci, Leonardo Da (1452–1519). *Thoughts on Life and Art.* 1906.

Vinton, Stallo. *John Colter Discoverer of Yellowstone.* 1926.

Viscount Grey of Fallodon. *Twenty-Five Years, 1892–1916.* 1925.

Vogel, Von F. Rud. *Das Amerikanische Haus das Amerikanische Haus.* 1910.

Volney, Constantin-Francois (1757–1820). *The Ruins or A Survey of the Revolutions of Empires* (Translated from the French). 1795.

Volpe Gioacchino. *La Storia Degli Italiani E Dell'italia.* 1934.

Von Bernhardi, Friedrich. *On War of Today.* 1913.

Von Glumer, Claire. *A Noble Name or Donninghausen.* 1883.

Von Kapherr, E. Frelherr. *Das Elchwid.* 1908.

Von Korinth. *Eine Spazlerfahrt im Golfe.* 1876.

Von Laszlo, Ph U. *Laszlo.* 1913.

Von Spix, Joh. Bapt, and C. F. Phil. Von Martius. *Travels in Brazil: in the Years 1817–1820* (2-vol. set). 1824.

Von Tautphaeus, Baroness. *The Initials: A Story of Modern Life.* 1850.

Voynich, E. L. *The Gadfly.* 1906.

Vrooman, Frank Buffington F.R.G.S. *Theodore Roosevelt, Dynamic Geographer.* 1909.

Waddington, Richard. *Louis XV et de Renversement des Alliances.* 1896.

Waddington, Richard. *La Guerre de Sept Ans Histoire Diplomatique et Militaire.* 1899–1914.

Wagner, W. *Romances and Epics.* 1906.

Wailly, M. N. De. *Geoffroi de Ville-Hardouin.* 1882.

Wakefield, John A. *Wakefield's History of the Black Hawk War* (A Reprint of the First Edition). 1908.

Waldo, S. Putnam. *President's Tour.* 1818.

Waldseemuller, Martin (1470–1521?), Franz Von Weiser (Knight) (1848–1923), and Joseph Fischer (1858–1944). *Waldseemuller's Cosmographiae Introduction.* 1907.

Waldstein, Charles, and Leonard Shoobridge. *Herculareum Past Present and Future.* 1908.

Waliszewski, K. *Ivan the Terrible.* 1904.

Walker, Dr. Thomas. *Journal of An Exploration in the Spring of the Year 1750.* 1888.

Walker, Horatio. *Exhibition of Recent Painting by Horatio Walker.* 1914.

Wallace, Alfred Russel. *The World of Life.* 1911.

Wallace, D. M., and L. Villari. *Russia* (Oriental Series), vol. 22–24. 1910.

Wallihan, A. G. *Camera Shots at Big Game.* 1901.

Walpole, Horace. *Letters of Horace Walpole,* vols. 1 to 9. 1866.

Walpole, Spencer. *The Land of Home Rule.* 1893.

Walsh, James J. *The Century of Columbus.* 1914.

Walsh, Thomas. *The Prison Ships and Other Poems.* 1909.

Walter, Ahto, and Tom Olsen. *Racing the Seas.* 1935.

Walton, Izaak (1593–1683). *The Lives of Donne, Wotton, Hooker, Herbert and Sauduson.* 1825.

Walton, Izaak (1593–1683), and Charles Cotton. *The Complete Angler.* 1823.

Wandell, Samuel H., and Meade Minnigerode. *Aaron Burr* (2-vol. set). 1925.

Ward, Artemus (1834–1867). *Artemus Ward, His Book.* 1862.

Ward, Artemus (1834–1867). *Artemus Ward in London and Other Papers.* 1867.

Ward, Henshaw. *Evolution for John Doe.* 1925.

Ward, Herbert. *Mr. Poilu: Notes and Sketches with the Fighting French.* 1926.

Ward, Mrs. Humphrey (1851–1920). *England's Effort.* 1916.

Ward, Mrs. Humphrey (1851–1920). *Marcella,* vol. 2. 1894.

Ward, Rowland. *Roland Ward's Records of Big Game.* 1914.

Warden, William. *Letters from Saint Helena.* 1816.

Ware, Eugene Fitch (1841–1911). *Some of the Rhymes of Ironquill.* 1899.

Warner, Anna B. *Gardening by Myself.* 1924.

Warner, Anne. *Seeing France with Uncle John.* 1909.

Warner, Susan (1819–1885). *Mr. Rutherford's Children.* 1853.

Warren, Edward Royal (1860–). *The Mammals of Colorado.* 1910.

Wartenburg, Count Yorck Von. *Napoleon as a General* (2-vol. set). 1902.

Washburn, Charles G. *Henry Cabot Lodge.* 1925.

Washburn, Charles G. *Theodore Roosevelt, The Logic of His Career.* 1916.

Washburn, Charles G. *Address on the Unveiling of Roosevelt Tablet.* 1923.

Washburn, Stanley. *Field Notes from the Russian Front.* 1915.

Washington, Booker T. *The Man Farthest Down: A Record of Observation A Study in Europe.* 1912.

Washington, George, and Jared Sparks (Editor). *Letters and Recollection of George Washington.* 1906.

Waterhouse, G. R. *Natural History of the Mamalia,* vols. 1–2. 1846–1848.

Waterton, Charles, Esq. (1782–1865). *Wanderings in South America.* 1891.

Watson, John. *The Mystery of the Downs.* 1918.

Watson, Thomas E. *Napoleon: A Sketch of His Life, Character, Struggles and Achievements.* 1902.

Wattles, Willard. *Lanterns in Gethsemane.* 1918.

Watts, Isaac, D.D. (1674–1748). *Divine and Moral Songs for Children.* 1836.

Watts, Louisa. *Pretty Poems for Little People.* 1854.

Wayland, Frances G. M. *Arnold Green.* 1927.

Weatherly, F. E. *Punch and Judy and Some of Their Friends.* 1897.

Webb, Alexander. *The Peninsula: Campaigns of the Civil War.* 1881.

Weeden, William B. *War Government Federal and State 1861–1865 in Massachusetts.* 1906.

Weekes, Alice Delano. *Life in an Oyster Bay Farmhouse before the Revolutionary War.* 1918.

Wegelin, Oscar. *Jupitor Hammon.* 1915.

Weigall, Arthur E. P. *Travels in the Upper Egyptian Deserts.* 1909.

Weir, Marion E. *Patience to Work and Patience to Wait.* 1859.

Weldseemuller, Martin (1470–1521?). *The Oldest Map with the Name America of the Year 1507.* 1507.

Wellby, Captain M. S. *Twixt Sirdar and Menelik: An Account of a Year's Expedition from Zeila to Cairo through Unknown Abyssina.* 1901.

Welling, Richard. *As the Twig Is Willing.* 1942.

Wells, Carolyn. *Idle Idyls.* 1900.

Wells, Carolyn. *A Satire Anthology.* 1905.

Wells, Carolyn. *Children of Our Town.* 1902.

Wells, Carolyn (Collected by). *A Parody Anthology.* 1904.

Wertenbaker, Thomas Jefferson. *Princeton 1746–1896.* 1946.

Wesley, John. *The Heart of John Wesley's Journal.* 1903.

West, Andrew E. *The Graduate College of Princeton.* 1913.

West, Charles, M.D. *The Mother's Manual of Children's Diseases.* 1885.

Westergaard, Waldemar. *The Danish West Indies under Company Rule 1671–1754 with a Supplementary Chapter 1755–1917.* 1917.

Wetherell, Elizabeth. *Queechy,* vol. 2. 1852.

Wetherill, J. K. *The Wandering Joy.* 1911.

Weyman, Stanley John (1855–1928). *The Castle Inn.* 1898.

Weyman, Stanley John (1855–1928). *The Long Night.* 1903.

Wharton, Edith (1862–1937). *The House of Mirth.* 1905.

Wharton, Edith (1862–1937). *The Book of the Homeless*. 1916.
Wharton, Edith (1862–1937). *Italian Villas and Their Gardens*. 1904.
Wheatley, Phillis (1753?–1784). *Phillis Wheatley Poems and Letters*. 1915.
Wheatley, Phillis (1753?–1784). *Phillis Wheatley*. 1915.
Wheeler, Benjamin Ide. *Alexander the Great (Heroes of the Nations)*. 1900.
Wheeler, Candace. *Content in a Garden*. 1901.
Wheeler, Maj.-General Joseph. *The Santiago Campaign*. 1898.
Wheeler, Post. *Russian Wonder Tales*. 1912.
Wheelock, Irene Grosvenor. *Birds of California*. 1904.
Whipple, Edwin P. (1819–1886), and James Thomas Fields (1817–1881). *The Family Library of British Poetry*. 1878.
White, Eliza Orne. *When Molly Was Six*. 1896.
White, J. William. *A Text-Book of the War for Americans*. 1915.
White, Reverend Gilbert. *Gilbert White's Selbourne*. 1900.
White, Robert. *Madeira*. 1857.
White, Stewart Edward (1873–1946). *Camp and Trail*. 1907.
White, Stewart Edward (1873–1946). *Speaking for Myself*. 1943.
White, Stewart Edward (1873–1946). *The Forest*. 1903.
White, William Allen. *Masks in a Pageant*. 1928.
White, William Allen. *God's Puppets*. 1916.
White, William Allen (1868–1944). *The Martial Adventures of Henry and Me*. 1918.
Whitehead, Charles E. *Adventures of Gerard the Lion Killer*. 1856.
Whitlock, Brand. *Lafayette*. 1929.
Whitman, Walt. *Leaves of Grass*. 1907.
Whitman, Walt. *Leaves of Grass*. 1891–1892.
Whitman, Walt. *Prose Works Complete*. 1892.
Whitney, Adeline Dutton Train (1824–1906). *Faith Gartney's Girlhood*. 1863.
Whitney, Caspar. *On Snow-Shoes to the Barren Grounds: 2800 Miles after Musk-Oxen and Wood-Bison*. 1896.
Whitney, Harry. *Hunting with the Eskimos*. 1910.
Whitridge, Arnold. *Critical Ventures in Modern French Literature*. 1924.
Whittier, John Greenleaf. *The Poetical Works*. 1882.
Whittier, John Greenleaf. *Illustrated Child Life*. 1873.
Whymper, Edward. *Travels amongst the Great Andes of the Equator*. 1892.
Widmann, Otto. *Birds of Missouri*. 1907.
Wied-Neuwied, Maximilian Prinz Von. *Reise Nach Brasilien Von Maximilian Price of Wied Newnied* (in 2 vols.). 1820–1821.
Wied-Neuwied, Maximilian Prinz Von. *Kopher Und --- (?) Der Reisena--(?) Brasilien* (Book of Pictures). c. 1817.
Wiffen, J. H., Translator. *The Jerusalem Delivered of Torquato Tasso (With A Life of the Author)*. 1851.
Wiggin, Kate Douglas (1856–1953). *The Birds Xmas Carol*. 1898.
Wiggin, Kate Douglas (1856–1953). *Penelope's Progress*. 1899.

Wiggin, Kate Douglas (1856–1953). *Penelope's Experiences in England*. 1930.

Wiggin, Kate Douglas (1856–1953). *A Cathedral Courtship*. 1901.

Wilbur, Hon. Curtis, and Dudley W. Knox. *Official Records of the Union and Confederate Navies of the War of Rebellion*. 1927.

Wilbur, Russell J. *Theodore Roosevelt: A Verse Sequence in Sonnets and Quatorzains*. 1919.

Wilde, Oscar (1854–1900). *The Ballad of Reading Gaol*. 1904.

Wilde, Oscar (1854–1900). *Lady Windermere's Fan*. Unknown.

Wilder, Thornton (1897–1975). *The Bridge of San Luis Rey*. 1928.

Wildfowler. *Shooting and Fishing Trips*, vols. 1 and 2. 1879.

Wile, Frederic William. *Men around the Kaiser / The Makers of Modern Germany*. 1914.

Wiley, John. *Modern Painters*. 1853.

Wilkinson, Marguerite. *New Voices: An Introduction to Contemporary Poetry*. 1928.

Willard, T. A. *The City of the Sacred Well*. 1926.

Williams, Gluyas. *Fellow Citizens*. 1940.

Williams, Roger D. *The Fox Hound*. 1914.

Williams, Roger D. *Horse and Hound*. 1905.

Williamson, H. C. *Random Rhymes*. 1918.

Williamson, Thomas. *Oriental Field Sports*. 1819.

Willis, Browne (1682–1760). *The New Whole Duty of Man Containing the Faith and Practice of a Christian*. 1756.

Willson, Forsythe. *The Old Sergeant and Other Poems*. 1867.

Wilson, Alexander (1766–1813). *American Ornithology or the Natural History of the Birds of the United States* (8-vol. set, vols.1, 3–9). 1810.

Wilson, Alexander (1766–1813). *American Ornithology: Wilson Plates*. N.d.

Wilson, Alexander (1766–1813). *American Ornithology*. 1812.

Wilson, Alexander (1766–1813), and Charles Lucian Bonaparte (1803–1857). *American Ornithology*. 1811–12.

Wilson, H. W. *Ironclads in Action / Naval Warfare 1855–1895* (2-vol. set). 1896.

Wilson, John. *Dies Boreales; Or Christopher under Canvas*. 1850.

Wilson, Mclandburgh. *The Little Flag on Main Street*. 1917.

Winchell, Alexander. *Preadamites*. 1880.

Wingate, Major F. R., D.S.O. *Mahdiism and the Egyptian Sudan*. 1891.

Winkler, John K. *Morgan the Magnificent*. 1930.

Wirt, William. *Wirt's Life of Patrick Henry*. 1836.

Wister, A. L., Mrs. *Why He Did Not Die? Or the Child from Ebraergang*. 1893.

Wister, Owen (1860–1938). *Philosophy Four: A Story of Harvard University*. 1914.

Wister, Owen (1860–1938). *Lady Baltimore*. 1906.

Wister, Owen (1860–1938). *Members of the Family*. 1911.

Wister, Owen (1860–1938). *The Beacon Biographies of Eminent Americans: Ulysses S. Grant*. 1900.

Wister, Owen (1860–1938). *The Story of a Friendship*. 1930.

Wister, Owen (1860–1938). *The Seven Ages of Washington*. 1907.

Wister, Owen (1860–1938). *The Pentecost of Calamity*. 1915.

Witcraft, John R. *Cornelius Jansen Clopper and His Descendants*. 1912.

Wolcott, Laura. *A Gray Dream*. 1918.

Wolf, Joseph. *Wolf's Wild Animals*. 1874.

Wolpole, George, Charles. *The Kingdom of Ireland*. 1882.

Wood, Arnold. *High Spots of Sicily*. 1931.

Wood, Casey Albert (1856–?). *The Fundus Oculi of Birds*. 1917.

Wood, General Leonard (1860–1927). *Our Military History*. 1916.

Wood, J. G., Rev. *The Illustrated Natural History: Birds*. 1867.

Wood, J. G., Rev. *The Illustrated Natural History: Reptiles, Fishes, Mollusks*. 1871.

Wood, Krie Fisher. *The Notebook of an Attaché*. 1915.

Wood, Robert Williams. *How to Tell the Birds from the Flowers*. 1907.

Woodberry, George Edward (1855–1930). *North Africa and the Desert: Scenes and Moods*. 1914.

Woodbury, John. *Harvard College; Class of 1880; Report 9, Fortieth Anniversary Report*. 1920.

Woodroffe, Paul. *The Little Flowers of Saint Francis*. 1905.

Woodruff, Frank Morely. *The Birds of the Chicago Area, Bulletin # 6*. 1907.

Woods, Frederick Adams. *The Influence of Monarchs / Steps in a New Science of History*. 1913.

Woolsey, Sarah L. (Editor). *The Autobiography and Correspondence of Mrs. Delaney*. 1898.

Worcester, Dean C. *The Philippine Islands and Their People*. 1899.

Worcester, Elwood. *Religion and Medicine*. 1908.

Worcester, J. E. *Worcester Sketches I*. 1823.

Worcester, Joseph E. *Dictionary of the English Language* (Spine: Webster's Dictionary). 1878.

Wordsworth, William (1770–1850). *The Poetical Works of William Wordsworth*, vols. 1–7. 1849.

Wordsworth, William (1770–1850). *Booklet of Poems*. 1917.

Wraxall, Sir Nathaniel William (1751–1831). *Wraxall's Historical Memoirs*. 1904.

Wright, Irene A. *Cuba*. 1910.

Wright, Julia McNair (1840–1903). *Sea Side and Way Side Nature Readers* (3-vol. set). 1891.

Wright, Mabel Osgood. *My New York*. 1930.

Wright, Richardson. *The Gardener's Bed-Book*. 1929.

Wyatt, Edith Franklin. *The Wind in the Corn and Other Poems*. 1917.

Wyckoff, Walter. *The Workers*. 1897.

Wyeth, A., John. *Life of General Nathan Bedford Forest*. 1899.

Wyss, Johann David (1743–1818). *The Swiss Family Robinson*. 1849.

Xenopol, A. D. *Histoire des Roumains de la Dacie Trojane* (2-vol. set). 1896.

Yeats, William Butler (1865–1939). *The Hour-Glass and Other Plays*. 1915.

Yonge, Charlotte Mary (1823–1901). *The Daisy Chain or Aspirations*. 1856.

Yonge, Charlotte Mary (1823–1901). *The Chaplet of Pearls / The White and Black Ribaumont*. 1869.

Yonge, Charlotte Mary (1823–1901). *The Little Duke*. 1894.

Young, Edward. *Night Thoughts*. 1805.

Young, James R. *Living Issues of the Campaign of 1900, Its Men and Principles*. 1900.

Young, Lafayette. *If I Were Twenty-One*. c. 1926.

Young, Martha. *Plantation Bird Legends*. 1902.

Young, Stanley P., and Edward A. Goldman. *The Wolves of North America*. 1944.

Young, Stark. *The Three Fountains*. 1924.

Younghusband, Major G. J. *The Philippines and Round About*. 1899.

Younghusband, Major G. J. *Indian Frontier Warfare*. 1898.

Youngs, Mary F. *The Rubaiyat of Gran'ma*. 1899.

Zimmern, Alice. *Greek History for Young Readers*. 1928.

Zimmern, Sir Alfred Echard (1879–1957). *The Greek Commonwealth*. 1911.

Zweile, Aulflage. *Die Hohe Jagd*. 1905.

~

Appendix

Toward the end of his life, Theodore Roosevelt compiled his last collection of personal essays, which he titled A *Book-Lover's Holidays in the Open*. Charles Scribner's Sons published this book in 1916. Most of the chapters deal with Roosevelt's various outdoor adventures in the American West and other places in the world where he went hunting or exploring, but chapter 9 is different. He called this chapter "Books for Holidays in the Open," but the title is a bit misleading. In the first paragraph, he wrote that the books he read while "on holidays in the open" are the same books that he enjoyed reading "when at home." The chapter is really a personal essay about his reading habits and some of his favorite books. As such, it provides insights into Roosevelt as a reader and lover of books.

Books for Holidays in the Open

By Theodore Roosevelt

I am sometimes asked what books I advise men or women to take on holidays in the open. With the reservation of long trips, where bulk is of prime consequence, I can only answer: The same books one would read at home. Such an answer generally invites the further question as to what books I read when at home. To this question I am afraid my answer cannot be so instructive as it ought to be, for I have never followed any plan in reading which would apply to all persons under all circumstances; and indeed, it seems to me that no plan can be laid down that will be generally applicable. If a man is not

Theodore Roosevelt reading with his dog Skip during hunting trip in Colorado, 1905.
Courtesy of Sagamore Hill National Historic Site, National Park Service, Oyster Bay, NY

fond of books, to him reading of any kind will be drudgery. I most sincerely commiserate such a person, but I do not know how to help him. If a man or a woman is fond of books, he or she will naturally seek the books that the mind and soul demand. Suggestions of a possibly helpful character can be made by outsiders, but only suggestions and they will probably be helpful about in proportion to the outsider's knowledge of the mind and soul of the person to be helped.

Of course, if any one finds that he never reads serious literature, if all his reading is frothy and trashy, he would do well to try to train himself to like books that the general agreement of cultivated and sound-thinking persons has placed among the classics. It is as discreditable to the mind to be unfit for sustained mental effort as it is to the body of a young man to be unfit for sustained physical effort. Let man or woman, young man or girl, read some good author, say Gibbon or Macaulay, until sustained mental effort brings power to enjoy the books worth enjoying. When this has been achieved the man can soon trust himself to pick out for himself the particular good books which appeal to him.

The equation of personal taste is as powerful in reading as in eating; and within certain broad limits the matter is merely one of individual preference, having nothing to do with the quality either of the book or of the reader's mind. I like apples, pears, oranges, pineapples, and peaches. I dislike bananas, alligator-pears, and prunes. The first fact is certainly not to my credit, although it is to my advantage; and the second at least does not show moral turpitude. At times in the tropics, I have been exceedingly sorry I could not learn to like bananas, and on round-ups, in the cow country in the old days, it was even more unfortunate not to like prunes; but I simply could not make myself like either, and that was all there was to it.

In the same way I read over and over again *Guy Mannering, The Antiquary, Pendennis, Vanity Fair, Our Mutual Friend,* and the *Pickwick Papers;* whereas I make heavy weather of most parts of the *Fortunes of Nigel, Esmond,* and the *Old Curiosity Shop*—to mention only books I have tried to read during the last month. I have no question that the latter three books are as good as the first six; doubtless for some people they are better; but I do not like them, any more than I like prunes or bananas.

In the same way I read and reread *Macbeth* and *Othello;* but not *King Lear* nor *Hamlet.* I know perfectly well that the latter are as wonderful as the former—I wouldn't venture to admit my shortcomings regarding them if I couldn't proudly express my appreciation of the other two! But at my age I might as well own up, at least to myself, to my limitations, and read the books I thoroughly enjoy.

But this does not mean permitting oneself to like what is vicious or even simply worthless. If any man finds that he cares to read *Bel Ami,* he will do well to keep a watch on the reflex centers of his moral nature, and to brace himself with a course of Eugene Brieux or Henry Bordeaux. If he does not care for *Anna Karenina, War and Peace, Sebastopol,* and *The Cossacks* he misses much; but if he cares for the *Kreutzer Sonata,* he had better make up his mind that for pathological reasons he will be wise thereafter to avoid Tolstoy entirely. Tolstoy is an interesting and stimulating writer, but an exceedingly unsafe moral adviser.

It is clear that the reading of vicious books for pleasure should be eliminated. It is no less clear that trivial and vulgar books do more damage than can possibly be offset by any entertainment they yield. There remain enormous masses of books, of which no one man can read more than a limited number, and among which each reader should choose those which meet his own particular needs. There is no such thing as a list of "the hundred best books," or the "best five-foot library."

Dozens of series of excellent books, one hundred to each series, can be named, all of reasonably equal merit and each better for many readers than any of the others; and probably not more than half a dozen books would appear in all these lists. As for a "five-foot library," scores can readily be devised, each of which at some given time, for some given man, under certain conditions, will be best. But to attempt to create such a library that shall be of universal value is foreordained to futility.

Within broad limits, therefore, the reader's personal and individual taste must be the guiding factor. I like hunting books and books of exploration and adventure. I do not ask anyone else to like them. I distinctly do not hold my own preferences as anything whatever but individual preferences; and this chapter is to be accepted as confessional rather than didactic. With this understanding I admit a liking for novels where something happens; and even among these novels I can neither explain nor justify why I like some and do not like others; why, among the novels of Sienkiewicz, I cannot stand *Quo Vadis*, and never tire of *With Fire and Sword*, *Pan Michael*, the *Deluge* and the *Knights of the Cross*.

Of course, I know that the best critics scorn the demand among novel readers for "the happy ending." Now, in really great books—in an epic like Milton's, in dramas like those of Æschylus and Sophocles—I am entirely willing to accept and even demand tragedy, and also in some poetry that cannot be called great, but not in good, readable novels, of sufficient length to enable me to get interested in the hero and heroine!

There is enough of horror and grimness and sordid squalor in real life with which an active man has to grapple; and when I turn to the world of literature—of books considered as books, and not as instruments of my profession—I do not care to study suffering unless for some sufficient purpose. It is only a very exceptional novel which I will read if He does not marry Her; and even in exceptional novels I much prefer this consummation. I am not defending my attitude. I am merely stating it.

Therefore, it would be quite useless for me to try to explain why I read certain books. As to how and when, my answers must be only less vague. I almost always read a good deal in the evening; and if the rest of the evening is occupied, I can at least get half an hour before going to bed. But all kinds of odd moments turn up during even a busy day, in which it is possible to enjoy a book; and then there are rainy afternoons in the country in autumn, and stormy days in winter, when one's work outdoors is finished and after wet clothes have been changed for dry, the rocking-chair in front of the open wood-fire simply demands an accompanying book.

Railway and steamboat journeys were, of course, predestined through the ages as aids to the enjoyment of reading. I have always taken books with me when on hunting and exploring trips. In such cases the literature should be reasonably heavy, in order that it may last. You can under these conditions read Herbert Spencer, for example, or the writings of Turgot, or a German study of the Mongols, or even a German edition of Aristophanes, with erudite explanations of the jokes, as you never would if surrounded by less formidable authors in your own library; and when you do reach the journey's end you grasp with eager appetite at old magazines, or at the lightest of literature.

Then, if one is worried by all kinds of men and events—during critical periods in administrative office, or at national conventions, or during congressional investigations, or in hard-fought political campaigns—it is the greatest relief and unalloyed delight to take up some really good, some really enthralling book—Tacitus, Thucydides, Herodotus, Polybius, or Goethe, Keats, Gray, or Lowell—and lose all memory of everything grimy, and of the baseness that must be parried or conquered.

Like everyone else, I am apt to read in streaks. If I get interested in any subject, I read different books connected with it, and probably also read books on subjects suggested by it. Having read Carlyle's *Frederick the Great*— with its splendid description of the battles, and of the unyielding courage and thrifty resourcefulness of the iron-tempered King; and with its screaming deification of able brutality in the name of morality, and its practice of the suppression and falsification of the truth under the pretense of preaching veracity—I turned to Macaulay's essay on this subject, and found that the historian whom it has been the fashion of the intellectuals to patronize or deride showed a much sounder philosophy, and an infinitely greater appreciation of and devotion to truth than was shown by the loquacious apostle of the doctrine of reticence.

Then I took up Waddington's *Guerre de Sept Ans*; then I read all I could about Gustavus Adolphus; and, gradually dropping everything but the military side, I got hold of quaint little old histories of Eugene of Savoy and Turenne. In similar fashion my study of and delight in Mahan sent me further afield, to read queer old volumes about De Ruyter and the daring warrior-merchants of the Hansa, and to study, as well as I could, the feats of Suffren and Tegethoff. I did not need to study Farragut.

Mahaffy's books started me to reread—in translation, alas!—the post-Athenian Greek authors. After Ferrero I did the same thing as regards the Latin authors, and then industriously read all kinds of modern writers on the same period, finishing with Oman's capital essay on "Seven Roman States-men." Gilbert Murray brought me back from Greek history to Greek litera-ture, and thence by a natural suggestion to parts of the Old Testament, to the Nibelungenlied, to the Roland lay and the *chansons de gestes*, to *Beowulf*, and finally to the great Japanese hero-tale, the story of the *Forty-Nine Ronins*.

I read Burroughs too often to have him suggest anything save himself; but I am exceedingly glad that Charles Sheldon has arisen to show what a hunter-naturalist, who adds the ability of the writer to the ability of the trained observer and outdoor adventurer, can do for. our last great wilder-ness, Alaska. From Sheldon I turned to Stewart Edward White, and then began to wander afar, with Herbert Ward's *Voice from the Congo*, and Mary Kingsley's writings, and Hudson's *El Ombu*, and Cunningham Grahame's sketches of South America. A re-reading of *The Federalist* led me to Burke, to Trevelyan's history of Fox and of our own Revolution, to Lecky; and finally, by way of Malthus and Adam Smith and Lord Acton and Bagehot to my own contemporaries, to Ross and George Alger.

Even in pure literature, having nothing to do with history, philosophy, sociology, or economy, one book will often suggest another, so that one finds one has unconsciously followed a regular course of reading. Once I travelled steadily from Montaigne through Addison, Swift, Steele, Lamb, Irving, and Lowell to Crothers and Kenneth Grahame—and if it be objected that some of these *could* not have suggested the others, I can only answer that they *did* suggest them.

I suppose that everyone passes through periods during which he reads no poetry; and some people, of whom I am one, also pass through periods during which they voraciously devour poets of widely different kinds. Now it will be Horace and Pope; now Schiller, Scott, Longfellow, Körner; now Bret Harte or Kipling; now Shelley or Herrick or Tennyson; now Poe and Coleridge; and again Emerson or Browning or Whitman. Sometimes one wishes to read for the sake of contrast. To me Owen Wister is the writer I wish when I am hungry with the memories of lonely mountains, of vast sunny plains with seas of wind-rippled grass, of springing wild creatures, and lithe, sun-tanned men who ride with utter ease on ungroomed, half-broken horses. But when I lived much in cow camps, I often carried a volume of Swinburne, as a kind of antiseptic to alkali dust, tepid, muddy water, frying-pan bread, sow-belly bacon, and the too-infrequent washing of sweat-drenched clothing.

Fathers and mothers who are wise can train their children first to prac-tice, and soon to like, the sustained mental application necessary to enjoy good books. They will do well also to give each boy or girl the mastery of at least some one foreign language, so that at least one other great literature, in addition to our own noble English literature, shall be open to him or her. Modern languages are taught so easily and readily that whoever really desires to learn one of them can soon achieve sufficient command of it to read ordinary books with reason able ease; and then it is a mere matter of practice for anyone to become able thoroughly to enjoy the beauty and wisdom which knowledge of the new tongue brings.

Now and then one's soul thirsts for laughter. I cannot imagine any one's taking a course in humorous writers, but just as little can I sympathize with the man who does not enjoy them at times—from Sydney Smith to John Phœnix and Artemus Ward, and from these to Stephen Leacock. Mark Twain at his best stands a little apart, almost as much so as Joel Chandler Harris. Oliver Wendell Holmes, of course, is the laughing philosopher, the humorist at his very highest, even if we use the word "humor" only in its most modern and narrow sense.

A man with a real fondness for books of various kinds will find that his varying moods determine which of these books he at the moment needs. On the afternoon when Stevenson represents the luxury of enjoyment it may safely be assumed that Gibbon will not. The mood that is met by Napier's *Peninsular War*, or Marbot's memoirs, will certainly not be met by Hawthorne or Jane Austen. Parkman's *Montcalm and Wolfe*, Motley's histories of the Dutch Republic, will hardly fill the soul on a day when one turns naturally to the *Heimskringla*; and there is a sense of disconnection if after the *Heimskringla* one takes up the *Oxford Book of French Verse*.

Another matter which within certain rather wide limits each reader must settle for himself is the dividing line between (1) not knowing anything about current books, and (2) swamping one's soul in the sea of vapidity which overwhelms him who reads *only* "the last new books." To me the heading employed by some reviewers when they speak of "books of the week" comprehensively damns both the books themselves and the reviewer who is willing to notice them. I would much rather see the heading "books of the year before last." A book of the year before last which is still worth noticing would probably be worth reading; but one only entitled to be called a book of the week had better be tossed into the wastebasket at once. Still, there are plenty of new books which are not of permanent value but which nevertheless are worth more or less careful reading; partly because it is well to know something of what especially interests the mass of our fellows, and partly because these books, although of ephemeral worth, may really set forth something genuine in a fashion which for the moment stirs the hearts of all of us.

Books of more permanent value may, because of the very fact that they possess literary interest, also yield consolation of a non-literary kind. If any executive grows exasperated over the shortcomings of the legislative body with which he deals, let him study Macaulay's account of the way William was treated by his parliaments as soon as the latter found that, thanks to his efforts, they were no longer in immediate danger from foreign foes; it is illuminating. If any man feels too gloomy about the degeneracy of our people from the standards of their forefathers, let him read *Martin Chuzzlewit*; it will be consoling.

If the attitude of this nation toward foreign affairs and military preparedness at the present day seems disheartening, a study of the first fifteen years of the nineteenth century will at any rate give us whatever comfort we can extract from the fact that our great-grandfathers were no less foolish than we are.

Nor need any one confine himself solely to the affairs of the United States. If he becomes tempted to idealize the past, if sentimentalists seek to persuade him that the "ages of faith," the twelfth and thirteenth centuries, for instance, were better than our own, let him read any trustworthy book on the subject—Lea's *History of the Inquisition*, for instance, or Coulton's abridgment of Salimbene's memoirs. He will be undeceived and will be devoutly thankful that his lot has been cast in the present age, in spite of all its faults.

It would be hopeless to try to enumerate all the books I read, or even all the kinds. The foregoing is a very imperfect answer to a question which admits of only such an answer.

Index

~

About the Author

Mark I. West, PhD, is a professor of English at the University of North Carolina at Charlotte, where he has taught since 1984. In addition to teaching, he has served in numerous administrative positions at UNC Charlotte, including the chair of the English Department, the director of the MA program in liberal studies, and the director of the American studies program. He currently holds the position of Bonnie Cone Professor in Civic Engagement. Before entering academia, he worked as professional archivist.

He has written or edited sixteen books, the most recent of which is *Shapers of American Childhood: Essays on Visionaries from L. Frank Baum to Dr. Spock to J. K. Rowling*, which he coedited with Kathy Merlock Jackson. His articles have appeared in various national publications, such as the *New York Times Book Review*, *Publishers Weekly*, *Americana*, and *British Heritage*, as well as many academic journals.